NOV 2005

641.692 LOWRY
LOWRY, DAVE.
THE CONNOISSEUR'S GUIDE
TO SUSHI :EVERYTHING YOU

✓

The
Connoisseur's
Guide to
SUSHI

WITHDRAWN

D0180120

The Connoisseur's Guide to SUSHI

EVERYTHING YOU NEED TO KNOW ABOUT SUSHI VARIETIES AND ACCOMPANIMENTS, ETIQUETTE AND DINING TIPS, AND MORE

Dave Lowry

THE HARVARD COMMON PRESS
BOSTON, MASSACHUSETTS

ALAMEDA FREE LIBRARY
2200-A CENTRAL AVENUE
ALAMEDA, CA 94501

The Harvard Common Press
535 Albany Street
Boston, Massachusetts 02118
www.harvardcommonpress.com

Copyright © 2005 by David Lowry
Photographs copyright © 2005 by Brian Hagiwara

All rights reserved. No part of this publication may be
reproduced or transmitted in any form or by any means,
electronic or mechanical, including photocopying, record-
ing, or any information storage or retrieval system, without
permission in writing from the publisher.

Printed in China

Printed on acid-free paper

Library of Congress Cataloging-in-Publication Data
Lowry, Dave.
   The connoisseur's guide to sushi : everything you need to
know about sushi varieties and accompaniments, etiquette
and dining tips, and more / Dave Lowry.
      p. cm.
   ISBN 1-55832-307-4 (pb : alk. paper)
   1. Cookery (Fish) 2. Sushi. I. Title.
   TX747.L74 2005
   641.6'92—dc22

                                        2005004385

ISBN-13: 978-1-55832-307-0
ISBN-10: 1-55832-307-4

Special bulk-order discounts are available on this and other
Harvard Common Press books. Companies and organizations may purchase books for premiums or resale, or may
arrange a custom edition, by contacting the Marketing
Director at the address above.

10   9   8   7   6   5   4   3   2   1

BOOK DESIGN BY DEBORAH KERNER • DANCING BEARS DESIGN

Dedication

For Dr. David McKinsey, who never quite got the shoes on/shoes off thing or the unisex public toilets, or wandering about in public in a bathrobe, but with whom I shared an astoundingly lot of sushi in Japan

CONTENTS

Introduction ix

PART I
THE BASICS 1

Rice 2

Nigiri Sushi (Hand-Pressed Sushi) 8

Maki Sushi (Wrapped and Rolled Sushi) 13

Chirashi Sushi (Scattered Sushi) 21

Oshi Sushi (Pressed Sushi) 27

Tane (Toppings) 32

Gu (Fillings) 38

Nori 46

PART II
FISH AND OTHER TOPPINGS:
An A-to-Z Guide 51

PART III
THE PRACTICE 195

On the Side: Condiments 196

Washing It Down: What to Drink with Sushi
and What Not To 211

Tableware and Utensils 216

Accoutrements and Furnishings in the Sushi-Ya 238

The Itamae 252

Sushi Ritual 263

Afterword 286

Index 288

Introduction

You aren't startled anymore at the chorus of "*Irrashai!*" roared in drill-sergeant decibels as you walk through the door of your local sushi place. You've patiently explained the difference between sushi and sashimi to friends and relatives, more than a few of whom imagine that the highlight of a sushi dinner includes snacking on quail eyeballs, or engaging in hand-to-tentacle combat with a writhing octopus resisting a soy sauce dunking. You've even gained some conversance in *sushi-ben*, the unique argot of the cuisine. You are not, by any reckoning, a sushi *monjin*—a complete beginner—anymore.

Congratulations. It's no small achievement. Penetrating even a little into the depths of any aspect of Japanese culture, even one like sushi, which seems to be available in restaurants all over the solar system now, is a challenge for those not born and raised in that country.

On the other hand, before you become too satisfied with yourself, consider the following tale: It's an incident that has passed into the legend of sushi gourmet folklore, spoken of in hushed tones and repeated the way balladeers in other times related epics like *Beowulf* or "The Night Grandpa Came Home Late and Grandma Thought He was a Burglar and Hit Him with a Nine Iron." It relates an encounter that all true sushi gourmands will swear they either witnessed or knew a colleague who did. It is the saga of Henri's fabled showdown at Yasu's Sushi.

If you live or dine in places like New York, L.A., Paris, or London, you know a restaurant like Yasu's. Rare is the major metropolis without a few of them. What city would be worth its culinary salt if it were lacking such an eatery appealing to the chic appetites of the hip-oisie, a restaurant where diners rate the experience as much by the heaping arrogance of the staff and the intimidation felt at just being on the premises as by the food.

At Yasu's only the seriously masochistic dared request seating at the sanctum of the sushi bar itself, in the actual presence of Masayo, the *itamae*, or master sushi maker. The pitiful neophytes who did and had no idea what or how to order were met with that sort of withering condescension reserved for, say, those who at a Sotheby's auction wonder aloud when the poker-playing pooch portraits go on the block. The wretches were desultorily served, then ostentatiously ignored for the remainder of the night, left for months with anxiety attacks triggered by just a whiff of pickled ginger.

Masayo was a terror, the Marquis de Sade of sushi. Holding court behind the counter at Yasu's, he had for months regularly reduced grown men to tears of frustration and humiliation. You didn't realize that only a troglodyte would order bonito in November? Masayo the Merciless rolled his eyes and suggested that appetites such as yours might be better satisfied down the street at Terry-Yaki-Ta-Go. For the philistine who pointed to the red clam *akagai* in the case but mistook it for *hokkigai* surf clam, Masayo could not even offer a response. He dismissed the boor with a wave of his hand and ordered one of his underlings to bring the poor fellow the tempura special.

When Henri slid onto the seat at the bar during his first visit to Yasu's, he asked, *"Kyo no osusume wa nan desu ka?"* ("What's good today?"). He was speaking, though, not just ordinary Japanese, but with the inflection used in speech in the Tsukuda Island section of downtown Tokyo. Tsukudajima is a little of what's left of old, prewar Tokyo. What London's East End is to the Cockney, Tsukudajima is to *Edokko*, the Tokyoite with a long generational string in that city that unwinds all the way back to the shogun era. Most important, Tsukudajima is probably as close to ground zero as you can get in plotting the birthplace of sushi. A more careful itamae would have read the subtle clue: Henri is not a man to be taken lightly in the rarified circles of sushi connoisseurship. Masayo's instincts, however, had become dulled. Lording it over the barbarians who edged haltingly into his realm on a nightly basis had lowered his defenses. Henri was, to him, merely another sushi parvenu in a long line, one more upstart boor to be put in his place.

"*Tai*," Masayo said. Sea bream.

Henri nodded and ordered a pair of *nigiri sushi* topped with it.

"How is it?" Masayo dismissively inquired after Henri had taken a bite, keeping it short, the better to give Henri more opportunity to praise his skill and the absolute freshness of the fish.

"Not bad for *ishidai*," Henri replied evenly, referring to the comparatively plebian parrot fish sometimes substituted for the more expensive true tai.

"What!" All traffic at Yasu's came to a halt at the sound of Masayo's raised voice, chopsticks poised in midair, waitresses froze, and spouted ewers of soy sauce went unpoured. "That wasn't ishidai! It was tai!"

At this point, the sushi amateur would have fainted, or at least backed down, buffaloed by the arctic, withering tone of Masayo's scorn. Henri, though, was in a class by himself. He simply pursed his lips, made a brief shrug, and said not a word.

At this point too, the wise sushi chef would have realized finally that he was dealing with a customer way out of the ordinary and backed off. Masayo? Masayo plunged right into the abyss. "What an absurd notion! I just filleted that tai an hour ago. A perfect *madai* type, as you could tell if you knew anything about fish. Want to see the carcass?" he sneered.

All conversation at the crowded sushi bar had halted. The mighty Masayo seemed to be on the verge of skewering yet another obstreperous upstart. But a few in the place sensed something in the air, and time hung suspended for a long moment, all eyes on Henri.

"No need," Henri responded with the kind of perfect, centered equanimity seen on the visages of both Buddhist statuary and couch-bound football fans in a post–Super Bowl coma. "Just bring me the dorsal fin."

The silence in Yasu's was like that of a mausoleum. No one was sure what was going on, but they were sure it was something.

"You know as well as I do," Henri continued calmly, "that a real tai has anywhere between ten and thirteen spines on the dorsal fin. All we have to do is count them and we'll know if it's a tai like you say or that ishidai that I'm tasting." He peered over the top of his glasses at Masayo. "Right?"

And thus it came to pass, so the legend goes, that the grass at Yasu's was, shall we say, convincingly and permanently clipped.

Let's face it; you want to be like Henri.

It wasn't always that way. You didn't always have such lofty aspirations of becoming a living legend in the sushi world like Henri. There was a time when just memorizing the Japanese words for a dozen or so of the fish on the menu—and being able to pronounce them with sufficient fluency that the itamae didn't burst into paroxysms of laughter when you ordered—was quite the accomplishment. Being able to wield a pair of chopsticks to polish off a full platter of nigiri sushi, your dipping saucer of soy sauce still a clear pool with nary a single flotsam grain of rice, was passing a milestone of culinary dexterity not unlike mastering the osso buco marrow spoon and an escargot fork and tongs at the same meal. The night that the itamae quietly slipped you a couple of pieces of *shimofuri*, the rare, fat-marbled lower flank of the best tuna, was as heady a moment as being escorted down to the cellar of Troisgros for a snort of the Lafite Rothschild that's been killing time there since the Truman era. But the more experience and expertise you gain in sushi bars, the more you're beginning to suspect there are more remote and esoteric levels of sushi connoisseurship to explore and enjoy. And you're itching to get there.

Those suspicions are entirely correct. Your aspirations are not to be denied.

You want to be a sushi snob.

And why not? There are wine snobs who delight in knowing—and letting everyone else know—that the vineyards in the St. Estèphe region got those terrible rainstorms back in '76, rendering all Medocs from that appellation, save for the Cos d'Estournel, barely drinkable. Barbecue snobs will spend an entire afternoon arguing about the comparative qualities of cumin versus paprika and debating the Memphis tradition of piling coleslaw on top of the meat as either blasphemy or the greatest union since Tristan and Isolde. Sushi is just as deserving of such rarified appreciation and connoisseurship.

If the appellation "snob" is personally offensive, think of it this way: If the world of sushi connoisseurship awarded belt ranks like judo or karate-do, you'd be knotting on a stiff, still-damp-with-the-dye black belt. Henri, though, is wearing a black belt so faded, frayed, and worn that it looks like a gray, threadbare rag. To some, there's little discernible difference; you and Henri are both sushi black belts and that's the end of it. You know better.

Sushi, even though you aren't awarded belts or certificates of ability, isn't a whole lot different from the martial arts, flower arranging, the tea ceremony, or any other Japanese discipline. Just when you think you have a grasp on what it's all about, you realize that despite everything you *think* you've learned, there's a whole lot more you still don't know about the basics. There is an enormous body of esoterica related to the enjoyment and appreciation of sushi as well. There are experts in these fields, and then there are *experts*.

This is a field guide for making your way through the world of sushi and establishing yourself as a sushi snob—or, if you still don't like that word, as a sushi *tsujin*, or in the more colloquial, a *sushi tsu*, a "sushi connoisseur." It is a book for the man or woman who wants to make his or her way through the intricacies of appreciating sushi, to recognize its lore, to find answers to the "whys" and "how comes" most others have not even thought to ask. By learning the lessons of this guide and absorbing the information here, you will impress the hell out of anyone sitting down to have a meal of sushi with you. You will impress even more the Japanese sushi itamae and waitresses you'll encounter, a goodly number of whom, let's be honest, are still vaguely amazed that Westerners eat sushi at all, never mind that they might have some authority on the subject. Those two reasons alone are worth the effort to become a sushi snob. It's good and great fun, and since you like sushi anyway, why not be an expert?

Beyond the fun, though, there is a profound sense of satisfaction in knowing a thing, knowing it as deeply and thoroughly as possible. So if your thing is sushi, read on.

A NOTE ON TERMS

Terms and terminology: You already know that there are a lot of them. And they are in Japanese. This is troublesome, I know, but it cannot be helped and should not be. If you want to be an opera snob, your vocabulary in Italian had better be more extensive than *stromboli* and *la Cosa Nostra*. Mention Austro-German existentialism and then mispronounce *Umwelt*, and your professor can hardly be faulted for assuming you couldn't find your Wittgenstein with a Schopenhauer. Sushi's the same. You can't tell the players without a scorecard (which this book is providing). But pronouncing and remembering those names—well, that's up to you. Buy a basic guide to Japanese that includes rules for pronunciation—it isn't tough and not all that different from Spanish in terms of the way vowels are sounded—and you're halfway there. The rest is just study and repetition. By the time you order *anago* for the fiftieth time, not only will your pronunciation sound like you were *Kyoto umare, Nara sodachi desu* (born in Kyoto and raised in Nara), you'll have enjoyed an awful lot of eel.

You will note, for good reason, a near dearth of Latin scientific names when it comes to describing the various fish and other seafood used in the sushi that follow. The scientific names for the various creatures described here are of value in narrowing down precisely what one is talking about, true. But they won't necessarily be of any great worth to you in a restaurant. Asking the itamae at your local *sushi-ya*, or sushi restaurant, for amberjack and then defining exactly what you mean by saying "You know, *Seriola quinqueradiata*," isn't going to make the cogs turn any faster in processing your order. He knows amberjack as *hamachi* or *inada* or about a dozen other names the species has, depending on local idioms, the age of the fish, and so on, and those are the words you'll need to use to be understood.

In translating Japanese terms for fish, I've tried to use the most common English equivalents. That isn't always easy, since names for fish here in America are often just as vague and local as they are in Japan. Mackerel, for instance, can refer to more than twenty different fish, and each of those can have half a dozen or more names. While the most common name for *Scomber scombrus* is "Atlantic mackerel," it's bought and sold as "Boston mackerel," "Spanish mackerel," "kingfish," "king mackerel," and "chub mackerel." Commercial fishermen, fishmongers and wholesalers, and grocery stores and specialty fish markets have all played fast and loose with these names, even making up some new ones to make the fish sound classier or tastier. The U.S. Food and Drug Administration crashed this little back-alley poker game to some extent a few years ago, issuing an official list of what each species of fish could be legally called when sold. (So much for peddling common smelt as "Adirondack Mountain troutlet.") It is that FDA guide that I've used in most instances to identify fish in English, but you should assume there will be some regional differences, depending on where you are.

SUSHI'S ORIGINS
AND HISTORY

Profligacy, in terms of food, has never been a prominent thread running through the fabric of Japanese culture. Famines in Japan were frequent. Food was precious. Maybe that's why sushi came about: the Japanese simply couldn't stand to see any food go to waste.

Legend credits the invention of sushi to an old woman who was worried that bandits might steal a pot of her rice. She shinnied up a tree and stashed the rice in an osprey nest until the threat passed. When she retrieved the rice, it had begun to ferment. She also discovered that some of the ospreys' fish scraps, which had fallen into the rice, were not only edible, but also, as far as comestibles left exposed to the elements in the living quarters of messy birds of prey go, rather tasty.

The fact is, using cooked, fermented rice as a preservative for fish is something that has been going on for a long time all over Southeast Asia. Without going into a protracted explanation that would accomplish little save causing you to relive the embarrassment of your high school chemistry class, it works like this: Once rice is cooked and begins to ferment, lactic acid bacilli are produced. The acid in the rice, assisted by a liberal dose of salt, promotes a chemical reaction that retards the growth of bacteria when the rice is packed around otherwise perishable substances, like fish. The rice works to pickle the fish, in a way. That's why, centuries later, the kitchen in a sushi-ya is still called a *tsuke-ba*, or pickling place. What distinguished this style of fish preservation in Japan from everywhere else in Asia was that the Japanese eventually (though not until the 19th century) decided to eat the rice in which they packed the fish.

If Granny Suzuki really did simultaneously save dinner from the banditos and discover sushi in the osprey nest, she may well have done it near Lake Biwa. For more than 1,000 years, crucian carp from the lake have been packed in salted rice to make *funa sushi*, the oldest meal that could, with an extremely elastic stretch of the imagination, be considered sushi-like. Critics observe that funa sushi is not only the oldest form of sushi around, but also actually tastes like the original batch. That's harsh. Even so, funa sushi does have an unmistakable pungency. It's been compared to an anchovy-and-goat-cheese bean dip left out on the patio in the sun for a couple of days in August in Georgia. And that's the kind of description you get from those who *like* it.

Funa sushi is, to be precise, a variety of *nare sushi*, in which rice and fish are compressed with some kind of a weight. But the use of a weight to spur the fermentation process is more than merely a curious footnote in the epic of sushi. When it was widely used, it sped up the pickling process considerably. "Considerably," mind you, is a relative term here. A batch of nare sushi still took about a year to be ready. Nobody minded the wait much. Nare sushi was affordable only to nobility and the wealthy in Japan from the 9th through the 14th centuries, and they weren't busy doing much anyway. That changed at the beginning of the 15th century, however, when Japan entered a long and bloody civil war that disrupted more than just dinner plans for the whole country. Cooks during that period discovered that adding more weight to the fish and rice reduced the fermentation time. Instead of a year, the fish was now ready to eat in a matter of months, rendering it, by previous standards, fast food. They also found that the fish did not have to be pickled nearly to the point of decomposition to taste good. (Who would have guessed?) Gourmets called the innovation *nama-nare sushi*, or raw nare-sushi, or *han-nare sushi*, half-pressed sushi.

If you've read James Clavell's *Shōgun*, you've got a reasonably good idea of what was going on in Japan from the 15th through the 16th centuries—except for the fact that relatively few shipwrecked Western navigators actually ended up soaking naked in hot tubs with the wives of high-ranking samurai. In 1600, the shogun Tokugawa Ieyasu managed to unite all of Japan politically for the first time in its history. Impressive, though the feat of course pales in comparison in the estimation of the sushi snob with the Tokugawa period's greatest contribution to civilization: the final steps in the evolution of sushi.

When Ieyasu moved the capitol from old Kyoto to Edo in 1606, he launched a process that was not entirely unlike the creation of Las Vegas. Instead of blooming almost overnight from a barren desert, though, Edo was built nearly instantly on swampland surrounding a shallow bay. Instead of garish hotels, clubs, and casinos, Edo soon gave birth to the Yoshiwara district, a neighborhood of brothels, bars, and gambling dens. Instead of attractions like Wayne Newton and Siegfried and Roy, Edo had . . . well, Edo didn't have anything that could be adequately compared with them. But it did have a bustling, lively *joie de vivre*, stimulated by the rise of the merchant class and that class's timeless skills at feeding popular appetites.

By the early 19th century there probably was not a city on the planet larger, in population or land size, than Edo. It was, all in all, *the* place to be in that part of the world, and the energetic atmosphere there was certainly conducive to working up a powerful hunger. Enter, at this propitious time, Hanaya Yohei. There are those rare individuals who come along at just the right moment in the unfolding drama of human civilization, making a unique contribution at the particular, alchemical instant it is appropriate, needed, and recognized. Einstein did it for our understanding of the physics of energy. Colonel Sanders did it for fried chicken. For sushi, this extraordinary individual was Hanaya Yohei. In 1824, Yohei opened Japan's first sushi stall, in the Ryogoku district of Edo. Nowadays, Ryogoku is best known as the site of the Kokugikan, the national sumo stadium. In Yohei's time, Ryogoku was, as the name means, "the place between two countries." It was at the edge of the city, along the banks of the Sumida River, with the countryside on the opposite bank. Yohei was canny enough to open his place right near one of the river's few bridges, so he had a constant stream of customers coming and going from the city. Location, though, was only the half of Yohei's genius. His second secret was packaging.

Way back around 1660, a physician experimented with a combination of rice vinegar and sugar that, when mixed in with rice, made the "fermentation" virtually instant. He'd struck upon the idea for making *sushi-meshi*, or sushi rice. But like the Chinese with their gunpowder or the Irish with their bagpipes, having once conceived of the idea, he really didn't know what useful or productive things he might do with it. It was Yohei who grabbed the physician's concept and ran with it. He envisioned sushi, with a fresh fish topping *and* the vinegared rice along with it, as a finger food, or in Japanese, nigiri sushi, or hand-pressed sushi. A nugget of rice was seasoned with vinegar and topped by a sliver of seafood fresh from the bay that was only a few blocks away. That's why a synonym for nigiri sushi is *Edomae sushi*: *Edomae* is "in front of Edo," i.e., the bay. And that was it: the creation of modern sushi.

This story, the sushi connoisseur must know, is not without its detractors. Some authorities have insisted that other sushi shops preceded Yohei's and that he is more accurately credited as sushi's first great marketer rather than its author. The objection may be valid. But they miss the point. Nubile models may have cavorted through exotic locales barely wearing miniscule beachwear in plenty of other magazines in the annals of journalism, but when we mention the "swimsuit issue" nobody gives credit to *Newsweek*, now, do they? Case closed.

If you could go back and work your way through the entire buffet line of the epicurean history of Japan, it wouldn't be until 1834 that you would recognize the same sort of sushi you're eating now—and it would have been a lot less expensive then. Mind you, though, if you did stroll across Edo's Ryogoku

Bridge and stop in for a bite to eat at Yohei-Zushi (you could have, up until 1930; the place lasted, unchanged in most ways, for nearly a century), the taste might be familiar. But the surroundings would have been noticeably different from any sushi-ya you'd frequent now. Then sushi was sold from moveable stalls, *yatai-mise*—"outdoor businesses," called just yatai for short.

That all changed on the first day of September in 1923. A couple of minutes before noon, there were hundreds of yatai being wheeled all over the city that had, by then, been renamed Tokyo. A couple of minutes after noon, there were far fewer yatai carts, and within 24 hours, fewer still. That's when the Great Kanto Earthquake struck. Vast sections of Tokyo were leveled. Land prices plummeted. It became economically feasible to move sushi into permanent *uchi-mise* (inside business) restaurants, though in most places it was merely a matter of the wheeled cart being moved inside. Patrons still stood at the counter to eat. Even so, permanent restaurants catering to the sushi trade became a fixture in the capital city of Japan. The era of the modern sushi-ya had arrived.

It is tempting for the sushi snob to long for the good old days and dismiss any recent developments as hopelessly nouveau. This is the general inclination of any snob. It works well when the object of one's snobbery is something like, say, wine. If you want to think that little sushi today is as good as the stuff Grandma hauled down from the osprey nest, fine. In broader perspective, however, the good old days of sushi began at about the same time as did the bikini and the vaccine for polio. We can mourn some of the changes wrought by the Allied occupation following World War II. The discouragement of mixed-sex bathing comes immediately to mind. Still, overall, sushi is better for it. Primarily for reasons of sanitation, Allied authorities put a quick end to the few remaining streetside sushi carts. That's not a bad thing; sushi as a cuisine really didn't benefit noticeably from the flies, dust, or sparrow crap that were a part of outdoor Tokyo. By the 1950s, sushi restaurants were exclusively indoor and served a dine-in clientele, with seats in front of the counter where the itamae worked. Postwar technology imported to Japan also spawned a boom in sushi throughout the country. Prior to the end of the war, sushi, or at least nigiri sushi in all its variety, was virtually unknown outside Tokyo. Other regions had their own specialties featuring fish and vinegared rice, as we'll discuss later. But cheaper and more efficient forms of refrigeration brought Tokyo's sushi to the rest of Japan. The same factors in transportation—cheaper and more efficient forms—also meant a wider selection of fish was available for the first time. Sushi today in Japan and everywhere else is fresher, safer, certainly greater in variety, and arguably tastier than it's ever been.

All of which is not to say that the story is over. The sushi snob cannot point to some golden age of the past where everything was better. You can't assume, either, that we've reached some sort of pinnacle of sushi perfection and that you've tasted the best that sushi is going to get. This is important. The urge for nostalgia is a powerful one whenever anything Japanese is the subject. There are those Japanophiles who imagine the country of their longing as a nation consisting primarily of tranquil gardens with pensive, kimono-clad beauties mincing daintily over half-moon bridges. If they would spend but 20 minutes in the sensory hell of a Shimbashi nightclub, surrounded by greasy-haired, chain-smoking geezers putting the make on young women with rainbow-colored hair and high heels that would test the balance of the Flying Wallendas, they would be swiftly disabused of those notions. They'd also have a reasonably good introduction to 21st-century Japan. *Madame Butterfly* it is not. To be sure, there is plenty of the past still around. The Japanese, though, have a genius for adapting the traditional to the modern.

Sushi, like the rest of Japanese culture, has never existed in a vacuum. Probably close to half the ingredients available for "traditional" sushi have become popular only since the end of World War II. Methods of transportation that allow delivery of fish within hours of its being harvested, along with cryogenic flash-freezing and other technology, and a willingness on the part of the itamae to experiment and innovate, has meant that sushi in Japan and the rest of the world continues to transform. The sushi connoisseur who fails to appreciate the ongoing evolution in the cuisine is missing an important part of the sushi experience.

Of course, at the end of the spectrum from the Japanophile who thinks sushi was perfected sometime in the distant past and should never be altered in any way is the sushi *arriviste*. This is the type who assumes sushi suddenly popped up in southern California about the same time as *anime*, who doesn't have any sense of the history and tradition of what he's putting in his mouth, and who figures his personal tastes are the only standards by which sushi ought to be judged. The preponderance of these people account for most of the mediocre sushi around today, along with the goofier extremes like deep-fried sushi or "Southwestern sushi" or, well, you get the idea.

The sushi snob, called in Japanese, remember, a sushi tsu— put your tongue right behind your back upper teeth and say "sue"—has to avoid both ends of this spectrum. You have to understand sushi's past as a means of getting a handle on its connoisseurship today. If you know where it's come from, what it is fundamentally supposed to be, you can be a better arbiter of the places sushi is going, and you won't be likely to fall for the fads to which sushi, like all foods, is susceptible. As a true sushi tsu, you have the adventurous spirit to try something you've never eaten before in a sushi-ya and the perspective to judge it by the standards long in place surrounding sushi appreciation—along with the good sense and decency not to dip it in ketchup.

PART I

The Basics

RICE

To observe that rice is an essential element to sushi is like pointing out that the Winter Olympics would be a whole lot less engaging without snow. No rice, no sushi: It's that simple, and that important. Here's what you need to know about it.

Although most of the rest of the world eats long-grain rice, and has for a very long time, the Japanese have been cultivating and eating short-grain rice. Because it contains more cellulose, short-grain rice is stickier. That stickiness is what makes sushi possible.

Japanese gourmets hyperventilate over the arrival of the season's new rice crop, called *shinmai*, which is special because the freshly dried grains are still at the point where they retain a lot of water. But as tasty as it is, new rice is not well suited for making sushi rice. Instead, the *itamae* uses older, more aged rice, which has lost a lot of its inner moisture. This "vintage" rice is called *komai*, a term that applies to any rice more than a year old. Rice prepared for sushi is, in Japanese, *sushi-meshi*. "Meshi" is the *kun*, or original Japanese pronunciation, of the *kanji*, or written character, for "rice." *Gohan* is the *on*, or borrowed Chinese reading, of the same character. (The *go* in "gohan" is an honorific, a prefix to make a word more polite.) Remember that some Japanese words sound more masculine, and some distinctly feminine. To native Japanese ears in most circumstances, "meshi" sounds more masculine. "Gohan" has a softer, more feminine sound to it. The *sushi-ya* has always been thought of as a man's world; some of the language used there reflects that. And so "meshi" is the word for rice that you will almost always hear and use. If you are a female, though, rest assured that you can use the word "meshi" without undue aspersions being cast upon your sexuality. When sushi-meshi is formed into the nuggets of rice for hand-pressed slabs of *nigiri sushi*, though, it's called *shari*. In normal parlance, "shari" refers to dry, brittle bones. It is used specifically to describe the tiny pieces of bones from the Buddha's body that were pulverized and distributed as relics after his death. The grains of rice, or maybe the nuggets of nigiri sushi themselves, were thought to resemble these pieces of bone. Today, you're likely to hear "shari" as a way of distinguishing the rice from the topping ingredients (*tane*—we'll get to this word later) of nigiri sushi.

To prepare sushi-meshi, the raw rice and water go into an automatic rice cooker. Because of the quantities needed, nowadays even a tiny sushi-ya uses a rice cooker, a little mechanized device that has revolutionized Asia. Rice is neither "steamed" nor "boiled," as it is often described in translation, in the cooker. It's prepared with a combination of both methods. Cooking rice is called *yudaki* in Japanese kitchen slang. The word in normal usage means a "hot water cascade." That's what the water and rice sound like, gurgling and bubbling away under the pressure of the steamer pot, hence the expression. Typically, near-equal parts of rice to water are the rule for cooking a batch of basic rice. For sushi-meshi, itamae may mess around with this equation, depending on the brand of rice and other factors, such as the humidity and the exact age of the rice. Good itamae will also mix brands to get just the product they want. Whatever the alchemy, what the itamae wants to avoid is a sticky, gluey gumminess, called *beta-beta* in Japanese, at one end of the bad rice spectrum, and grains not entirely cooked and *kochi-kochi*, hard inside, at the other end. Sushi rice has to be just glutinous enough to stick together, but with each grain retaining its own identity, kind of like kids at a junior high school dance. Good sushi-meshi has a pleasant firmness of texture in the mouth that is *shiko-shiko*.

Freshly cooked rice, for sushi or any other meal, should meet three criteria: It should have a glowing luster (*tsuya*), a pleasant stickiness (*nebari*), and the correct taste (*aji*). Tell an itamae, or any Japanese cook, that his rice exemplifies these three terms and he will lay down his life for you. You can complain in a sushi-ya about the mean waitress, the bad seating, or the mistreatment of Japan's Korean minority, and the itamae is likely to take it all in stride. You insult the quality of the rice, however, at your own peril. Any criticism at all will be taken very, very seriously.

Once cooked, rice is transferred to a wooden tub (*hangiri*), then fanned to cool it; at the same time, a seasoning is drizzled over it. The seasoning—*awase-zu*, or coming together vinegar—is more or less standard among itamae and consists of rice vinegar, sugar, and salt. Awase-zu is also referred to as *su-mezu*. (The combination of vinegar, salt, and water that the itamae uses for moistening his hands to keep the rice from sticking to them while he fashions shapes for nigiri sushi is called *te-zu*, or hand vinegar.) From an aesthetic point of view, the sugar and vinegar add a pleasing luster to the rice. The grains look fat and glossy, an appearance that's helped along by the fanning, which moves cool air over the hot rice to make the surface of the grains more amenable to absorbing the salt-and-sugar liquid. In more scientific terms, the vinegar, in addition to its historical role in sushi as a preservative, temporarily dissolves much of the stickiness of the freshly cooked rice, allowing the dissolved sugar to coat the grains, which, in turn, makes them sticky again. Salt balances this exchange and highlights flavor.

Sushi-ko, a dehydrated, more concentrated version of awase-zu, makes homemade sushi a lot easier. A good sushi-ya shouldn't let the stuff even come through the door, however. That's because sushi rice changes slightly—or should—according to both the season and the specific kind of sushi for which the rice is being made. The variable is the amount of sugar used. When you think about tastes that go great with fish, especially raw fish, a Saturday-morning-cereal type of sweetness isn't at the top of the list. So don't think of it that way. Instead, consider this: Sugar mitigates the sourness of the vinegar. By varying the sugar, the itamae doesn't so much add sweet as calibrate the amount of sour. Premixed sushi-ko concentrates coat the rice so that any extra sugar added in will not adhere properly. That, aside from a simple pride in making his own vinegar-and-sugar concoctions, is why the itamae holds dehydrated sushi-ko in low esteem.

Changing the amount of sugar in awase-zu gives an itamae three distinct versions of sushi-meshi:

Usu-aji (thin taste) sushi rice contains the least amount of sugar; in other words, it is the most vinegary or sour. Usu-aji is used almost exclusively with nigiri sushi.

Ama-kuchi (sweet mouth) is the sushi rice used mostly for sushi specialties like *inari sushi* and some *maki sushi*. It has comparatively more sugar than usu-aji.

Kokuchi-aji (thick taste) has the most sugar of any rice used for sushi. It is used mainly with scattered, or *chirashi*, sushi.

In general, the farther south you go in Japan, the sweeter the sushi-meshi tends to be. People in most regions of southern Japan are stereotyped for liking sweet tastes more than their more northern cousins. Something else to consider is temperature. Nigiri sushi's rice should be, according to sushi lore, the same temperature as the skin on your cheek; slightly cool. The rice should be slightly warmer for chirashi sushi, since you want the flavors of the toppings to blend in, which they do better with warm rice.

Alas, a lot of itamae have gotten sloppy, even in Japan, and they'll use the basic awase-zu recipe to flavor the rice in all kinds of sushi. If a sushi-ya pays attention to this important detail, though, it is nearly a foolproof hallmark of an outstanding establishment, as is the itamae who lightens up on the sugar in sushi-meshi during the summer.

Nigiri sushi eaten during the summer has traditionally had more of a sour kick to the rice. It is a practice that undoubtedly comes from sushi's earliest days, when the vinegar was working to keep the fish from spoiling; in warmer weather, naturally, more vinegar would have been added. But it also has to do with a Japanese folk belief that if a diet is balanced between the five tastes (sweet, sour, salty, hot, and bitter), the body will run smoothly. Lose that equilibrium, and it's like saying "Heidi-ho, come on in and make yourself at home" to bacteria, viruses, evil humors, and heaven knows what else is out there to afflict one. In hot weather, according to these beliefs, we naturally eat more salt to offset what is lost through perspiration. The increase in salt intake can threaten the intricate interplay of the five tastes, and it can be countered, in part, by increasing the sour. Sure, the AMA probably doesn't endorse all this. But that is why more vinegary foods, like pickled vegetables, are associated with summertime Japanese cuisine, and it is why nigiri sushi-meshi in the hotter months will have more vinegar than in the winter. Or it will if the itamae knows what he's doing.

In addition to his other duties, then, the itamae can be riding herd on up to three different pots of rice. Even keeping one ready isn't a job for amateurs. If the rice for sushi gets too cold and is reheated, it gets slippery and squishy and won't hold together. A worse fate awaits if it is chilled, as many a neophyte sushi enthusiast has learned after bringing home leftovers and sticking them in the refrigerator. The grains get hard and chalky, virtually inedible. So a towel goes over the tub of cooled rice to keep it at the ambient temperature as long as possible. A competent itamae and his staff will have a constant supply during the sushi-ya's hours of operation, and it will be consistent in quality. If it is not, the sushi snob's response is merciless, swift, and decisive. The *sushi tsu* must always be gracious and reasonable in expectations in most areas of a sushi meal—except when it comes to sushi-meshi. You should still be gracious, of course. But if the rice in your sushi is in any way inferior, do not return. Standards for other matters of sushi snobbery can vary in some instances, but not with rice. There's no excuse for any place calling itself a sushi-ya to present any-thing but excellent sushi-meshi. Come on, it only takes five ingredients: rice, rice vinegar, sugar, salt, and water. The rest is up to the itamae. Ineptly combine them, combine them any way but perfectly, in fact, and you've got, to use an architectural metaphor, the culinary equivalent of an LBJ-era trailer park home sitting directly in the path of a West Texas tornado. Arrange those ingredients as they should be, and the sushi-meshi is a little bite of epicurean Bauhaus, my friend, the taste of perfection.

NIGIRI SUSHI
(Hand-Pressed Sushi)

Eating with our hands is good. We learn this very early in life. The delights of a good nap, the cathartic value of a splenetic tantrum now and then, and the stoking of the internal furnaces with fuel delivered there directly with our hands: We carry all these childhood lessons with us long after we've given up the apartment on *Sesame Street* for more sophisticated digs. The rewards of finger foods explain, in part at least, the popularity of sandwiches, beer nuts, and week-old lime Jell-O cubes, and it's one reason why nigiri sushi is what most people think of when they hear "sushi."

A 3rd-century text from China, the *Wei zhi*, notes that the "People of Wa [Japan] eat with their hands." About 1,300 years later, when sushi emerged as the sort of cuisine we're still eating, those people of Wa had pretty well perfected that particular habit. That it was a meal a hand's length away might even account for the explosion of sushi as a meal for the masses during the Edo period. If you've ever eaten a garden tomato in August, standing over the kitchen sink, you know: There's a pleasant intimacy in stuffing dinner directly into your face without any intermediary utensils, which transcends cultures and time. Maybe it's the elemental act itself. Maybe it's the addition of the tactile sensation, touching the food at nearly the same instant as tasting it. Maybe it's the sensual nature, the Tom Jones–ish food-as-sex metaphor. And maybe you're not reading this book to entertain my ruminations on life and food. You can eat nigiri sushi with chopsticks. You'll lose something in the process, though.

Since sushi—at least nigiri sushi—is kind of the ultimate handmade food, you can expect every itamae to have his own individual way of shaping the rice for nigiri. There are, nevertheless, some standard *kata*, or shapes, for the rice used in nigiri sushi. Learn them.

Koban-gata

The casual sushi aficionado may have seen only this shape, a rounded nugget like a big, unshelled pecan. The name comes from a *koban*, an old Japanese gold coin of similar, oblong shape. It's the easiest to mold; prepackaged nigiri is always koban style. In middle-level and even in a lot of better-class sushi-ya outside Japan, *koban-gata* is how nigiri sushi is always made.

Tawara-gata

This is nearly identical to koban style; in the lexicon of some itamae and sushi-ya, it's actually just another term for the same shape. A *tawara* is a bale of tightly woven straw that was used in earlier times to store newly harvested rice. The form of the rice nuggets resembles the bales.

Hako-gata

A *hako* is a box; the form is a neat rectangle. It's tricky to mold sushi this way by hand. If your regular sushi-ya commonly serves *hako-gata* and the itamae suddenly departs when you're there one evening, it might be because the batch of rice came out a little harder than usual. Hako-gata can't be made at all with rice that isn't of a perfect texture.

Suehiro-gata

This type is a folding fan shape. It's also called *jigami-gata* or *ogi-gata*. It looks, in cross section, like those fans with ribs that splay out when they're spread. *Suehiro-gata* sushi is rare. In profile, it looks like an arch—the bottom flat, the top curved over—so it is appropriate for displaying a particularly good-looking topping. But it's easier to get the proportions of rice and topping wrong with fan-shaped sushi than with any other shape. If the fan is too thick across, the taste of the rice over-whelms the piece of sushi. If the topping is sliced or prepared too thickly, it droops over the arch and ruins the effect. When you get to know an itamae well, ask him to demonstrate suehiro-gata for you and see how well he does it.

Funa-gata

This sushi is shaped like a boat (*funa*), flat on the keel with the bow and stern curving up. *Funa-gata sushi* is rare; there isn't any great advantage to shaping the rice this way other than to show off the tane or the skill of the itamae. But you might see it when he's in an expansive mood and wants to strut his stuff. If an itamae can consistently and quickly make a funa-gata shape, it's a reasonably reliable sign he's gotten some fairly advanced and intensive training. It isn't a shape the average sushi maker would even recognize, let alone be able to make correctly.

Kushi-gata

The translation is "comb shaped." If you could take one of those cream-filled Hostess Sno Balls, the mere sniffing of which can send one into insulin shock, and kind of stretch it out into a longer oval, that's what *kushi-gata sushi* would look like. The "comb" here, incidentally, refers to the type worn by upper-class women during the feudal period. And it's *kushi*, not *kuchi* (mouth). Kushi-gata is the second most common way of form-ing the rice for nigiri sushi after the koban style. It's compara-tively easy to make and the flat bottom keeps the serving from sliding around on the plate. It's also called *Rikyu-gata*, named for the tea ceremony master of the 16th century, Sen no Rikyu. More specifically, it's named after a sweet cake confection he liked to serve during the ceremony. So the Sno Ball analogy has a nice symmetry to it, don't you think?

Whatever the shape, a chunk of coal is just a nonrenewable energy source without the pressure required to squeeze it down into a couple of carats, so beloved by De Beers and fiancées alike. Nigiri sushi is the same. "Nigiri" means "to grip." Watch the itamae crafting nigiri sushi and you'll see, of course, the lump of rice get squeezed with his left hand. Keep an eye on his right. With his first two fingers extended, he presses the rice into shape. The two fingers look like the Cub Scout salute. In Japan, it looks like a *mudra*, one of the ritual gestures of the esoteric Shingon sect of Buddhism. The first and second fingers extended and gripped with the fist of the other hand forms the *chi-in ken*, the "adamantine diamond fist," which symbolizes deep or profound knowledge to practitioners of that faith. So among sushi cognoscenti, chi-in ken or *chi-ken* is a slang expression for the act of making nigiri sushi.

Nothing is more important in the construction of nigiri sushi than its ability to hold together properly. The shari, or rice, and the tane, or topping, must bind as perfectly as a prosecution-proof alibi. A topping sliding off its rice, assuming the sushi-ya isn't being struck by an earthquake and you're not juggling the sushi, is unforgivable for an accomplished itamae. A big part of his preparation is to match the tane with the shape of the rice, laying it on and covering the rice sufficiently so the sushi hangs together during the normal course of handling it as you eat. That's relatively easy for a competent itamae when he's working with a lot of tane that are uniform in shape or cut. If he is working with toppings like clams or cockles or fishes or their relevant parts that are oddly shaped and slippery, that's when you might see the itamae, if he's got the talent, resort to pressing different shapes of shari. It can be a real challenge for him. If you notice an unusual shape, take a look to see if you can surmise why. Maybe he's just demonstrating his nigiri virtuosity; maybe there's a practical reason.

Like diamonds, candy bars, and strike zones, the size of nigiri sushi has shrunk from its original size. During the Edo period, the typical bite of sushi was actually about a bite and a half, or *hitokuchi-han*. Now it's more like a single, though for some mouths an admittedly large bite, or *hitokuchi*. Which leads to the question, do you jam a whole serving of sushi into your mouth at once or do you bite it off? The variations of oral capacity in our species being what they are, it is impossible to expect everyone to polish off a piece of nigiri sushi at one go. Remember, it's *hai dozo*, "yes, please," to a sushi meal but *iye kekko desu*, "thanks, not necessary," to the Heimlich maneuver. If you must bite nigiri sushi into two or more pieces—using a knife is *not* an option here for the sushi tsu—try to do it in such a way that the topping isn't dragged off the rice and left dangling between your teeth. There is no elegant way out of this, so avoid it. We could probably work up a chart illustrating the exact incisor compression necessary to cut through the various toppings of nigiri sushi. But that's a little too weird, even for the sushi snob. Practice will be the best and most delicious instruction on this delicate matter.

The same practice will give the sushi tsu a perspective on the correct proportions of rice and topping. Low rent is the sushiya that dresses a slab of rice the size of a jumbo Snickers bar with a slice of topping skimpier than a Hershey's Miniature. Just as inappropriate is the itamae who, responding apparently to the carnivorous Western appetite for protein, blankets a pathetic nubbin of rice with a coverlet of fish the dimensions of a New York strip steak. Any kind of sushi has to be a balance, though by "balance" we don't necessarily mean a 50-50 break. Think of the ideal proportions of nigiri sushi as the best a Fortune 500 company CEO could expect in a divorce split from his second wife: about 60-40, with her larger share representing the rice and his smaller share the fish. Fortunately, hitting this balance is a lot more frequent in the sushi-ya than in the divorces of those gouged CEOs. And unlike the woeful CEO, your circumstances are not mandated by the judicial system. Exercise your choice by patronizing those sushi-ya that get the proportions of sushi and topping correct.

MAKI SUSHI
(WRAPPED AND ROLLED SUSHI)

The history of wrapped sushi rolls, or *maki sushi*, goes back to the vegetarian cookery that evolved in 13th-century Kyoto temples. Buddhist monks there lived lives of piety, austerity, and rigid discipline, but they were not averse to a decent meal. They created the technique of wrapping or rolling foods in sheets of dried nori seaweed.

Futo-maki, *hoso-maki*, *temaki*, and *no-no-ji-maki* are the four main kinds of maki sushi, along with a few subcategories that I'll also mention. The first two are the most common varieties. See page 16 for a discussion of the latter two kinds.

Futo-maki

Futo means "thick" or "fat." There aren't any legal statutes governing the exact size necessary to qualify as a thick roll of sushi. In general, futo-maki are nori-wrapped sushi too big to eat in one bite. They range in diameter from roughly the size of a BMW tailpipe (don't ask how I know) down to the circumference of a roll of pepperoni. Infrequently, futo-maki will have only a single *gu* (filling) inside in addition to the rice. Most, though, feature a combination of fillings. Sometimes, usually away from Tokyo, you might hear futo-maki called *chu-maki*. The *chu* here means "in the middle." *O-maki* (big roll) is another term.

Hoso-maki

Hoso, "thin" or "narrow," maki are bite-size wrapped sushi about as big around as a slug for the quarter slots at Harrah's. While some futo-maki are "inside out," with the rice on the outside (we'll get to that in a minute), hoso-maki nearly always have a nori wrapping around them.

Both thick and thin maki sushi are made the same way. A square of nori is spread atop a flexible bamboo mat called a *makisu*. A layer of sushi rice is laid on, with a furrow pressed in for the ingredients to be added. The whole bundle is then rolled up in the mat to make it firm and get it into the right shape. It is cut into four, six, or eight neat pieces, and dinner is served. Do you want to know, incidentally, if your itamae is from western or eastern Japan? Look at his *sashimi-bocho*, the long knife he uses. If it is sharp on the tip, it's a *yanagiba-bocho*, which is preferred in Osaka and much of western Japan. Blunt on the end and it's a *takobiki-bocho*, the most popular style of sashimi knife in Tokyo and the eastern part of the country.

There are some specialties of wrapped sushi that deserve special mention:

ANAKYU-MAKI ▼ This is hoso-maki with a combination of cucumber and eel.

HIMOKYU-MAKI ▼ This is a hoso-maki with *himo* and cucumber inside. A himo is a cord or thong: here it refers to the stringy fringe of some clams, which is a sushi delicacy.

KANPYO-MAKI ▼ This is maki sushi with strips of a cooked gourd, *kanpyo*, in the center. Kanpyo-maki is also called *teppo-maki*, or gun barrel maki, because it looks like the business end of a rifle.

KAPPA-MAKI ▼ A *kappa* is a predatory water sprite of Japanese folklore that attacks and sucks out the entrails of his victims. When not dining in that singular fashion, kappa feast on cucumbers. They crave 'em. And so, a roll of maki sushi made with a center gu of *kyuri*, or cucumber, is a kappa-maki.

OSHINKO-MAKI ▼ *Oshinko* is a pickle. Maki sushi with a center gu of *takuan*, or pickled radish, are oshinko-maki. The *ko* of oshinko comes from an old word for *miso* (soybean paste). Since vegetables have long been pickled in miso, they were once called, especially in rural regions, *ko o mono*, "bean paste things." The *shin* means "new." The implication is that a new food has been made out of an old one through the pickling process.

TEKKA-MAKI ▽ Tuna scraps left over from the carving process, wrapped in rice and nori, make tekka-maki. In the slang of the Edo underworld, gambling dens were *tekka-ba*. Legend credits a compulsive gambler who wanted a snack and didn't want to stop throwing the dice. He needed food that could be eaten without getting his fingers sticky, and was inspired to wrap sushi rice and cheap cuts of tuna in nori.

UMEKYU ▽ This wrapped sushi is made of cucumber and *neri-ume*, a paste made of tart pickled Japanese apricots, which are often mistaken in Japanese cookbooks for plums. The taste is puckery. Some sushi connoisseurs like to finish a meal with umekyu because they so efficiently cleanse the palate.

The world being what it is today, all sorts of experimental maki sushi are being created. A reliably good sign that they are not for the serious sushi tsu is the use of the word "roll" when describing them. You know, like the "Detroit roll," or "Miami roll," or "Encino roll." Every city with more than three sushi places in it seems to spawn a unique kind of roll. None seem particularly memorable. Here are a few of the more common Frankenstein-type rolls you will encounter out there.

AVOCADO ROLL ▽ This is self-explanatory. Equally self-explanatory should be the obvious, that avocados belong in guacamole and not in sushi.

SPIDER ROLL ▽ This is maki sushi with fried soft-shell crab in the center, along with perhaps some kind of spicy mayonnaise sauce. Spider rolls are to real sushi what William Shatner's roles are to serious acting. They're fun and diverting, but they aren't going to be putting any Oscars on the mantelpiece, now are they?

HAWAIIAN ROLL ▽ Hawaiians consume more Spam per capita than people in any other state in the Union and anywhere on earth, for that matter. So it was only a matter of time before Hawaiian sushi makers played around with the idea of sticking Spam into maki sushi. Should you be eating sushi in Hawaii and offered Spam sushi, it will probably be useful for you to know that the Hawaiian word for "atrociously stinky" is *pilau*.

CALIFORNIA ROLL ▼ Of course, no treatment of maki sushi would be complete without mention of the California roll.

Okay, now here are a number of less common types of maki sushi that you may be lucky enough to come across.

Temaki

These are sushi rolls (maki) wrapped by hand (*te*). They look like ice cream cones. The itamae rolls a horn of nori around rice and other fillings. *Temaki* aren't only made by hand; they have to be eaten that way too. This is one kind of sushi that doesn't lend itself to chopsticks at all.

No-no-ji-maki

In the shorthand *kana* syllabary that covers all the spoken sounds of Japanese, the character for *no* is written like a flopped, backward, lowercase "e." If the sheet of nori is tucked into the rice or the gu inside as the itamae begins to wrap, in cross section the nori in the piece of maki sushi resembles that no. *No-no-ji-maki* has always been more popular in the Kansai region, around Osaka, than in Tokyo. Some Tokyo itamae disdain it, since technically it is a little easier to wrap maki sushi that way, and they regard it as a product of the lesser-skilled craftsman.

Ura-maki

This inside-out sushi is not really a separate form of maki sushi; it's a little razzmatazz take on wrapped sushi that is popular here and in Japan, even though it can be somewhat difficult to eat neatly. *Ura-maki* are sometimes called *naruto-maki*. The reference is to a renowned tidal whirlpool at Naruto, in southern Japan. Cut to reveal a swirled center, with darks strips of nori set against the white of the rice, ura-maki are reminiscent of the whirlpools. An older term for inside-out sushi is *kawari sushi*. *Kawari* means a "change" or "something different from the usual." Another oddball term you might encounter is *mehari sushi*, or needle-eye sushi. It's just a way of describing any kind of maki sushi wrapped so the rice, or white of the eye, surrounds a dark pupil of ingredients.

Saiku Sushi

Saiku can mean "craftsmanship" or "handiwork," but not coincidentally, it can also be written with characters that mean "artifice," "faked," or "lovely to look at but not necessarily all that great to eat." Saiku sushi are elaborate forms of maki sushi, cleverly wrapped so that when they're cut, the pieces look like figures or even letters or fancy geometric patterns. The rice is often dyed to accentuate the artwork. They're fun and impressive, but taste-wise, they're usually nothing to write home about. A couple of classic saiku sushi the sushi tsu is likely to encounter are "coin roll" and "four seas roll." The coin roll, or *bunsen-maki*, is round, shaped like a feudal-era coin. The middle gu is typically cut square, with four curved bands of nori separating the rice, all bent in the direction of the center of the roll. The *shikai-maki* is similar, but it's typically square on the outside. The four curved bands of nori look like ocean waves coming from four directions (*shikai*), aimed at the island of ingredients in the middle. Saiku sushi is also known as *kazari sushi*, or decorative sushi.

Tomoe Sushi

This can be thought of as a form of saiku sushi. It's an arrangement of maki sushi rolled so it looks, in cross section, like the Taoist yin-yang symbol. A more complicated version has what looks like three comma shapes chasing one another around in a circle. This is a *mitama sushi*. Three jewels, or *mitama*, are, along with a sword and a mirror, the three sacred regalia of Shinto, and the triple-comma shape figures in a lot of family crests and other decorations.

Gunkan Sushi

Gunkan sushi is a common cousin of maki sushi. A pressed mound of rice is encircled with a vertical wrap of nori, leaving a hollow space on top to be filled with sea urchin or salmon roe or some other topping that would be too goopy to hold its shape without the nori enclosure. A *gunkan* is, in Japanese, a warship. Gunkan sushi are also called *funamori* (boat-shaped) sushi or *kakomi* (surrounded) sushi.

Konbu-maki

This sushi is pretty rare in this country, a pity since it offers a completely different taste. *Shiraita konbu* is a pale, yellowish-white species of kelp that's dried for eating. Sheets of it are used instead of nori to wrap sushi-meshi and other ingredients into maki sushi, after boiling them with water, rice vinegar, and sugar has softened them.

Konnyaku Sushi

This is an odd version of sushi popular mostly in Kyushu. Sushi-meshi and other ingredients are stuffed inside pouches of *konnyaku*. Konnyaku is a uniquely Japanese food. It comes from a plant called elephant's foot or devil's tongue, which is indigenous to Japan. The root is boiled down and the result, formed into slabs, is a gelatinous, rubbery substance that looks like grayish, slightly firm Silly Putty, and is even less appetizing in appearance. The taste of konnyaku isn't memorable. It is, like so many Japanese foods, eaten for the texture.

Hana Sushi

This means "flower sushi," but it almost always refers to maki sushi that's squeezed on one side to produce a teardrop shape.

When these are lined up side by side, they look like a branch of *fujiwara*, or wisteria leaves, so it's also known as *fujiwara sushi* or *fuji-no-hana sushi*.

Sasa-maki Sushi

Not uncommon in Japan, this is rare here. It's just sushi wrapped in *sasa*, aromatic bamboo leaves. The leaves aren't eaten. They're a container, peeled away before you dig in.

Shinoda Sushi

Shinoda sushi is a maki sushi wrapped with *abura-age*, or sheets of fried tofu, instead of nori. Supposedly, an itamae named Shinoda created this variation; it is sometimes called, for obvious reasons, abura-age maki sushi, but don't confuse it with inari sushi, explained on page 20.

Fukusa Sushi

A *fukusa* is a cloth folded over into an envelope shape to make a bag. *Fukusa sushi* is formed with a patty of rice in the center of an egg omelet that's then folded around it and tied off, usually with a strip of kanpyo. The rice may be seasoned with bits of cooked carrot, toasted nori, or any of the ingredients mentioned below in the section on inari sushi.

Chakin Sushi

Chakin are small cloth purses. *Chakin sushi* is made exactly like fukusa sushi, except the omelet is shaped into a pouch, drawn together at the mouth after it is filled with rice, then tied off with kanpyo, a strip of omelet, or the stem of an herb like *mitsuba*. Inari chakin sushi is the same, only with abura-age, or fried tofu, used as the "cloth."

Hamaguri Sushi

This clam-shaped sushi is made basically the same way as fukusa sushi or chakin sushi, but with the omelet folded over and tucked under so that it resembles a *hamaguri*, or common clam in its shell.

Date-maki Sushi

Date is a dated Japanese expression for a fop or dandy. All maki sushi was once called *date sushi* because they were considered the fanciest sushi of the cuisine. Today, the word refers specifically to maki sushi in which a thick egg omelet is used to wrap the rice and ingredients.

Inari Sushi

Inari, usually pictured as an old man with a pair of rice sacks and accompanied by a pair of foxes, is the god of rice in Japan. Because pockets of abura-age, or fried tofu, stuffed with sushi-meshi look like the rice bags carried by Inari, they're called *inari sushi*. They are also known as *age sushi* (*age* means "fried," referring to the tofu pouches), or *o-inari sushi* or *o-inaribukuro* (inari stuffed in a sack) or *kitsune* (fox) *sushi*.

Inari sushi, popular with Japanese children, makes a perfect snack or light lunch, but it isn't common in sushi-ya. You're most likely to encounter them in prepackaged lunch box–type sushi. Sushi-meshi for inari sushi can be plain or it can be mixed with slivered carrots or shiitake mushrooms, or sprinkled with black or white sesame seeds; any number of garnishes are used to add to the taste and appearance.

The sushi tsu prefers Kansai-style inari sushi, where the seasons dictate a series of garnishes mixed in with the sushi-meshi. In the spring, it is tiny chopped leaves of peppery *kinome* picked from *sansho*, or Japanese prickly ash. In summer, *shiso* leaves are diced and tossed into the rice. Ripened buds of sansho are added to inari sushi rice in the autumn; in winter, it's grated zest of tart, lemony *yuzu*, the Japanese citron. There may be other seasonal ingredients added to Kansai-style inari sushi: *benitade* (a spicy water pepper) or *tonburi* (the seeds from a species of cypress) in summer; *asanomi* (hemp seeds) in the fall.

CHIRASHI SUSHI
(Scattered Sushi)

hirashi sushi is a natural adaptation of mixing rice with whatever odds and ends are around the kitchen, common in Japanese home-style cooking. Perhaps because of this ordinary foundation, or maybe because chirashi sushi evolved outside the capital city and is thus more a dish of the bourgeois countryside, it has a pedestrian standing in the world of sushi. Whatever the reason, nigiri and chirashi sushi are respectively the Zsa Zsa and Eva Gabor of the sushi world. You know, Zsa Zsa had all the glamour, all the headlines in the gossip columns, all those great afternoons chatting with Mike Douglas on his show. But it was Eva who had the steady pay, who turned the role of the ditzy Hooterville hausfrau into a beloved TV icon. Eva *was* Lisa on *Green Acres*. The nigiri sushi of the *Edomae* tradition is what most people think of when they think of sushi. It has a lot of élan and connoisseurship that is decidedly more refined, or at least a whole lot cooler, than the chirashi style of presenting sushi. Even so, if you want a lot of sushi and don't want to spend a lot of money, and if you want to sample several kinds of toppings at your leisure without ordering each from the itamae, chirashi sushi is a good choice.

There are two varieties of chirashi sushi: Kansai and Kanto styles. Both are bowls or lacquerware boxes of sushi-meshi topped with ingredients and eaten with chopsticks. Both should have a ratio of two-thirds rice to one-third topping ingredients. Both styles of chirashi sushi use rice—or should, if they're being made properly—that has a little more vinegar and a little less sugar than is used in the sushi rice for nigiri sushi. Much beyond that, the differences between them become more apparent. *Kanto-fu*, or Kanto-style chirashi, is by far the most frequently served in sushi-ya in this country. If your order of chirashi sushi comes with a bed of sushi rice and a layer of toppings, you're eating it Kanto style, as it is made in Tokyo and its environs. The toppings (called gu in chirashi sushi and not tane as they are in nigiri sushi) are cut pretty much as they would be for nigiri sushi, with a few exceptions: Instead of a rectangle, the egg omelet might be cut on a slant, just for appearance's sake. Octopus in chirashi sushi is sliced smooth instead of with the wavy crinkle cut of a nigiri sushi tane, since it doesn't need that rougher surface to keep it from falling off the rice. Fresh Japanese cucumbers are often cut or carved in an array of patterns to decorate the dish. These are mainly aesthetic differences.

As far as what comes with this type of sushi, there isn't any legislation regulating it, but if *torigai* (cockles) and shrimp weren't included among the gu for chirashi sushi Kanto style, diners would react much the same way patrons at your local pub would if the cashews were gone from the nut dishes on the bar. They are just expected. In the United States, the cockles may or may not be there, but the shrimp is a standard. There is no set number of toppings that must be used, but traditionally, Kanto chirashi sushi has nine ingredients in it, not including the rice; the number has a fortuitous connotation about it. Whatever the composition, Tokyoites tend to view chirashi sushi as just another way of getting sushi rice and fresh fish and other such ingredients together. It is thought of as Edomae sushi in a bowl.

In Kyoto, Nara, and other places around the Kansai region, chirashi sushi is seen as a completely separate kind of meal from nigiri sushi. In Kansai-fu chirashi sushi, the rice is stirred in with the ingredients; it is more like what Westerners might think of as a rice salad (although the typical rice salad at, say, the Bloomington, Illinois, Second Baptist Church potluck social probably would not have chopped eel in it). Arguably, this method of preparation takes more skill than the Kanto version. That's because the key element to all chirashi sushi is the disposition of the rice. It may seem that a couple of fistfuls of sushi-meshi have been simply tossed into the bowl. Not so. Examine that rice carefully. You'll see it's been packed into the bowl just tightly enough to make a firm base, but not so firmly that it forms a solid mass. Rice placed in chirashi sushi too loosely, which tends to fall apart in ugly clumps, or too tightly, is the sign of an amateur maker. In Kansai chirashi, this procedure is even more difficult since the ingredients are mixed in with the rice itself. An itamae who can put together a bowl of Kansai-style chirashi sushi knows his business well.

Along with the differences in the way the rice and the gu are combined come other distinctions between the Kanto and Kansai styles. In Tokyo, a typical order of chirashi sushi can have nine or more toppings, as noted. That's because Kanto folks want plenty and don't want to be bored, and it's why Kanto chirashi sushi is a good buy when you want a variety. Kansai chirashi sushi is noticeably more limited in this regard. Four or five gu at most will be included, with the latter a kind of unofficial standard, which is why another name for scattered sushi from Kansai is *gomoku* sushi, or "five-ingredients sushi." There aren't any hard-and-fast rules as to what those five ingredients have to be. But just as cockles and shrimp are considered essential for real Kanto-style chirashi sushi, eel is something of a must in the Kansai kind. Another standard for Kansai chirashi sushi, and a quick way to distinguish it even at a glance from the Kanto version, is that *kinshi*, a *tamago* (egg) omelet that's been shredded into fine, thread-like slivers, is a frequent addition. Kanto uses the same kind of tamago as in nigiri sushi, the larger and thicker slabs of omelet.

In the Kansai climes, it's more a matter of appreciating the flavor and texture of the rice; the other stuff is mainly there to provide some contrast. Kansai-style chirashi sushi celebrates the rice and not what's with it. The same sorts of vegetarian additions as are found in chirashi sushi from the Kanto are in the Kansai version, such as marinated shiitake mushrooms, julienned carrots, and whole or chopped shiso leaves. But in a bowl of scattered sushi from Kansai are also some delicious tidbits that would be too subtle for Tokyo tastes. These include tiny, curled fresh *warabi* ferns in season, fragrant sprigs of kinome (prickly ash leaves), and spicy crumbles of benitade (water pepper). These savory snippets of Japanese greens and herbs add a unique zing to the meal.

Here are some variations on the theme of chirashi sushi:

Bara Sushi

Bara sushi is a term frequently used in the Kansai region, often as a synonym for chirashi sushi. *Bara*, or *bara-bara* in its more onomatopoeic form, means the same as chirashi—"scattered" or "random." The sushi tsu, though, should know that in Okayama Prefecture, in the far southern part of Honshu and right across from the island of Shikoku, bara sushi is a classic dish in which ingredients are woven into intricate patterns across the top of the rice. Okayama bara sushi looks like a mosaic. It is one of Japan's most luxurious dishes, available in its correct form only in the above-mentioned locations.

Mushi Sushi

"Steamed sushi" is another Kansai variety. The sushi-meshi and toppings are prepared in a bowl and placed in a *mushiki*, or steamer, for about 15 minutes just before serving. Since the steaming process would cook most raw fish, most *mushi sushi* is vegetarian and is sometimes made with kinshi, the slivered omelet just mentioned on the previous page. But sometimes it's made with eel that has already been cooked and will bear the steaming without any ill effect. Mushi sushi does not sound particularly appetizing; its appeal grew out of the long damp winters of Japan, when sushi sounded good but it was too cold to truly enjoy the temperature of chilled raw fish.

Tekone Sushi

This is definitely what's for dinner if you find yourself out at sea with a crew of Japanese fishermen hauling in a catch of bonito. *Tekone* is "hand-mixed" sushi, an impromptu presentation using bonito and whatever else is on board that day. Sushi rice is prepared and a bonito is filleted, then quickly marinated with fresh ginger juice. Those are the basics. Tekone sushi might have sesame seeds, shiso, pickled ginger, or other odds and ends thrown in, and then it's all hand stirred and served in a bowl with a side of nori. A few sushi places in Japan serve tekone sushi; most of them are near shores where bonito are landed. A dinner of tekone sushi has an outdoorsy feel to it, or at least an out-to-sea feel. Hungry fishermen created tekone sushi, serving up the catch of the day only a few moments after it had been hauled out of the deep. If you can get past the mental picture of a fisherman's bare fingers kneading through your meal, it's a marvelous dining experience for any sushi tsu.

Sake Sushi

Sake sushi has an even more colorful origination than tekone sushi. It comes from Kagoshima Prefecture. Kagoshima is at the southern tip of Japan's southernmost main island, Kyushu. Next stop south of Kagoshima, if you miss Okinawa, is the Philippines. Kagoshima was the southern frontier of old Japan. Its people lived hard and played harder. During the feudal period, one of them, a wealthy and extravagant *daimyo*, celebrated the cherry blossom season with a full-blown, stagger-into-the-gutter bout of debauched revelry. Most of the partygoers were too wasted to know their own names, never mind clean up after themselves, so it wasn't until a few days after the cherry-viewing bash that they'd recovered sufficiently to commence salvage operations. They found that the remains of their chirashi sushi had been soaked with spilled sake that had begun to ferment in the warm weather. In many places in the world, such a discovery would lead cleanup crews to suddenly get very busy elsewhere, in the hopes that they wouldn't have to tackle the mess. In Japan, it led to an inevitable question: what do you suppose that tastes like?

The answer was, not bad. Thus was born sake sushi. It's still made essentially the same way: Layers of fish or vegetables are piled in between layers of rice; the whole thing's drenched in sweet sake and allowed to ferment just slightly, then it's topped with shrimp and *kogayaki*. The latter is a pan-fried omelet made with eggs, grated mountain yams, and oboro fish flakes. It wouldn't be cherry blossom season in Kagoshima without sake sushi.

And before leaving the subject, there are a couple of other dishes that look like chirashi sushi, and they are identified by the suffixes *don* and *ju*. *Tekka-don* or *tekka-donburi* is as simple as a sushi-related meal can get. Chunks of the lowest grade of tuna, maguro, are arranged along with small squares of nori over a bowl of sushi-meshi. *Una-don* is the same preparation, only made with eel. These same two dishes might also be advertised as *tekka-ju* or *una-ju*. In some sushi-ya or other Japanese restaurants, the difference is that the "ju" versions will have just ordinary steamed rice while the "don" have sushi-meshi, but this isn't a universal categorization by any means, so if you're in the mood for this type of dish, you'll need to ask which kind of rice you're getting.

O saka's best-known contribution to the sushi party is the sumptuous *oshi sushi*, or pressed sushi. Oshi sushi's origins harken back to the early history of sushi, when fermented rice was used to preserve the fish pressed into it. Using wooden forms to compress and combine these ingredients allows for some intricate combinations of flavor and texture. Of the triumvirate of sushi—nigiri, chirashi, and oshi sushi—the last, Osaka's contribution, has the widest potential for creativity. There are several kinds:

Hako Sushi

"Box sushi" is formed with an *oshi-waku* (push-frame, a wooden rectangular mold) and is practically synonymous with oshi sushi. It's what most Japanese will think of if you mention sushi Osaka style. It's even called *Osaka sushi* sometimes, though some sushi tsu, particularly those from the Osaka region, insist there are actually two different kinds of *hako sushi*. The first is just called oshi sushi or hako sushi. The second is *battera sushi*. The distinction has to do with the construction. In hako sushi, sushi-meshi is packed into the mold lightly and whatever toppings are going to be used are put on top of the rice; then the top is pressed down to seal tane and rice together and the "sushi brick" is slid out. Hako sushi is almost always cut into squares or rectangles for serving. That's why a very early term for hako sushi is *kiri sushi*, or cut sushi.

Battera Sushi

Granted, the words "superpower" and "Portugal" are not often paired today, unless the subject is wine cork production. But in the 16th century, Portuguese shipping fleets dominated international trade, especially with the Japanese. The Portuguese arrived in Osaka around 1545 in galleons, or *bateira*. Even though this method of sushi preparation existed for hundreds of years before the Portuguese ships appeared on the scene, that's where battera sushi gets its name. The molds used for making it look like the Portuguese galleons.

The distinction between battera and hako sushi is that battera is made upside down. It begins with a layer of *baran* (aspidistra leaves), which, while inedible, act like a coating, which makes it easier to pop the sushi out of the mold. On top of the baran goes whatever fish or other tane are going to be in the sushi, then the rice. The mold is flipped and a whole "loaf" comes out, to be cut into squares for serving.

The standard fish used as a tane for battera sushi used to be *kohada*, or gizzard shad. By around 1900, mackerel had replaced shad as the most common ingredient, a substitution that continues today. Neither fish is exactly known for its delicate flavor. They're both strong and oily. That's why, for many Japanese, battera sushi conjures up a decidedly "fishy" image. If you get that reaction when talking about battera sushi, it means whoever you're talking to is thinking of the *saba*, or mackerel, used for a lot of battera-style sushi. *Saba sushi* is a synonym for this kind of battera sushi, though it literally means "mackerel sushi." It would not do, however, to think of battera sushi in such a limited way. A very popular battera sushi, for instance, is made from shrimp. In this case, the shrimp are boiled, then laid out in a radiating circle, in the bottom of a circular pan like the ones used to bake cakes, their tails touching at the center. The rice is added and pressed, with a layer of nori sometimes added, then the whole thing is flipped over and sliced like a pie. This is *ebi no marugata sushi*, or round shrimp sushi. One of the great classic oshi sushi dishes of Osaka is made with *tai*, or bream. Fillets of the fish are seasoned first with apricot juice, then wrapped in konbu kelp along with rice and pressed in a mold. This *tai no oshi sushi*, or *shime-dai no oshi sushi*, was reputedly a favorite of the imperial family back when they were calling the shots from Kyoto. Several restaurants in that city now claim to have been the original purveyors of the dish, or have the original recipe, or to be descendants of someone who was a really, really good friend of a dishwasher in the Imperial Palace, or some such. A variation is *kodai suzume sushi*. It is one of the most attractive presentations of any sushi: palm-sized triangles of rice with fillets of young bream, or kodai, pressed on top. The shape of this sushi resembles fat little sparrows perching, hence the name *suzume* (sparrow).

Battera sushi is available at grocery stores all over Japan. It is a perennially popular item for a quick dinner, often picked up by husbands on their way home from work. It has the added advantage of staying fresh for several days. A principal reason pressed sushi evolved in the Kansai region was that places like Kyoto and Nara were far inland. Oshi sushi made it possible to keep transported fish edible for longer periods than would otherwise be possible.

Finally, there is a bit of cultural frisson the sushi tsu will want to know about regarding the distinction between hand-formed Edomae, or nigiri sushi, and the pressed Osaka version. It has to do with the different societies in Osaka and Tokyo we mentioned earlier. Osaka's was a mercantile culture. The merchants ran the show there, more so than in any other part of Japan. We often think of Japan as being ruled by the military class, the warlord daimyo, the shogun, and all their sword-slinging samurai. That's not an unrealistic view of feudal Japan, but it isn't a complete one either. Farmers, since they fed the whole country, exerted tremendous influence. Tax revolts were frequent during some periods, and in nearly every revolt, throngs of ax- and rake-wielding farmers kicked the stuffing out of the professional warrior samurai class. Merchants too had a major role in the economy and culture. What separated these two groups from the samurai was that they learned to be more private in their work and in their pursuits of pleasure. They kept a low profile because they learned that was a good way to keep the head that was a big part of the profile. Make too public a spectacle of yourself enjoying things, and you could get whacked for being obstreperous, or just uppity, or just because you got noticed.

You can see the results of that behavior by comparing Edomae sushi with Osaka's pressed sushi. Edo—later Tokyo— produced sushi that almost seems to explode with color and vibrant patterns when it's arranged and presented. The sushi is a reflection of the freewheeling attitudes of the capital city, as well as an example of the cuisine of a military and political power that was large and in charge and didn't care who knew it. Meanwhile, in places like Osaka, the merchants were more private. That meant they were subtler. They preserved their fish and created and enjoyed their own forms of sushi and, for the most part, kept quiet about it. The fashionable displays of Edo-style sushi contrast with the quiet, subdued look of the sushi from Osaka. There's no value judgment to be made here. The reputation of the modern sushi tsu will not rest on preferring one over the other. It is simply worthwhile for you to be aware of such cultural distinctions in sushi and to appreciate the differences.

Other Pressed Sushi

Along with the rectangular or round shapes of hako sushi and battera sushi, pressed forms of sushi can be made into long bars. There are two kinds.

BO SUSHI ▼ This is best translated as "stick sushi." The character for *bo* means any kind of long stick or pole. *Bo sushi* is just sushi pressed into a long shape, like a candy bar. Any kind of topping that would do for any other form of oshi sushi is used; mackerel is a very common form of bo sushi. The length of the sushi is made by pressing it in a bamboo mat, as with maki sushi. It is then cut into bite-size pieces.

TAZUNA SUSHI ▼ This is the second form of bar sushi. There isn't anything different about it from bo sushi, except the toppings are laid on the rice at a slant. When two or more toppings are layered, the top looks like a barber's pole or a candy cane. The derivation of the word is interesting. *Tazuna* are reins on a horse's bridle. The samurai decorated their mount's reins with alternating colors of silk, thus producing that candy-cane look.

HA SUSHI ▼ This is a specialty of Nara, though it can be found all over Japan. It is a favorite *omiyage*, or travel gift, brought back to the folks who stayed behind. It should be sold in boxes with "My Friends Went to Nara and All I Got Was This Delicious Ha Sushi" printed on the top. *Ha sushi* is sushi made with a variety of toppings and sushi rice with a layer of leaves, typically persimmon, pressed in on the bottom or on top. Sometimes ha sushi is made like an upside-down cake, with the fish first, then the rice, then the leaves wrapping it all up. The leaves may also be cherry or some other, preferably nontoxic, plant leaves. They add a very faint acidity to the sushi-meshi, but mostly they're for looks. Ha sushi (leaf sushi) is attractive to many Japanese because of its rustic, countrified appearance, which evokes memories of the old home place, the little country village out of which their grandparents couldn't migrate fast enough.

TANE
(TOPPINGS)

The general word for topping is tane, and there are five more specific words to describe the toppings for nigiri sushi. These are terms you want to know.

The word "tane" means, literally, "materials." Whatever tops the rice in a serving of nigiri sushi is its tane, or *neta*. The words mean exactly the same thing and are the same characters, just reversed. Some sushi itamae say it one way; some the other. Here's a general rule: "Tane" is the most common pronunciation in and directly around Tokyo. That's the one used throughout this book. "Neta," if it's used at all, tends to be used by itamae from other parts of Japan. And "tane," remember, when it is combined with another word, usually becomes *-dane*. So, "The mere sight of sushi tends to make my boyfriend gag, but he finds the white meat fishes, or *shiromi-dane*, particularly repulsive."

There are five kinds of tane, the two most prevalent of which are *akami* and *shiromi*.

Akami

This means, literally, "red meat." *Akami-dane* are the toppings for nigiri sushi that are red or darkish in color. As you will see on page 142, in the section on tuna, akami has become synonymous with that fish. Some itamae may even assume you're talking about tuna if you mention akami. That's a loose and inaccurate usage, since akami can also describe bonito, but don't be a pedant about this. If the subject is akami, the fish in question is a tuna in nearly all cases.

Shiromi

Shiromi-dane are white-fleshed fish like bream, sea bass, and yellowtail.

Here's a metaphor to illustrate an important aspect of the differences between akami-dane and shiromi-dane: Season tickets to an NHL team may cost about the same or even be slightly more expensive than season tickets for the city's symphony. Even so, and while it might be difficult to describe to someone from another culture, two distinct images emerge if we describe the new neighbors as having either season tickets to hockey or season tickets to the symphony, right? The same goes for the distinction between akami-dane and shiromi-dane. Shiromi-dane are thought to be classier than akami, just as they were in the Edo period. One possible reason is that white-meat fish like flounder or bream or amberjack have a light, clean flavor, a delicateness that elevates them, in the estimation of Japanese sushi cognoscenti, to a different level. You don't have to agree. You just want to know the distinction exists.

So, in terms of fish, about one-third of all of them on or in your sushi are going to be red or white, akami-dane or shiromi-dane. We'll get to the other two-thirds in just a moment. What's vital for the sushi tsu, as always, is to know just a little bit more than this. You must learn a little something about these two basic classifications.

Akami and shiromi are fundamentally different in taste and texture because they are from different fish that have different needs for the particular muscles in question. The *aka* (red) of akami comes from the hemoglobin in the muscle tissue of fish living near the water's surface, fish that have to move a lot and for long distances. They're the sprinters and the cross-country runners of the sea. Their meat has a lot of hemoglobin in it to process oxygen more efficiently and more quickly during that fast traveling. A flounder, lolling around near the ocean bottom, doesn't need to travel around that much. Like your spouse's deadbeat cousin who shows up for meals every holiday, he's a grazer. Instead of quick bursts of speed to avoid those links above him on the food chain, he hides or makes himself inconspicuous (unlike the deadbeat cousin, who takes the sofa right in front of the TV after dinner). His meat—the flounder's, not the cousin's—is white. That's why akami and shiromi-dane taste different and have different textures.

Before leaving the subject, we ought to mention briefly the notion of just how fresh akami and shiromi ought to be. For the latter, freshness is always a primary consideration. All shiromi begin to degrade in texture and flavor as soon as they die. For some shiromi, this degradation is slower and less obvious in taste than in others. But in general, all of them must either be served very fresh or be frozen soon after their demise to be at their peak. Ideally, shiromi would be *ikijime*, eaten as quickly as they can be taken out of the water, butchered, and slapped on rice. However, the same cannot be said always of akami. The case in point of tuna is a good one. This being a book on sushi and not a medical textbook, I will not be overly graphic. The sushi tsu, however, understands that within hours of a fish shuffling off the mortal coil, it begins the process of firming up known as rigor mortis. It is caused by proteins jelling, which firms and stiffens the flesh. With a few exceptions, we recognize that when it occurs in say, people, pets, or sandwich bread, rigor mortis is a bad sign. In an akami like tuna, on the contrary, you actually want this process to set in quickly and to linger. That's because on a cellular level, rigor mortis works to soften fibers while simultaneously adding a denseness to the tissues of the meat, which makes it more palatable. The faster rigor mortis sets in, the better it is for the meat. That's why commercial fishermen go berserk after a big catch, getting it roughly butchered and into the refrigerated hold of the boat, and it is why, in *The Perfect Storm*, the biggest problem for the men on the *Andrea Gail* (other than that big wave) was when their ice-making machine crapped out. It is after rigor mortis is finished that another process sets in, one less desirable and known technically as "rotting." Getting freshly caught fish packed in ice and keeping it that way determines how long the fisherman can maintain rigor mortis in the catch. The size of the fish will have something to do with it as well.

An expert fisherman with the right equipment can keep a big tuna chilled for up to a week. All this time, the fish is aging. That's different from—see above—rotting, as you know if you like aged beef. Once the tuna or other akami is thawed is when the critical moment arrives. As quickly as you can eat it after this thawing, the better the taste and texture will be. This is eating it *nojime*.

So what would a hunk of tuna taste like if you had it moments after it had been landed? Some think it would be delicious, but most would find akami that fresh noticeably gamy or wild tasting. So, while gills-still-flapping freshness is a concern for the sushi connoisseur when considering the condition of shiromi-dane, don't become obsessive when evaluating akami's quality.

Now, let's move on to the other two-thirds of the tane in sushi.

Hikari-mono

Hikari-mono are "shining things." These are smallish fish, ranging in size from a few inches up to a couple of feet, that would, though it is possibly impolitic to make too much of it, be considered little more than bait among many fishermen. Gizzard shad, sardines, sea bream, mackerel, and a few others make up the hikari-mono category of tane. All are served with a little or a lot of their skin left on for taste, and most of them require some kind of brief preparation to bring out their full flavor. They are either soaked in or spritzed with rice vinegar or salted.

Nimono-dane

The *ni* of *nimono* means "boiled," or more precisely, "slow-simmered." A long, slow boil, often with an *oshibuta*, or weighted lid dropped directly on top, is a preferred method of cooking in the Japanese kitchen. It was adapted to some sushi-tane for several reasons: Some tane were more easily digestible after they'd been cooked for a while. Others had an odor that, while not indicative of any kind of spoilage, just wasn't all that appetizing. Finally, simmering some tane kept them edible for a longer period of time. Clams, abalone, squid, and several other tane were once prepared nimono style. Culinary trends along with superior methods of refrigeration have conspired, however, against this. Today the only nimono-tane you'll find in most sushi-ya are eel, mantis shrimp, and octopus. What makes nimono-dane is not just the boiling, though. It's the application of *nitsume* after the tane's been cooked.

Here's a quick primer on nitsume: You can bet that if one of the fast-food chains could figure out a way to mass produce a nitsume palatable enough to a sufficient demographic, we'd soon be seeing commercials for eel croissandwiches or something equally clever. Nitsume is sushi's special secret sauce, although Thousand Island dressing does not figure in it. Nitsume was originally a more complicated preparation that began with the proper broth, the essential ingredient. If an itamae were making nitsume for, say, clams, he would toss a couple dozen clams in a stockpot with lots of water and start boiling. He'd strain that broth off, then boil it again, and keep on reducing it until the broth was lip-smackin' strong and concentrated. He would then blend it with some seasonings, producing a unique nitsume to brush on the clam sushi that day. If it were eel nitsume, he'd start the broth with eel and reduce it the same way, and so on for any other nimono-dane. About 50 years ago, nitsume was simplified, and eel broth became the standard base. The other ingredients in nitsume are shoyu (Japanese soy sauce), sugar, mirin, and *shochu*, a kind of Japanese vodka.

A few itamae still mess around with other broths, as in the old days. They're few and far between in Japan, and finding one in the United States would be a dream come true for the sushi tsu. Most will rely on eel-broth nitsume, and that's acceptable. Less so are the itamae who use bottled nitsume. The prepackaged sauce is okay for lower-end and even middle-level sushi-ya. And even some well-trained itamae may swear by it and defend the practice, pooh-poohing any objections voiced. If they try to tell you it's as good as the made-from-scratch nitsume, though, they're either shining you on or they're not as expert as they should be. Nitsume correctly used in the sushi-ya has to be concocted in-house because, like sushi rice, it varies seasonally. Summertime nitsume has to be thicker than in wintertime because with warmer weather, a less viscous sauce will run off the tane. Nitsume, by the way, is also called *nikiri* and *tare*. The first is an accurate synonym. The latter is misleading. In Japanese, tare is a sauce used for dipping grilled or stewed dishes.

Hokanomono

This isn't a true category. It's just "other things." There isn't any specific term to cover these tane. If something on or in your sushi isn't red, white, shiny, or boiled, assume it's in the "other" category. Several kinds of fish eggs, sea urchin, and shrimp—and generally all crustaceans and mollusks—fall into this category.

GU
(FILLINGS)

The slice of tuna atop your nigiri sushi is a tane, as we've already established above. Stick a tane inside a sushi roll or in a bowl of chirashi sushi and it transforms. It's called gu. All ingredients in rolled sushi other than the rice, whether animal or vegetable, are gu. The word's etymology is interesting. The old Chinese pictograph for "gu" is a pair of hands holding a kettle. It originally meant having the means to do something, and in China, there wasn't a much more important something than having a meal. So the kettle in hand symbolized the ability to accomplish a task, the means to get the job done. Gu has evolved to mean a "tool" or an "implement" or an "ability" and, with the exception of its use in the sushi-ya, gu is rarely used as a word on its own; it's almost always a suffix or prefix. If you get tired of calling yourself a sushi tsu, you can use the word *gugansha*, a person (*sha*) who has a discerning eye (*gan*) for the important gu. A complete rendition of possible gu used for sushi would read something like a toxicology report on Johnny Cash. You could get through it, but it would be so long you would need a nap or two before you finished. Technically, all of the toppings in Part II can be used as gu, though tradition has always indicated that some, like most shellfish, are not. There are some other gu, though, that tend to be specialties of wrapped and scattered sushi. The most frequently encountered of these follow.

DENBU See *oboro*.

GOBO is an edible burdock, a plant that is a noxious weed in most of the rest of the world, although the Chinese use it as a medicinal herb. On the grocery shelf it looks like a long, skinny, and dirty horseradish root. Prepared properly, the brown skin is scrubbed off rather than peeled, to avoid losing a lot of the taste that is just under the surface. It is used in many ways in Japanese cuisine. In the sushi-ya, gobo will almost always be encountered as *yamagobo*, boiled with chile peppers until it is bright orange and quite spicy. It ends up looking like small, skinny carrots. Yamagobo is found in maki sushi or chirashi sushi. The average sushi enthusiast, eating yamagobo, munches it down as he would a carrot, starting at the tip and working his way back. The sushi tsu knows, however, that these are best enjoyed the opposite way, starting at the fat, tender top, whether it's served on the side or in rolls.

GOMA are dried sesame seeds. They are sprinkled atop maki sushi, especially if eel is an ingredient, and also stuffed into inari sushi. *Kuro-goma*, the black seeds, have a more pronounced flavor than *shiro-goma*, or white seeds. The white seeds exude more oil.

HASU is lotus root, also called *renkon*. The Japanese were lotus eaters a long time before the Greeks of legend, though unlike the Greeks, they weren't ingesting them to get mellow and have a good excuse for blowing off work the next day. Lotus tubers are cut into sections that reveal a pattern of holes inside. Dull white in color, the tubers look like big snowflakes. They are preserved in a light vinegar solution and have a crunchiness that feels like a jicama or raw potato. Hasu are used in chirashi sushi and some other kinds of mixed sushi, like sake sushi.

HORENSO, or spinach, is more popular as an ingredient in maki sushi in the United States than it is in Japan. Leaves are parboiled and are a common element as a gu in futomaki. Horenso is also seen in *o-hitashi*, a common salad or side dish made of steamed or boiled spinach leaves soused with shoyu, mirin, dashi, or other ingredients. An order of o-hitashi goes well with most sushi, and it is a good way to get your greens in.

KAIWARE are the young shoots of either daikon or *kabu*, a Japanese turnip. They look something like large alfalfa spouts and have a very faint touch of heat. Kaiware are a standard ingredient in temaki sushi. You will also find them scattered on top of some nigiri sushi.

KANPYO are the dark brown things that look like shoelaces in maki sushi. They begin as a gourd called *yugao* or *fukube*. Along with strawberries and mushrooms, these soccer ball–size round green gourds are grown in Tochigi Prefecture, north of Tokyo. It is a mountainous, forested region, kind of like the American Northwest, only without spotted owls or Starbucks (as of this writing). If you took a drive through Tochigi in the late summer, you'd see, in front of dozens and dozens of homes all over the prefecture, hundreds of racks of drying gourd that have been peeled and sliced into strips. It is a cottage industry there. After drying, the kanpyo is packaged and sent to wholesalers, more than 200 tons of it a year. Some of it ends up in your maki sushi after it has been boiled to soften, then boiled again with sugar, shoyu, and other ingredients. Kanpyo is what adds the sweetness you should taste in a lot of futo-maki.

KOGAYAKI is a type of omelet used only for sake sushi. Don't be surprised if itamae or sushi tsu from places other than the Kagoshima region in Kyushu have never heard of it. Eggs are beaten and mixed with crumbled tofu, grated yam, and ground fish paste to make a firmer omelet than the standard tamago-yaki. This omelet is then sliced and added to the scattered form of sake sushi.

KONBU is giant kelp. In dried forms, it is used for flavoring soups and many other Japanese dishes. In the sushi-ya, konbu appears mostly as *oboro konbu*. Sheets of dried konbu are soaked in vinegar and then sliced into thin, nearly transparent ribbons that are used in place of nori strips, sometimes to tie ingredients on top of nigiri sushi, and sometimes to hold wrapped sushi together. Don't confuse oboro konbu with *tororo konbu*, which might show up in the sushi-ya as a side dish, by the way. Tororo konbu is soaked the same way, but it is cut into tiny threads and is eaten with rice.

KOYADOFU is freeze-dried tofu. Not content just to prepare and eat tofu in about 103,000 different ways, the Japanese, 10 minutes after refrigerators were introduced there, started experimenting with freezing the stuff. They found that tofu that was frozen, then dried, then reconstituted with water had a spongy consistency, kind of like angel food cake. That's koyadofu. Koyadofu soaks up other flavors like, well, like a sponge. The grayish, cube-shaped stuff in the middle of your maki sushi is almost certainly either koyadofu or a chunk of sponge. If it doesn't taste of dishwater, assume it's the former.

KYURI, often sold in Asian grocery stores as "Japanese cucumbers," have their botanical roots in the Himalayas, from where they spread westward. They're grown all over Asia. The Japanese hybrid version is small by our cuke standards and covered with warty bumps. The skin is thicker than our native cucumbers and the seeds are much smaller and less numerous. The texture of the flesh is firmer and crisper. Skinned and sliced into long strips, kyuri is the gu for kappa-maki. Outside Japan, other kinds of cucumbers may be used in lesser-quality sushi-ya, but the good ones will always have real Japanese kyuri.

MITSUBA is a kind of wild chervil. Mitsuba means literally "three leaves," the Japanese equivalent of its name in the west, "trefoil." Mitsuba is used as an ingredient in maki sushi. The flavor is subtle, to say the least. Since it is not grown commercially outside Japan, it has to be imported, and only a better-grade sushi-ya will use it. In terms of its taste, think of a cross between parsley and celery.

NATTO is something you'll either love or loathe. If you love it, you will be hard-pressed to explain why. If you hate it, you can go on for hours about it. Fresh soybeans are soaked, then steamed along with rice straw and bacteria that induces fermentation. The result is a mucilaginous slime that coats the beans. Pick up some natto with a pair of chopsticks, and sticky threads will hang down in a most unattractive way. Natto used to be sold door-to-door, and many older Japanese from Tokyo and other cities in the Kanto region have fond memories of the natto salesman calling out his presence, moving through the neighborhood in the mornings.

If you eat in sushi-ya or Japanese restaurants of any kind long enough to interact with the staff or other regular diners, sooner or later you will be confronted with the question, "Do you like natto?" Many Japanese are convinced that no foreigner could possibly eat the stuff. Even if you don't like it, it is fun to watch their reaction if you tell them you do. Some Japanese cannot stand it either. Until about 50 years ago, there were a lot more people in Manhattan eating grits than there were people in the Kansai region eating natto. People in Kyoto and Osaka held it in contempt. If the subject comes up and they touch fingers to their nose, they are making the inevitable comparison to *hanashiru*, a slang term for what comes out of that orifice during a bad head cold.

Natto appears in temaki sushi as part of the other ingredients and stars as the featured gu in natto-maki. You may also find it in misoshiru. Natto is supposed to lower your blood pressure and it is full of vitamin B_{12}, calcium, and potassium. If the thought of eating it causes your blood pressure to rise and you don't care if it is packed with enough vitamins and minerals to sustain the entire crew of a shuttle mission to Mars, here's how to play your status as a sushi tsu and not lose face: When you are asked if you'd like to try natto in sushi, ask what kind of natto. It comes three ways: *otsubu* (with large beans), *kotsubu* (small beans), and *hikiwari* (chopped beans). No sushi-ya is going to have all three varieties, and you can claim to be such an aficionado of whatever kind it doesn't have that you cannot bear soiling your palate with the kind it does have. But at least try natto first and see if you are a fan.

NINJIN is carrot. Japan has both the Bugs Bunny–fare Western style and two native species. One of them, the *kintoki*, is about the same size as our carrots, though more of a dark orange. The other is the *takinogawa*, which is the same dark shade of orange as the kintoki, but longer and thinner. Assume the carrots in your maki sushi are the ordinary American kind, but don't hesitate to take a bite and thoughtfully muse aloud and within earshot of the itamae, "Why, this ninjin is so good, I'd swear it was a kintoki."

OBORO is interesting. Take some cheap, white-fleshed fish, like cod. Boil it. Shred it to the consistency of sawdust. Dry it. Season it. Add a little flavoring and dye it either white or pink, or both. You have oboro. You wonder why, and that is a reasonable question. Oboro, also called *denbu*, is eaten for its texture as well as for its looks. The taste is mild, very similar to *surimi*, or processed fish cake, which is often sold in the United States as "imitation crabmeat" or "seafood salad." Oboro is the flaky pink or white stuff found in a lot of maki sushi.

SAYAENDO are snow peas, which are slivered to decorate chirashi sushi. You may also hear them called *kinusaya*.

SHIITAKE are the best known of Japanese mushrooms. They grow on logs of *shii*, a species of chestnut. The mushrooms are commercially raised in the more forested regions of Japan, especially around Oita and Miyazaki Prefectures. Shiitake are picked when they are at the stage growers call *donko*, with the caps still slightly curled under. Then they are dried and will keep nearly as long as Keith Richards has. Shiitake are reconstituted with water, then boiled in a mixture of shoyu, sugar, and mirin. They are sliced and put in maki sushi or, if they are small, left whole and added to chirashi sushi. When they are whole, they might have a star shape cut in the top of the mushroom, to look nicer. That is *hoshi* (star) shiitake.

SHIRASU are young, dried sardines. They are crunchy and salty and are most commonly eaten along with sake as a snack. But they are also sometimes added to temaki sushi. *Chirimenjako* is the term used for them in western Japan.

SHISO goes by a couple of names in English, "beefsteak" and "perilla." It is botanically a member of the mint family. There are two kinds of this plant, red and green. It is the saw-toothed leaves of green shiso, or *aojiso*, that adorn chirashi sushi, and may be used with nigiri sushi as well. The leaves aren't just decorative; they are very aromatic, a cross between sweet basil and mint, and they're meant to be eaten. Shiso is also called *oba* in some parts of Japan.

TAKENOKO are young bamboo shoots. Bamboo is a grass. It is a hell of a large grass, but a grass nonetheless. It starts growing in central Japan in March and reaches maturity in just over a month, so there isn't a lot of time to get the young shoots harvested. Takenoko is used in maki sushi and some kinds of scattered sushi, and is always seasoned first by boiling it in shoyu, mirin, sugar, and some kind of stock.

TAKUAN is pickled *daikon*. Takuan Soho was the flakiest Buddhist monk of 17th-century Japan. If you know anything of the eccentric Buddhist clergy of that period, then you know that was no small feat. He was the youngest abbot ever appointed to head the most famous Zen temple in Japan, Kyoto's Daitoku-ji, then he left after less than a week in office. He taught tea ceremony and Zen to the emperor and knew several of the major political figures of his day. He wandered all over the country and gained numerous disciples, and irritated them all when he refused to give any of them an official transmission of mastery. He also refused to write a traditional deathbed poem, instead tracing with his finger in the air the character for "dream" and leaving it up to the rest of us to decide whether he meant he was just waking up from a long one or was looking forward to one even longer. His grave is decorated with a big stone daikon because he is credited with creating the pickled daikon, named after him.

To make takuan, daikon are pulled up and left hanging to dry for a few weeks, then packed in salt and *nuka*, a rice bran. (That is why takuan are known generically as *nuka-zuke*, or nuka pickles.) Takuan is the result. Everyone who has eaten in a Japanese restaurant is familiar with takuan. It is usually served in slices as a *tsukemono*, or pickled vegetable side dish. Takuan is also the sole ingredient in oshinko-maki. Today, takuan is often dyed with the same coloring used for painting the double no-passing stripes on highways. Actually, that's not true, though it seems that way because the yellow of takuan sold in packages is excessively bright. Good itamae use takuan with little or no artificial dye, so if you are in a place that serves these apparently pale versions of takuan, don't complain, and instead compliment this discerning choice.

NORI

After months of negotiation, whining, and threats, you've finally dragged your friend into a Japanese restaurant, sedated him with a sake-tini or a plum wine kamikaze. And you were actually able to broach the concept of eating raw fish without worrying he's going to Code Red into a full-blown, six-cylinder, nine-cats-in-a-bag conniption fit. You made the soothing point that some sushi, like, say, for instance, these tasty maki sushi here, stuffed with perfectly normal cucumbers, don't even have anything of the uncooked seafaring sort at all in them. And then your friend asks, "Gee, what's that green stuffed wrapped around it?"

"That's, um, nori." Like that's going to forestall the inevitable.

"Yeah, but what is it in English?"

"Uh, seaweed."

And then your friend *does* have the conniption.

There is no way around it. If you are eating sushi for very long at all, chances are you are going to ingest some seaweed, though why this should discomfit so many is hard to understand. Seaweed in one processed form or another figures in everything from French vanilla ice cream to the gel capsules for Prozac. In the cuisine of sushi, it appears most prominently in nori, usually translated as *laver*, a Latin term for "water plant." Nori is only nominally a seaweed. More accurately, it comes from one of a few different kinds of algae. Making this distinction would probably not have assuaged your friend; algae is not a quantitatively more appetizing notion as a foodstuff than seaweed. It's also unlikely he would have been placated by the knowledge that nori has more calcium and iron than almost any dairy product.

Nori is such a near-indispensable element of the Japanese diet that it is hard to believe it wasn't always so. It isn't just used to make sushi in Japanese cuisine. Nori strips the dimensions of a business card are eaten along with rice for breakfast; nori crumbled into flakes is sprinkled on rice for lunch; it is rolled around balls of rice for dinner. It can be roasted or seasoned with salt or teriyaki sauce. Various forms of seaweed have been eaten in Japan for at least the past 1,500 years. Until the late 17th century, however, nori was reserved for the wealthiest classes.

Nori doesn't grow naturally in those flat sheets, as you may have guessed. Instead, it collects in little dark green Vandyke beards on rocks or other objects ranging in depth from the tideline to about 25 feet below the surface of the oceans all around Japan. Collecting it from the sea was difficult and even a little dangerous until the 17th century Tokugawa era, when the shogun Tokugawa Ieyasu decided he wanted fresh fish served to him on a daily basis. He assigned the fishermen of Shinagawa, a town at the mouth of the Sumida River on the southeast edge of what is now Tokyo, the task of providing the fish. The fishermen built weirs to keep a steady fish supply on hand. Before long, they noticed the wooden struts of the weirs were sporting lush bushes of algae, tasty algae of the sort that had previously been harvested only in the wild. Thus was born nori aquaculture, which made this tasty treat more affordable.

Today the algae that go into nori are grown in much the same way, on underwater frames in several places in seaside Japan. They are also farmed in Korea. Of the 20 species of norilike seaweed, only two are harvested to make the sheets you see and eat in the sushi-ya. The growing season goes from about November through March. In the spring, the algae are scraped off and washed, then dried, roasted to concentrate the flavor, and finally pressed into sheets.

Kept sealed in plastic, the thin, flat, notebook-size sheets of nori have a lifespan longer than Katharine Hepburn's. It keeps similarly well if, once a package has been opened, the uneaten remainders are kept in flat tin boxes in the refrigerator. Leave them out on the counter overnight unprotected, however, and they go stale, limp, and gummy faster than a rerun episode of an '80s sitcom. They are so desiccated in the preparation process that they act like a sponge, happily sucking up any humidity in the air.

Some nori is sold pregrilled. If not, it must be held over a heat source like a stovetop for a few moments. Skip this step—even an average itamae would have to be deranged to do so, because it is fundamental to sushi making—and the nori is tough and nearly tasteless.

Along coastlines in some regions of Japan, the algae for nori are still collected from the wild. Harvesters wait for the tides to go out, and then, timing their approaches with the waves, they scamper back and forth across rock beaches to pick bits of algae where they are exposed. There are better ways to make a living. Still, the occupation persists, as much out of the nostalgia for the old Japan it evokes as for the superiority of the resultant product. This *isonori* (beach nori) is dried on racks and pressed into sheets by hand. It is expensive, rarely seen outside Japan, and used there mostly as an omiyage, a gift brought to the folks back home when you've been traveling in an area where isonori is made.

Much like an Andy Warhol print, commercially produced sheets of nori have two sides. Unlike the Warhol, it is possible to reliably distinguish one from the other. There is a dull side and a shiny one. Look on the dull side and you can see indentations made by the racks where the nori was dried. It is that side where the rice and ingredients for wrapped sushi go; the shiny side faces out.

Color is a reliable indicator of the quality of nori the sushi-ya is using. With the ruthlessness of a South Miami coke dealer, unscrupulous nori processors may cut their product with lesser varieties of algae that haven't as much flavor. To hide the deception, they dye it. If the nori is a dark, uniform black or purple, it has probably been adulterated with pigments. It won't kill you, of course. It just doesn't taste like good, top-of-the-line nori. There are three kinds of nori you will encounter in the sushi-ya. All go under the name of *Asakusa nori*. Asakusa has been a neighborhood in Japan's capital since not long after Tokyo was first built, and it has always been home to all the major nori wholesalers. Japanese nori used by all but the cheapest sushi-ya comes from one of three locations; they differ from one another a little in taste and, more noticeably, in color.

Tokyo Bay, in Chiba Prefecture, close to where nori was originally farmed, still supplies a hefty percentage of Japanese nori. Though pollution there drastically reduced the crop for decades, more recent and massive reclamation projects have restored many areas of the bay, and nori farmers there have increased their harvests substantially. Chiba nori, a bright emerald green flecked with jade, has a subtle tang of salt.

In Hyogo Prefecture, the bay that joins the Japan Sea and Seto Inland Sea around the city of Kobe produces a nori that is thicker and darker than the Chiba product. Hyogo nori is the strongest tasting of the three. Some sushi tsu complain it has a mineral flavor that interferes with the rice and other ingredients when it is used to make maki sushi. Others wax poetic about it, insisting that Hyogo nori's "taste of the sea" is a perfect accompaniment to wrapped sushi with fish in it. Itamae with less training or experience often prefer Hyogo nori because it is comparatively thicker and stronger than other nori and therefore easier to work with.

In Saga Prefecture, a nori is manufactured from very delicate leaves of the algae that are indigenous to the Ariake Sea there. Saga nori is glossy and is colored a rich mossy green, mottled with flecks of black. Wide fluctuations in tides allow the algae daily exposure to sunlight, which imparts flavor and a unique consistency. This nori is fragile, with a lacy look when held up to the light, a texture almost like cellophane, and an aroma praised as "sweet" by its fans.

If you go nori shopping, you might see packages labeled *tezukuri nori* or *maki sushi nori*. This is mostly advertising hype. Aside from being cut to different dimensions that may make the sheets easier to handle, they are the same as any other kind of nori sold for sushi.

PART II

Fish and Other Toppings

An A-to-Z Guide

ork chops are out. So far, at least, Twinkies may safely be excluded from the list. Overall, though, it would almost be easier to list edibles that haven't been used in or on sushi than to completely catalog those that have. Even if one confines the list to seafood, it's a lot. If its mailing address is the ocean and it can be grabbed, hooked, netted, plucked, or speared, chances are it has been paired in some way with rice for use as a tane or gu in sushi.

What follows, then, is not a full rendering of the ingredients featured or found in various forms of sushi. It is reasonably comprehensive, covering almost all those the sushi tsu is likely to encounter outside Japan. There are lots of fish and shellfish used for sushi in Japan that never make it onto the sushi-ya menus in the States, or do so only rarely. I've included some of these because the dedicated sushi snob may have an opportunity to sample them someday and needs to be prepared. And because even if you don't ever eat, say, young bream, you ought to know about it and as many other tane and gu as possible. Longing for the difficult to obtain is a spectacularly enjoyable aspect of snobbery, sushi or otherwise.

The ingredients are listed alphabetically, using Romanized English versions of their Japanese names, since that's how you are most likely to see them translated on a menu.

AJI 🐟 HORSE MACKEREL

Take hair, for example. Women's hair. In Japan. During the Heian era, women wore it long and straight, pulled back, all the way down to their hips. Later on, the bouffant coiffures of the sort we associate with the geisha came into vogue, in part because they showed off the nape of a woman's neck. Want an obscure word in Japanese to add to your vocabulary? Try *tabo*. It means the bundle of hair at the nape of a woman's neck. When a kimono is worn properly, it's *nuki-emon*, with the back of the collar loose and low. To the discerning eye of the kimono expert, the tabo should look like it's just resting on that part of the collar. Anyway, the point is that fashions change in Japan just as they do elsewhere. That goes for sushi as well. We've already laid to rest the myth that sushi as we eat it today has some eons-old history in Japan. It's fairly modern in terms of Japanese cuisine. Furthermore, many of the ingredients we might consider essential to it are even more modern. Some tane—most, in fact—have come into culinary fashion only since the end of World War II. But a few others that were once popular have faded. *Aji*, or horse mackerel, is one such tane.

The characters for "aji" are written with a combination of "fish" and "three" because the season for aji begins in March, the third month. In English, the big, horse-like eyes probably account for the "horse" part of "horse mackerel"; the "mackerel" half of the name is nonsense. Aji aren't mackerel. They are in the same big family as pompano and jacks and trevally. Because of their tendency to gather in large schools, another term for aji is "scad." In Japan, two types of aji figure in sushi. Yellow aji, or *ki-aji*, so called because of a pale, lemony hue along its back, swims in bays. Black aji, or *kuro-aji*, keeps to deeper, open-ocean waters. The latter is much easier to harvest but it is less flavorful and consequently less desirable as a tane. The yellow aji is also called *ma-aji* (horse aji), and in western

Japan, sometimes "little" or *ko-aji*. Most aji have a protruding lower lip that makes them look perpetually *monkutare*, as the Japanese would say: "pouting."

Back in the old days, aji was to kisu (see page 129) as Budweiser is to Rolling Rock. Kisu was considered "high-class"; aji was for the common folk who were pinching their yen. Kisu is still as classy as an ad in the back of *The New Yorker*, while aji's reputation in sushi has settled even further into the proletarian, sometimes regarded as so common that it isn't even offered on sushi-ya menus outside Japan. That's unfortunate for the snob who, of course, wants to experience as wide a range as possible in sushi, even the tane equivalent of cheese macaroni. If you bring up a desire to try aji among Japanese sushi enthusiasts, they may look at you the same way you would look at a Japanese who comes to the United States and professes a desire to sit down at a restaurant specializing in tuna casserole. That said, Mom's tuna casserole with the potato chip crust has a niche in the hearts of many an epicure, and in Japan, in spite of its bourgeois status, there are legions of sushi tsu with a tender regard for this ordinary fish.

Although aji are found in temperate waters around the world, if you have the fish in a sushi-ya here, it almost certainly was caught and frozen in Japan. (To be more specific, it's harvested most heavily in the waters of western Japan from March to May, and in eastern seas from June through the middle part of the summer.) They grow to a little more than a foot long, but for sushi, much younger, smaller aji are used, so that each whole fillet can be used as a tane. Aside from its big, Betty Boop eyes, it is a ridge of rough, spiky scales running along its centerline that distinguishes the otherwise pedestrian aji in appearance. In the slang of Japanese cuisine, these scales are *zen-go* (front to back, since they seem to be laid in the opposite direction from the rest of the scales). They have a prickly feel a lot like shark skin and they have to be scraped off completely, usually with the back edge of a knife blade, during the cleaning process. As with other hikari-tane, the aji's skin is left on. When the fillets are soaked in vinegar, the itamae lays them back-to-back so the flesh is exposed to the solution as much as possible.

≋ **By Any Other Name:** Other regional names for this fish in Japan include *mure-aji*, *seki-aji*, and *katsu-aji*. *Tenzen-aji* is a colloquial expression used by some fishermen. *Tenzen* or *ten-no-shite* means "nonchalant." It's a reference to the fish's wide-eyed expression, which seems to say, "Who, me?" In English, aji is also known as "saurel."

≋ **Watch For:** Aji is now increasingly served completely raw, without any of the customary vinegar baths of hikari-tane. A standard presentation for it this way, *aji-tataki*, is to coarsely chop the fillets, then heap them and serve them gunkan style, topped with a dab of grated ginger and a sprinkle of finely diced chives. *Tataki* means "to hit into pieces." Note, though, that when you see the word in reference to *bonito* (*katsuo*), it doesn't mean the same thing. *Katsuo-tataki* is thicker cuts of bonito just flash-seared so the inside is still raw. Some Japanese restaurants serve beef or tuna this way as well.

≋ **Ask the Itamae:** When it's served as a tane for nigiri sushi, aji is usually served with the same grated ginger and finely chopped green onions or chives as in aji-tataki, but ask the itamae if he'll pour you a little saucer of citrusy *ponzu* with your order. Ponzu is a citrus juice used for flavoring lots of Japanese foods. Just touch the tane with that before you eat it. Ponzu's citrusy smack complements the taste of the fish, which can otherwise charitably be called bland.

≋ **Trivia:** "Aji" is a synonym for "taste," so there are lots of puns in Japanese restaurant conversations involving the name of this fish and tastes of all kinds, or lack thereof.

AKAGAI ⟿ RED CLAM

With a round dark brown or black shell about the same circumference as a cocktail glass, *akagai* roam the sandy bottoms of most of the coastal waters of Japan. The greatest concentrations of them are centered at the mouths of rivers emptying into the sea. "Roam" might be an ambitious verb. Japanese fisheries researchers have discovered that the average free-range akagai rambles in foraging during its lifetime over territory about the size of a billiard table. Such inclinations make collecting akagai a less-than-strenuous undertaking. Once in hand, though, the red clam (*aka*, "red"; *kai* or *gai*, "clam") proves a tough customer to crack. Forget about prying it open like an oyster. Its shell has to be cracked or carefully split at just the right spot, the adductor muscle slit before the clam can be opened, and the meat extracted.

The flesh of the akagai explains the name. For much of the year, it's a healthy, bright reddish, baby-tongue pink. The color comes from the hemoglobin in the clam's primitive circulatory system. Its texture has a rubbery crunchiness that makes it the most popular of all shellfish for sushi in Japan. In the United States, akagai has to be imported frozen. We just don't have an equivalent among our many mollusks. That doesn't factor against ordering akagai when the opportunity presents itself. The clam meat doesn't lose much at all in the way of taste and texture during the deep freeze or the trip. What does matter is the season in which akagai is harvested. This shellfish has a much more definite and noticeable change in taste, depending on when it is taken, than do most of its bivalve relatives. Think of your holiday drinking season, which commences about Columbus Day and culminates on St. Patrick's Day, as the prime time for akagai. Sushi tsu use the term *hon-akagai* or "true akagai" to describe it during this period. The hue of the meat deepens to a vibrant peach during the winter.

That's when it is at its peak flavor. *Shiro-akagai*, or "white akagai," is the description used for summer's red clams, a thin and pallid version by comparison, the flavor markedly poorer. If you had a handy akagai color chart at your disposal, a wallet-sized card, say, it would show dramatic changes in the color of the meat between summer and winter. Lacking that, you just need a lot of exposure to akagai to see the difference. That is not an easy task, since this tane is not readily available in Western sushi-ya. If it appears on the menu, it's a must try.

Akagai meat comes out of the shell looking like a biology experiment gone very, very wrong. It's an ugly sight best left to the professionals. The itamae uses the end of his knife to snip and clip to produce a tane that resembles, depending on your particular mental state, either the pointed leaves of an iris blossom or a Rorschach inkblot of slugs mating. Either way, even if you're a sushi snob, it won't be among the most attractive of tane. The itamae also scores the akagai to make it easier to chew and to help hold the meat on the rice. As for the leftover scraps, do you think they're discarded? Please. This is a cuisine that's found a way to use fermented fish entrails. (They're called *shiokara*, a favorite snack to go along with sake.) The scraps from akagai aren't going anywhere except on somebody's plate. Know enough to order *hashira* or himo, and that somebody could be you. The hashira, or pillar, since that's what it looks like, is the clam's adductor muscle, the one that keeps the shell closed tightly. The "strings" of flesh that attach the clam to its shell are the himo. Both find use as tane, the latter braided roughly into a rectangle; both are considered the best parts of the akagai.

≋ **By Any Other Name:** Akagai is also known as ark shell or cockle.

≋ **Ask the Itamae:** In sushi-ya before World War II, akagai was customarily served after it had been thoroughly rinsed in rice vinegar. The odor of fresh akagai was thought to be a bit strong. Today, about half the sushi-ya in Japan still bathe akagai, and the other half prefer it just as it comes from the shell. If akagai is available, be sure to ask if it's had the vinegar treatment or is being presented strictly in the raw, so that you'll know exactly what you're tasting.

≋ **Watch For:** Even among shellfish, which are notoriously perishable, akagai can start breeding bacteria very quickly after being harvested, rendering the meat more virulent than Tijuana ditch water in just a matter of a few hours. The temptation to order akagai when you see it listed on the menu is strong and as I said, you should try it, *providing* you know the reputation of the sushi-ya to be sterling. On the positive side, few but the best sushi places are likely to have akagai on their menu, and those places are likely to be scrupulous in observing a keen sense of freshness and sanitation to keep you safe and satisfied. Also be aware that akagai, as mentioned above, has a famous texture among sushi tsu. "Crunchy" would be a neutral way to describe it. "Crunchy," though, can run the textural gamut from a crisp, slithery slice of fresh summer cucumber all the way to the sensation of biting into a hunk of chicken bone cartilage. Akagai's crunchiness definitely leans toward the latter. You are forewarned.

≋ **Should Have Been Expected, Vulgar, Sexist Genitalia Reference Trivia:** The color and shape of akagai flesh cause the name to be used as common Japanese slang for a mature woman's vulva.

ANAGO ⤳ CONGER EEL

Before Westernization, Japan used a method for counting years, months, and days based on a zodiacal rotation of 12 animals. It so happened that one summer on the Day of the Ox, in the mid-1800s, the naturalist and renowned calligrapher Harada Genai was in the mood for eel. Harada's gastronomic yearning would possibly have slithered through the storm drain of history except that the owner of his favorite eelery needed a signboard and name for the newly opened place. He prevailed upon Harada to write a name in his distinctive hand. Harada thought for a moment, then wrote the characters for "Today is the Day of the Ox" on the shop sign.

The likely truth, that Harada was just hungry and whipped out the first words that came to mind, was less appealing to the patrons than the notion there must be something significant about the words of this sign. Before long, customers were lining up around the block on every Day of the Ox.

It's an interesting tale for you to relate when the subject of eel comes up, which happens, admittedly, more often among sushi aficionados than in ordinary circles, where eel discussions are perhaps less frequent. Note that there are two different kinds of eel in Japan: Harada's sign was written for a restaurant specializing in unagi, the freshwater eel, which is eaten in all kinds of dishes, usually grilled. *Anago* (conger eel), its saltwater cousin, is the variety used for sushi in Japan, and it should be found at better sushi-ya elsewhere. In the United States, unagi is often substituted, which we'll get back to in a minute.

Anago grow to be about three feet long, and slimier than a South Side Chicago ward boss. While it makes them imperfect pets for cuddling, the slime does allow them to survive for periods out of water, when they're hustling across the countryside looking for their spawning grounds. (*Hanashi ga anago*, to "talk like an eel," is a dated though evocative expression to describe someone who never gets to the point in a conversation.) Eels are also palindromic. Point this out to your sushi-eating buds and one will certainly correct you, noting that "eel" is not the same spelled backward or forward. Correct *them*, since this word refers to the eel's ability to swim backward as readily as it goes forward. The skill is important to the sushi tsu, because it means that almost the entirety of the anago's body is muscular and thus fair game for sushi tane.

To put it mildly, live anago destined for sushi depart the station in a gruesome fashion. A spike goes through their heads into a chopping block. Still wriggling, they're eviscerated. I mention this because there's a neat bit of trivia attached. In the Kansai region and in much of the rest of Japan, eels are gutted with a slit all along their bellies. In Tokyo, though, they're always cleaned from the dorsal side. The reason: The concentration of samurai in the old capital of Edo (Tokyo) were understandably cool on the idea of anything being cut through the belly, what with the quaint tradition of *hara-kiri* being so prevalent. In deference, cooks there went the dorsal-side route. Oh, and one other note of equally macabre proportions: The rear of the kitchen in an eel restaurant is supposed to be one of the spookiest places around, because of the "eel music" that can be heard there. Eel music happens when business is good and eels are being filleted one after another, their heads and attached spines tossed into a bucket out back. The nearly skeletal eels continue to writhe against each other and the bucket for a while, making a whispery, slithery, *gasa-goso, gasa-goso* "music."

Gutted and cleaned, anago is chopped into manageable pieces and boiled with nitsume sauce. Once upon a time, all this would have been done in the sushi-ya, and it might be done occasionally today. Chances are, though, that the eel will be prepared up to this point at a factory, then frozen. So the old sushi admonition that anago could be ordered to get a sense of the skill of the itamae, given that each of them would have different methods of preparing the nitsume, isn't very reliable anymore.

While anago are farmed commercially, freshwater unagi are much easier to raise that way, so they're cheaper, which is one reason they will often show up in sushi-ya outside Japan. You'll taste the difference. (You'll also notice a difference in American-bred eels; the taste is not as rich.) Unagi have more fat in them, which explains why they grill so nicely. Anago for sushi are meatier, the flavor a little more pronounced, and they tend to be larger. The Inland Sea around Miyajima, an island in Hiroshima Bay, is supposed to have the tastiest anago. Another "supposed to" commonly believed by Japanese gourmets is that you can tell a wild anago from a farm-raised one by the yellow racing stripe all along the ventral side of the eel. Not so. Both kinds may have the same yellow. Sushi itamae who still prepare their own look for *gin-anago* (silver eels) with lines of white spots along the flanks.

Of course, your order of anago arrives slathered in nitsume. Here's how to tell if the itamae is a good one: If your order was made from the top half of the eel (thicker and wider), it should be skin side up. The lower piece (it tapers toward the tail) should be served skin side down.

≋ **Trivia:** Anago have more than 100 times the vitamin A of any other fish.

≋ **More Interesting Trivia:** Anago and unagi are never supposed to be eaten along with *umeboshi*, pickled plums. This is part of *tabeawase*, a compendium of folk beliefs about which foods belong together and which don't. Another tabeawase taboo is tempura and watermelon.

≋ **Possibly Less Interesting but Definitely More Fun Trivia:** Both anago and unagi are favorite foods for combating the dissipations of summer's heat. They're supposed to provide energy during that time of year when, not coincidentally, they're caught in abundance. They are also believed to jump-start a sputtering sex drive in males. So Japanese wives will serve eel for dinner as a little hint that the action on the futon has been less than electrifying of late. Ordering anago sushi might elicit some ribald comments from the itamae, and if everyone speaking Japanese around you is snickering, that probably explains why.

AOYAGI 〜 TROUGH-SHELL CLAM

B *aka* (idiot) is the best known of Japanese epithets outside Japan. That's a pity, since there are better ones, like *sukan-tako*, "an unlikable octopus." Or there's *deba-game*, "a bucktoothed turtle," which for some reason is what Japanese Peeping Toms are called. Or there's *doko no uma no hone da ka waranai otoko*, "a horse bones from who-knows-where person," which serves as an imaginative though prolix description of a person whose past is questionable. Written with part of the characters for "horse" (*ba*) and "deer" (*ka*), "baka" derives, according to legend, from an especially stupid court noble. Looking out over a pasture near his mansion, he supposedly wasn't smart enough to tell the former from the latter. Wherever it came from, the word "baka" has a low-class connotation. Gangsters and truck drivers might use it, but teachers and nurses wouldn't. That's why the *bakagai*, "the idiot shell," is more politely known in the sushi-ya and most other places as *aoyagi*.

The original name may have come about because this shiny, bright yellow bivalve looks very much like the more common, thick-shelled hamaguri clam, but, unlike the latter, which is sturdy, the aoyagi's shell crushes easily. So it "fools" you. Another explanation is that the "foot" of the clam, its meat, lolls out of the shell like the tongue of a drooling idiot. The more genteel name, aoyagi, comes from Aoyagi-mura, an old seaside village north of Tokyo in Chiba Prefecture, where these clams reside in abundance.

Aoyagi is only so-so as a sushi tane. In its favor, the meat comes in a big piece that makes a satisfying mouthful. The flavor, though, is probably nothing you'll want to tell the kids about. In addition to its very ordinary taste, however, the aoyagi is beset with more warning signs and potential dangers than a stretch of Pacific Coast highway during heavy fog. While it can be eaten raw, many itamae will serve aoyagi only after it's been parboiled. That's because when raw it can be crawling with *Enteritis vibrios*, a pestilent bacteria that can turn your intestinal tract inside out and back again. Boil it too long, however, and it smells really bad, inside-a-Dumpster-in-midsummer bad. Oh, and the mantle and some of the viscera are also mildly poisonous and must be completely cut away before serving, to prevent the possibility of an after-dinner retch-a-thon.

If this extravagant endorsement of aoyagi leaves you with the impression that the idiot-shell clam is beneath your esteem unless your idea of fun includes a date with the stomach pump at the ER, think again. The best part of the aoyagi isn't the meat; it's the adductor muscle. Or muscles, since there are two. The larger is the *oboshi* (big hat); the smaller is the *koboshi* (small hat), or, as it's better known in the Osaka area because of its pink color, *baraboshi* (rose hat). The flavor of these is exquisite—distinctly sweet and firm. Both are succulent and juicy, with just enough resistance in their texture for a satisfying chewiness. These little pink knobs are typically served gunkan style, atop shari that's been wrapped in nori.

≋ **Watch For:** Sushi lore provides a standard of measurement for judging the freshness of the aoyagi's adductor muscles. They should feel like and respond as a stimulated nipple. It's a putatively sexist analogy, true. Even so, the aoyagi's *boshi* being too hard and resistant are a near-sure sign they've gone bad. The itamae will almost certainly check for any spoilage with this very perishable tane. Even so, it's a trick you ought to know.

≋ **Ask the Itamae:** Sushi-ya in the West sometimes substitute very small bay scallops, or the adductor muscle of the larger sea scallop, for aoyagi boshi. This isn't a deception meant to cheat. Scallops are almost as expensive as the aoyagi and they're an excellent tane in their own right. They are also more readily available outside Japan than are aoyagi. Still, you should be sure of what you're served if you want to develop the sushi snob's taste for the real thing. So ask, as politely as possible, if this is actually aoyagi or *hotate-gai* (scallop). In the West and in Japan, the boshi of the *shiofuki*, or wedge-shaped surf clam, are also occasionally substituted for aoyagi boshi. Here the taste is clearly inferior and there can be no excuse for the switch. Also be aware that you'll hear the term *kaibashira* as a generic one to describe these tasty muscles in any bivalve. You'll have to ask specifically what kind of kai, or clam, it is.

AWABI ⇨ ABALONE

National Geographic magazine issues of the 1930s and '40s provided the West with some of the first widely circulated views of Japan. For about half of the readership, the most memorable of those views wasn't Mt. Fuji or Kyoto temples or cherry blossoms. It was the nubile, young, bare-chested *ama* diving for *awabi*—abalone. Superior lung power and an efficacious distribution of insulating body fat, along with remarkable courage, qualified women for this dangerous job. For hours at a time, day after day, they dived, stripped to the waist, more than 100 feet down in chilly ocean waters, prying abalone loose from rocks. When they resurfaced, they were so depleted of oxygen that their inhalations came as long, soft whistles audible for considerable distances over the water. In a survey, readers of one Japanese newspaper ranked the ama's whistle as "the most unmistakable sound of the True Japan."

Neoprene wetsuits spelled a truly lamentable end to the aspirations of many a young male tourist bent on examining this quaint aspect of Japanese tradition. Technological advances aside, it's still frightfully difficult, dangerous work. Awabi thrive several hundred feet below the surface. Once down among them, the diver has to be careful, since abalone are fragile. Unlike nearly every other shelled creature consumed by the sushi enthusiast, bivalves all, abalone are single-shelled uni-valves. (*Awabi no kata-omoi* is an old-fashioned way to describe a one-sided love.) Think of them as oceangoing snails, only bigger, ranging in size from the palm of your hand to nearly big enough to serve as a hubcap for a sports car. And they are as tenacious as a personal-injury-suit lawyer with a fat retainer. Awabi are forcibly scraped from rocks with smooth iron pry bars. If they're cut at all during the process, they bleed to death by the time they're brought up because they lack the ability to clot. Though abalone farming has made harvesting easier, awabi, because of both its deliciousness and the difficulty of procuring it, remains one of the more expensive sushi tane.

Four kinds of awabi are eaten in Japan: *Megai* (red abalone) has the softest flesh; it is steamed or boiled and goes in a vari-ety of dishes besides sushi. *Madaka-awabi* is a little firmer. Its brown-skinned meat is luscious, with a chewable texture that makes it a favorite for sushi tsu, but it's found in only a few places in Japan and doesn't travel much to other parts of that country, never mind outside it. Although before World War II all awabi for sushi was steamed or boiled, *kuro-awabi* (black awabi) and *Ezo-awabi* were the two species firm enough to be eaten raw, as they are today. Kuro-awabi is the second-best choice of readily available abalone in Japan for sushi. The sur-face of the flesh is a mottled blue-black; the meat is a cloudy gray. The Audi of awabi-dom is the Ezo, named after an old word for the prefecture of Hokkaido, where it is most com-mon. Sushi tsu in the United States eat one of eight species: black, white, red, green, pink, threaded, flat, and pinto—all firm enough for sushi, and all taken off the Pacific Coast. The most commonly served used to be the largest, the red abalone. Experts disagree, but our red abalone is either the same species as the Japanese megai or a very close cousin. Depleted stocks of red abalone mean that some others might appear in sushi-ya here; there isn't enough difference in taste to fuss about. Note, though, that Western aquaculture is experimenting enthusiastically with abalone. Ezo-awabi are cultivated successfully in Iceland and are shipped to the United States now, though they are still much more expensive than other varieties.

No matter what the species, all awabi has to be alive and feisty or flash-frozen Popsicle-hard for use as a tane. Alive, the abalone is force-fed a dose of salt that causes the meat to pucker and tighten so that it can be cut away from the shell and sliced diagonally for nigiri sushi. It's still quite tough, though, and has to be thoroughly pounded with a mallet before it goes on as a tane. If it is frozen, awabi chunks are placed in a steamer going full blast until they are thawed, and then they are steamed again, more slowly, with salt water.

Awabi is a quintessential early summer food; for many Japanese, the word alone calls to mind the month of May or June, the way watermelon conjures idyllic scenes of midsummer in the West. Most other shellfish are at the peak of flavor in the winter, which is another reason the abalone is such a beloved summer tane. In the old days, it was nearly always a nimono-dane (see page 35), served with a brushing of nitsume on top. It is rare to find that now; awabi is almost always served raw to appreciate the flavor more fully. You'll notice at better-quality sushi-ya a series of scored slashes along the length of the meat, making the awabi look like a measuring ruler. The cuts are, as you might guess, to make the meat easier to chew.

≋ **Watch For:** *Mushi-awabi* is abalone that has been steamed, then cooked long and slow in a broth. If awabi is used as a tane after it's been steamed this way, it will be served with nitsume sauce. It is quite rare, but this is a taste of Edo-period Edomae sushi.

≋ **Ask the Itamae:** There's a flat disk of muscle on top of the meat that holds the abalone to its shell. If the awabi is large enough, the itamae can slice this piece off horizontally for you, then cut it into nigiri-size servings. It's the best part of the awabi. If you're kind to your regular itamae, he might suggest you try it if he's got any on hand. Also, male awabi have more flavor than female, so much so that some top-flight sushi-ya in Japan won't even offer awabi as a tane unless it's from a male. Lord knows the sushi tsu would never object to that sort of epicurism, but you'll also want to be sure you're not being had. Here's how to tell: The itamae—or anyone—has to have the entire abalone body on hand to sex it. He looks for the large, crescent-shaped gonads. They are cream colored in Ken abalone; gray or green in Barbies. If a sushi-ya advertises male awabi, it had better be able to *habeas* the *corpus*.

≋ **Trivia:** Dried, flattened awabi, called *noshi-awabi*, has a long history in Japan. Samurai on campaigns originally carried it since it was portable, light, and protein rich. Later, it became a ritual gift offered on special occasions. A fake version of noshi-awabi is still a gift presented at weddings. Shinto priests continue to make and use the real stuff in their religious ceremonies.

AYU SWEETFISH

Imagine a Japanese version of the TV game show *Jeopardy!*, and you are a contestant. (Japanese game-show audiences adore having foreigners on; they are as endlessly fascinated with the novelty of non-Japanese being able to speak the language as we would be in having a chimp on Sunday-morning TV doing political analysis.) If the answer for Final Jeopardy is "It's the only freshwater fish eaten as sushi," then for heaven's sake, bet every last yen you've got. Scrawl out your answer for Alex-san to read. "What is the *ayu*?"

They resemble a trout, but ayu are actually members of the salmon family. They are that part of the salmon family, however, that has, in a sense, left the fold to join a commune in northern California. That is to say, ayu are vegetarians. While other salmon pursue predatory and carnivorous lifestyles, gobbling the flesh of anything alive that will fit in their mouths, ayu are content to swim about freshwater streams, placidly nibbling algae. Probably because of their earth-friendly diets, the flesh of the ayu is decidedly sweet and very lean, making it a favorite of fly fishermen whose ecosensitive interpretation of living simply so that others may simply live does not preclude the occasional morning spent snagging an ayu and then cooking and eating it. Life has certain ironies. A vegetarian fish ending as a main course is among them.

Japanese fishermen are just as nutty as their counterparts anywhere else in the world, and ayu are a particular passion for them. One method of angling, *tomoturi*, or friend fishing, used during the spring spawning season, is clever and takes advantage of the male ayu's propensity for defending his territory against interloping ayu by biting them on their bellies. The fisherman uses a light nylon silhouette of an ayu with a hook in its middle. Casting into a male's turf, he waits for the ayu to attack, then reels it in. In addition to their value as a sport fish, ayu are now commercially farmed, and they're available frozen in the United States. Ayu appear sometimes in more authentic Japanese restaurants here, usually grilled whole. They are used in sushi in two ways, one obscure, the other really obscure.

Ayu sugata sushi is made with the whole sweetfish, which is stuffed with sushi rice. Ayu grow to be about a foot and a half long; but for this method the itamae uses a much smaller one, about the size of a tube of toothpaste. The fish is scaled and gutted, then the insides are lightly sprinkled with a combination of rice vinegar and sugar. The cavity is stuffed with sushi rice and then cut into nigiri-sized pieces and arranged with the head and tail in place, so that it looks as if the fish is still intact. This kind of sushi rice–stuffed ayu is popular at sushi-ya in mountain resorts or hot springs. You may find an itamae who can make it; if you're in Japan and staying at one of the many mountain resorts there, be sure to look for it. And as long as you've gone that far, you might as well go down to Gifu Prefecture and make your ayu sushi experience complete by watching the *ukai*.

You've probably seen photographs of ukai, the tradition of fishing with trained cormorants. These trained birds have rings placed around their necks so they can dive and capture fish but not swallow them. The fish is most often ayu. Cormorant fishermen who work on the Nagara River in Gifu Prefecture, in southwest Japan, have a special sushi they make with ayu each fall. It's a nama-nare sushi. The whole ayu is packed in sushi rice and allowed to ferment. There are several different recipes used locally; the best are considered those that call for the fermentation process to continue through December, so the dish can be enjoyed as part of the New Year's celebration. Ayu *nama-nare sushi* is a step back in time in the evolution of sushi making (remember the chapter on sushi's history?) when the rice was used as a way of fermenting and preserving fish. If your travels take you to Gifu, this form of ancient sushi is a must for any sushi tsu, needless to say.

Ayu is farmed commercially. If you need to know the difference between wild and domestic, according to rural Japanese, look at the chin. Wild ayu are supposed to have long, sharp chins, the better to help them root out algae from the riverbed. Farm-raised ayu are alleged to have soft, rounded chins.

≋ **By Any Other Name:** An old, poetic name for ayu is *kogyo*, or spring fish. *Waka-ayu*, or young sweetfish, is a seasonal phrase used in haiku and other Japanese poetry to evoke late spring. Anglers in England have fished for centuries for a close relative of the ayu, which they call a crake.

≋ **Watch For:** You will, as noted, be more likely to see ayu served grilled in a Japanese restaurant than any other way. Again, it is grilled whole, as in innards and all. The balance between its sweet, succulent flesh and the bitterness of the viscera makes grilled ayu a classic of Japanese cookery. The very best version of ayu prepared in this fashion is *ochiayu*, a female sweetfish taken later in the season and ripe with eggs.

≋ Trivia: Two characters are used to write *ayu*. One is "fish"; the other is *uranai*, or fortune-telling. The story is that the semi-mythical early 3rd-century Empress Jingu caught an ayu as she was contemplating an invasion of Korea. She interpreted this as a sign the attack would be successful, which it was.

EBI 🐟 SHRIMP

Frozen fish sticks aside, shrimp were probably your first taste of seafood as a child. So it is that *ebi* may be the most nostalgic of sushi ingredients for the sushi snob. It does not come as you may have initially tried it, fried with a side of ketchupy cocktail sauce—though we might be giving some of those avant-garde itamae some ideas.

The shrimp clan is larger than the Osmond family. There are almost 2,000 varieties sporting merrily in nearly every ocean on earth: cold-water shrimp, warm-water shrimp, deep-water shrimp, freshwater shrimp, and sand shrimp. There are pink, brown, and white shrimp, and just to make it more inter-esting, "whites" can actually look green, blue, or gray. There are tiger, Malaysian, Bay, Mexican, and Chinese shrimp. Don't have a conniption over this. Sushi-ya in Japan almost always serve warm-water whites or pinks, which are called in Japanese *kuruma-ebi*, or wheel shrimp, since they curl into that shape when they're cooked. With a couple of exceptions we'll get to in a moment, your order of ebi will be whites or pinks or a species in taste and texture very close to the Japanese version, for a good reason: The Japanese get the bulk of their sushi shrimp from the same place we do: the waters off Mexico.

A preliminary word of warning: If you notice an iodine taste at all in your order of ebi sushi, you've got (a) the cheapest brown shrimp commercially harvested, not suitable for sushi at all, and (b) to find a better class of sushi-ya right away. Even very fresh brown shrimp have a distinct smack of iodine in flavor; pinks may have a nearly undetectable trace; whites will have none at all. Here's an impressive trick if the situation ever presents itself: Pinch the last section of the shrimp's shell between your fingernails. If you can feel a groove, it's a pink or brown. A lack of grooviness means it's a white, though please, let us not succumb to stereotypes here.

Interestingly, itamae rarely talk about the various species of shrimp. Instead, the nomenclature of the sushi-ya regarding shrimp is all about size. Ebi that are about two inches minus the heads are *sai-maki* or *ko-maki*. *Chu-maki* are around four inches; *maki* go up to about six inches. Though not really up to NBA standards, the giants of the shrimp world are *o-guruma ebi*, up to 10 inches long. Very similar monster-size species include what are colloquially called *taisho-ebi* (probably named after the Japanese word for "general" or "commander") and the darker *kurai-ebi* most abundant in Korean waters. All these usually meet their doom deep-fried in tempura batter. It's the smallest-size shrimp that usually appear in sushi-ya in Japan and abroad.

Life being what it is, and given the preponderance of fabulously annoying people in it, there will be among the sushi tsu's cohort the odd person who goes into a dither about the whole raw fish nonsense when you mention sushi. Ebi are a good way to at least keep people like this from making unpleasant gagging noises if they accompany you for a sushi dinner, since you can reassure them that not all sushi is raw fish. This perfectly normal shrimp sushi, for instance, is cooked thoroughly, you can tell them. Ebi is also a good choice for these types because the shape is recognizably shrimp-like, and this will be comforting.

The Japanese are fond of the idea of the shrimp being presented looking something like it did in nature. That's the main reason the tail is left on when it's served as sushi tane. Not incidentally, these tails, plucked or snipped off between the teeth and left scattered on a plate, are a certain mark of the sushi amateur. The snob *always* eats the tail. (Though not the whole tail; there's a little spiky part in the center section that's deftly clipped off by the itamae before the shrimp is served. Since it looks like a spear point, in the slang of the kitchen this process is called *yari-kake*, or snipping the spear, a necessary task to avoid customers getting the sharp point caught in their throats or cutting their mouths.) Shrimp tails provide a little dose of calcium, and their crunchiness adds a nice contrasting texture. Occasionally, the ebi head will be presented stacked alongside the nigiri sushi. Sometimes, it will have been lightly battered and deep-fried as tempura. Dip it in a dish of shoyu and touch it to a lump of *wasabi* and it's a spicy, crunchy treat as well.

Odori, or dancing, shrimp, is how raw ebi are described. It's not entirely accurate. Real *odori ebi*, gulped still wriggling when they go down, isn't part of the sushi repertoire at all, but rather a specialty of *ikesu*, restaurants featuring seafood served so superbly fresh it is still moving around. But the experience of fresh shrimp, still alive when they're beheaded and shelled—sometimes just the tail is dipped into boiling water for an artistic effect—and served as a nigiri tane, is one every sushi tsu should try.

Spring through summer used to be the best time to eat ebi, just as they were spawning. Winter sent them so deep into the ocean they were beyond the reach of the fisherman's net. Now shrimp are farmed commercially and readily available throughout the year. You will notice, though, that they taste best in the autumn. Ebi are used almost exclusively on top of nigiri sushi or chirashi sushi. If they're among the ingredients in the latter, they are the first one many Japanese sushi tsu will eat. It's a nod at the ebi's symbolic association with venerable age (see "Trivia" on page 74).

≋ **Other Shrimp:** In his travels, the sushi tsu must be eternally on the lookout for *ama-ebi*, or sweet shrimp. These diminutive delicacies are mostly from off the coast of Maine and are one of the most recent additions to sushi-dane. Wild ama-ebi harvesting has also started off Hawaii's privately owned island, Niihau. The average size is about three inches. Wild ama-ebi are at their peak from December through March. If they appear on a sushi menu, and they do, increasingly, rest assured you will be paying top dollar. Ama-ebi are shelled, and then kept individually wrapped in plastic in the sushi-ya's counter case. If you have a chance to see them before preparation, look for the sharp little point on the third joint of the shell, a positive indicator of the species. They are always served completely raw and have, as the name suggests, a slightly sweet flavor. It is a sushi tradition that the head of the ama-ebi, rich in fat, is always fried, with or without tempura batter, and served with an order of this shrimp. It is meant to be eaten, eyes, antennae, shell, and all.

Far rarer is the *botan-ebi*, the "peony shrimp" that's found only in northern Japan, up around Hokkaido. Like the ama-ebi, the peony shrimp is never boiled, and it's so delicate that it sits in its shell until needed. The itamae will peel it and use it only for nigiri sushi. Customarily, it is slit from the backside instead of the belly. You're only going to find this preparation up north, in the far Tohoku region or around Hokkaido, where it is harvested. Shirobotan-ebi and Toyama-ebi are a couple of other names for closely related botan-ebi species. If you are up that way, just incidentally, you'll also hear of hokkoaka-ebi and shiba-ebi, a couple of regional favorites that may occasionally pop up in sushi-ya in this country, though I wouldn't hold my breath. Just remember the names, especially if you run into an itamae from that region, because you'll have something to talk about. That is, he can tell you how great they taste and you can tell him how envious you are that he's had them and you haven't.

≡ **Watch For:** The average itamae prepares ebi by boiling the shrimp after skewering it to keep it from curling. Then he splits it on the belly side and presses it out like an opened book. This is noshi style, or flattened. The ebi then goes into the case along with the other ingredients. If you're in a place where a handful of ebi are sitting in a bamboo strainer, order up. It's an indication that the itamae has taken the additional steps that add a lot of flavor. After the initial boiling, he's refrigerated the split shrimp until an order comes in. Then he's taken them out to give them a quick bath in a solution of rice vinegar, sugar, and mirin. They drain in the basket and then go into or on top of the sushi, and the difference in taste is noticeable.

An attractive twist on ebi is to take a pair of small ones, flatten them, then slit their tails lengthwise and lace them together to achieve a bow-tie effect in a tane for nigiri sushi. It's called *saimaki-ebi*.

≡ **Trivia:** In poetic Japanese, ebi are the "old men of the ocean." It's because they have that hunched-over look and those long whiskery antennae, giving them a distinctly aged appearance. Hence *ebigoshi* is the word meaning "bent with age." You'll see ebi used prominently in various decorations for the Japanese New Year as a symbol of longevity.

HAMACHI 🐟 YELLOWTAIL

Think of that part of the Yellow Brick Road that leads the Oz-bound Dorothy to the edge of a forbidding, haunted forest. Trees are festooned with dire warnings to "Turn back now!" Even the most serious and dedicated sushi tsu at times feels he's reached that part of the freeway on his long journey to expertise. Such a moment is upon us when we attempt to chart the way through the jungle of terms for the yellowtail. There's nothing to be done about it but to step into those magic slippers before gathering our determination and starting out.

Here's the story. Yellowtail, about three feet long when they're adults, also do business in English as "jacks" and "ambers" and, just to make it complete, "amberjacks." There are at least half a dozen species worldwide that are known as yellowtail, and they are called a lot of other things as well, which is the problem. It's the pantload of names given to yellowtail in Japanese alone, many of them in common use in the sushi-ya, that so confuses matters. Consider: An adult yellowtail in Japanese is a *buri*, a word rarely heard in the sushi circles, since by the time the fish is three feet long, he's simply too fatty for good sushi. *Warasa* and *mejiro* are also names for mature yellowtail. *Wakashi*, used around Tokyo, and *tsubasu*, in the Kansai region, both describe adolescent yellowtail. Yellowtail in piscine prepubescence are called *fukunagai* in northern regions of Japan, *kozokura* in the south, and *kando* on the far western side of Japan that faces the Asian mainland. All these are still too old to be suitable for sushi. *Mojako* (about six inches) are too small. Sushi-size yellowtail are anywhere from one to two and a half feet or so in length. In Tokyo, they've long been called *inada*. Around Osaka, they're *hamachi*. Usually, dialectal terms from other areas of Japan are replaced with the Tokyo standard, but in the case of yellowtail the process has been reversed. Although some itamae insist that "hamachi" refers to any sushi-size yellowtail that's been farm-raised and "buri" is the term for the same fish caught in the wild, in general, "hamachi" refers to yellowtail in the sushi world.

Keeping up? Okay. There are still a couple of tricky curves ahead. Although "yellowtail" is by far the most common term in English for this fish, and it is the one preferred by sport fishermen, the U.S. Food and Drug Administration officially classifies this fish as an amberjack. Legally, however, it and its various closely related pals can be sold in the United States as "yellowtail," "bonito," "jackfish," "kingfish," "coronado," "king amberjack," or "madregal," and doubtless under a few other *noms de plume*.

Before wading through a list of aliases longer than the one maintained by the Witness Protection Program, I probably should have addressed a more pertinent issue: is the damned thing worth eating? Yes. Pink and firm textured, hamachi's meat is often compared to the richer cuts of tuna. Some sushi tsu prefer it to tuna. Commercially raised hamachi are reared on a specific diet that accentuates the buttery lushness of their flesh. As with some other shiromi-dane, scales are removed with a thin knife, leaving just a sliver of skin on the meat, which adds another dimension to the flavor. Hamachi is the oiliest by far of all the white-meat tane. Consequently, the sushi beginner might find the taste a little overpowering. There is no doubt, though, that hamachi is among the best of the shiromi-dane in reputation. It's a favorite with Japanese sushi snobs as well as their Western counterparts.

Even with all the closely related species we have, the best hamachi still comes from Japan. It is frozen, of course, and not every sushi-ya will have it. If you've had good Japanese hamachi and try the other fishes that sometimes are sold under that name, you will quickly learn to taste the difference. Most sushi tsu agree that non-Japanese hamachi is leaner, without the same richness or complexity of flavor. Imported hamachi fillets are now marketed in the United States. If they've been properly frozen, they're suitable for sushi, but look for that silvery membrane of skin along one side of the fillet to be sure the fish has been cut correctly.

Though it isn't part of sushi cuisine, to not mention hamachi *kama* would be nearly criminal. "Kama" is a slang expression that refers to the jaw or "collar" of the yellowtail. Lightly salted and stuck under a broiler, the bony kama is loaded with meat. Good Japanese restaurants will have it, though it may not be on the menu. Ask for it by name if you're in the mood for an exquisitely simple meal.

Like tuna, hamachi is filleted into blocks, or *cho*. Although, as with tuna, the fattier sections are those cut closest to the belly, there isn't as much variation in the taste of the meat among various hamachi cho as there is with tuna. There are, though, a couple of exceptions. The first is those pieces for sushi tane taken at the upper cho of the yellowtail. They have a streak of very dark meat, the *chiai*, or bloodline, very much like the one found in tuna. Unlike the chiai in tuna, though, the hamachi chiai is edible. A lot of sushi tsu relish it. Others, and those without much sushi experience, find it entirely too "fishy" and strong. If you want to try it, you'll have to ask the itamae specifically, since he's not going to serve it to those who don't appreciate the singular taste. Note that when hamachi is very fresh, this streak is very bright red. It soon turns a darkish brown as the meat of the fish begins to show some unwanted signs of age.

The second special cut of hamachi is the *suna-zuri*, which means "sand rubbing." It's the bottom of the belly that, again like a tuna's, is full of fat and creamy, rich flavor, with a discernible smoky undertaste. The suna-zuri portions of a yellowtail are not going to be handed out by the itamae to the average casual customer. Either marry one of his children or spend some time courting him to get in on this exquisite tidbit.

Hamachi's season is midwinter. The colder the season, the better hamachi tastes, goes a Japanese saying. There's even a term, *kanburi*, that's used to distinguish hamachi harvested at this time. That's not to say it is going to be shabby during the summer; hamachi does not suffer from a wide range in seasonal palatability, as do some other shiromi-dane. It is, nevertheless, fixed in the Japanese mind as a wintertime tane.

≋ **Watch For:** *Negi-hama-maki* is a treat. The dark meat along the hamachi's lateral line is sometimes chopped into small chunks and mixed with *nakaochi*, the leftover pieces of tuna that don't look nice enough to serve as nigiri sushi. To this mixture is added some finely chopped *negi*, Japanese onion. This is wrapped in nori for a delicious maki sushi.

Another treat that often shows up on the plate of a sushi-ya regular during the latter hours of the evening is a grilled yellowtail skeleton with bits of meat still clinging to it. The itamae isn't trying to get rid of leftovers. The grilled carcass of a hamachi is another rare treat, to which only favorite customers are privy. The day one appears on a platter in front of you is a sign that you are either the object of affection of the itamae or you have been recognized as a serious sushi snob. Even if he's really cute, hope for the latter.

≋ **Ask the Itamae:** Given its eating habits, which include a lot of small crabs and other crustaceans, the yellowtail has evolved a long, very muscular pyloric section separating the stomach from the intestines, which grinds up the leftover shells from its lunch. Not surprisingly, given the eating habits of the Japanese, they've found a way to cook it, usually grilled. It's called *hamachi-cho* or *hamachi-i*. If you establish a good relationship with your itamae and tell him you want to try it, he may be able to grill up a mess of it or point you in the direction of a chef at a local Japanese restaurant who can satisfy your craving.

≋ **Trivia:** Along the coast of northern Japan, late winter storms can include thunder and lightning along with blizzards. Locals call the storms *buri-okosu*, "yellowtail awakeners," since an increase in the catch of this fish often coincides with the storms.

HAMAGURI ⇨ CLAM

Like a lot of other primitive civilizations, the Japanese of the Jomon era (about the 3rd century B.C.) left behind enigmatic mounds of shells. Ethnologists suspect these were a kind of votive offering. Uh-huh. Sushi snobs know better. Those shell mounds are the remains of some terrific clambakes.

There are several species of clams in Japanese waters. *Hamaguri* is Japanese for "beach chestnut," the generic term for a clam. Most of the clams that appear on sushi menus as hamaguri in the United States are Pacific clams, also called Manila clams. They are a little smaller than the soft-shelled New England beauties that are fried and steamed and made into chowders; the best size for harvesting hamaguri is about an inch across, when the meats are close to the size of an English walnut.

Back in the good old Edo days of the 18th century, hamaguri was a hot item for sushi. It's since gone the way of hula hoops and movies where couples wore pajamas to bed. Hamaguri as a sushi tane is rare now, though certainly it is still around in Japanese sushi-ya. If you see it listed, it's a possible sign that the place caters to a lot of Japanese sushi lovers, probably from around the Tokyo area. It is always worth a try. Some sushi tsu develop a real affection for hamaguri; the meat is almost sweet and it serves as a palate cleanser, a good choice between bites of oily fish.

Hamaguri is a nimono-dane. It isn't going to be served raw. Or if it is, the wise sushi tsu isn't going to be eating it. Once shelled, the whole clam viscera are boiled the same way *menrui*, or noodles, are prepared in a Japanese kitchen: plopped into a pot of water just beginning to boil. Once the water reaches a full, roiling boil, the cook adds a cup of cold water to bring the temperature down, and repeats the process two or three times. If they're kept at a full boil for too long, hamaguri become as hard as pencil erasers and less tasty. What the itamae is looking for in doneness is the condition of the black alimentary canal he can see underneath the meat. When the entrails are springy and firm against a poke from his finger, the meat's done. After cooling, the guts are removed, and the hamaguri is marinated in a nitsume syrup of soy sauce, mirin, and sugar. Hamaguri is usually brushed with an additional swoosh of nitsume before becoming part of nigiri sushi.

≋ **Watch For:** There are, you must know, itamae who regard the above method of preparing hamaguri in the same way that Texas cooks look at beans in chili: with a combination of near-equal parts of disdain, pity, and disgust. They will tell you that hamaguri can never be boiled. *Tsukkomu* or *tsukikomi* is the only way to prepare clams as a tane, they insist. Both mean the same thing: "to put into" or "stick in." In a culinary sense, they have the connotation of something gently poached. Hamaguri treated this way aren't cooked at all; they're covered in a reduction sauce of boiled shoyu and mirin and just enough sugar to make the solution *neba-neba*, or slightly sticky. The sauce is allowed to cool a bit before the clams are added for a few hours, until they have completely absorbed the flavor and "cooked" ever so slightly.

≋ **Ask the Itamae:** If your itamae does have access to hamaguri or even fresh littleneck clams, and he comes from Osaka or thereabouts, ask him to make *hamaguri shioyaki* and battera sushi for you sometime. You can read about battera-style sushi on page 27. It's a favorite in the Kansai region, which includes Osaka and Kyoto, and in many sushi-ya there a standard accompaniment to battera sushi is hamaguri shioyaki. Even if the itamae can't make it, he'll recognize you as a sushi tsu; this isn't something an amateur will know. It is arguably the greatest method ever invented for preparing clams. The dish is simple: The itamae starts with clams still in their shells. The small, protruding ligament where the clam's shells are connected has to be snipped, since you don't want them opening as they're grilled. That minor surgery performed, the clams are wiped with a damp cloth just to moisten them, then rolled in a bowl of rough salt. (*Shioyaki* means "salt-grilled.") They're carefully placed directly on a grill and covered with foil. In a couple of minutes, they've steamed in their own juices. They're taken off the grill, and the diner carefully lifts the top shell, swills the aromatic liquid, then enjoys the clams. Half a dozen hamaguri shioyaki by themselves, juices slurped and meats savored, are an epicurean glimpse of paradise.

≡ **Trivia:** Hamaguri is a key ingredient in *sumashi*, or clear soups served on Girl's Day, Hina Matsuri. They are also typical fare at Japanese weddings, with the clams served still in their shells. If the clam shells are still attached at the hinge when they arrive in the bowls of the bride and groom, it's a sign the union will be equally strong and bonded.

HATAHATA ⋙ SANDFISH

atahata, the sailfin sandfish, is to northern Japan what the catfish is to the southern United States. It is eaten all over Japan grilled, fried, and in other ways, in addition to sushi. The Japanese of Akita and Yamagata, the northernmost prefectures of the main island of Honshu, though, have a particular affinity for hatahata, a food source that has many times throughout history meant the difference between their survival and starvation.

Hatahata are handsome, chrome-silver fish about a foot and a half long. Their scales are so fine they're nearly invisible, making the sandfish very slippery. They run in schools and for much of the year confine themselves to the deeper waters far offshore. In winter, hatahata start swimming into the shallow waters around Akita and Yamagata. They once came in such numbers that the beaches would be littered with them and, according to a folk saying of the region, "even the cats won't eat them." Humans weren't as picky once upon a time. Hatahata were a reliable form of protein well up into the 20th century. They were eaten fresh and were dried under the eaves of homes to be used in leaner months, which in that part of Japan was a big chunk of the calendar year. Even with the enormous harvest, there were sandfish left in the sea. A feudal lord named Satake was sent to rule the lands that are now Akita, and cleverly exploited the hatahata catch, drying them and exporting them all over Japan as food and as a cheap fertilizer. He was so efficient that hatahata were once known as "Satake fish."

The good times never last. By the 1960s, the sandfish catch began dwindling markedly. It got so bad that for a couple of years during the '90s, the Japanese government banned all hatahata fishing. The populations have begun to recover, aided by some still-experimental commercial farming of the species. And sandfish are also imported to Japan from Korean fisheries. It's good news for the cats of Akita, who have learned, we hope, not to take the fish for granted. It's good news, too, for the Japanese sushi enthusiast who had to pay dearly for sandfish even when he could get it. The bad news is for the sushi tsu outside Japan. Hatahata numbers are still not healthy enough to export them in any numbers. It is very rare to find them in sushi-ya in the United States, and there aren't any equivalent species that can be substituted, even though in small numbers the subspecies Ezo hatahata is found in the oceans off far northern California and up into the Bering Sea.

If you run across it, hatahata is a shiromi-dane, one of the fattier ones. Hatahata flesh is luscious and rich. It is a tane for the midwinter, just before the fishes begin to spawn. Hatahata tane should be raw and cut a little thicker than most other shiromi-dane, to really appreciate the flavor and texture. Amateurs may find it too fishy; the sushi snob knows this is a tane that is matched beautifully with shoyu. The salty tang of the soy sauce plays off the taste of the sandfish to near perfection.

The sandfish's arrival in the shallow fishing waters of Akita and Yamagata coincides with strong thunderstorms that rake across this part of Japan each winter. *Heikireki* is a medieval word for "thunder," one that, in the dialect of northern Japan, was pronounced "hatata" or "hatahata." That's where the name came from, since the fish showed up in greatest abundance along with the thunderstorms. It was once called *hatahata-gami*, or fish of the God of thunder, since it was believed to be an emissary of that deity.

≋ **By Any Other Name:** Hatahata is also called *shirohata*, *kahata*, and *kaminari-uo*. The last name means "thunder fish," another reference to the hatahata's arrival in northern Japan during the storm season.

≋ **Ask the Itamae:** Again, hatahata is a rare occurrence in sushi-ya outside Japan. If it's on the menu, the sushi snob will be thrilled to try it as a nigiri tane. But don't leave well enough alone. If you see sandfish offered, consider bringing up the subject of *hatahata sushi-zuke*. It's an Akita sushi specialty. Sandfish fillets are pressed into a mixture of *koji* and rice and left to cure. Koji is the mold that causes rice to ferment to make sake. The process works best when quantities are generous, so sometimes 40- or 50-gallon tubs are filled with rice, mold, and fish. The results, after anywhere from a week to up to a few months, are served together. That's sandfish sushi-zuke. Let me pause here to add that if you think about it, there are any number of things in the world the bare-bones description of which sound less than seductively attractive. Sushi-zuke is among them. On the odd chance your path may someday cross with an itamae from Akita, you will solidify eternally your reputation as a sushi snob in his estimation by knowing about this kind of sushi. Another term for sushi-zuke is *ii sushi*. Note that while the name of the ingredient usually comes first, as in *ika sushi*, people from Akita and thereabouts will almost always say *sushi-hatahata*. It's a curious inversion and no one knows why they do it. But it's a sure sign that the speaker is from that region.

≋ **Trivia:** The vinegar produced during the pickling of the hatahata sushi-zuke doesn't go to waste. It's bottled as *shottsuru*, a Japanese version of the fish sauces that are popular in Vietnam, Thailand, and other parts of Asia. There is a whole repertoire of foods cooked in or with shottsuru, most of them originating in Akita or its environs.

HATA ⟨⟩ GROUPER

A fried-fish emporium in a small Illinois city was the setting for the encounter. It was one of a nationwide chain that shall remain anonymous, save to observe that its name comes from a famous fictional pirate. The Japanese businessman was in Illinois to check out the soybean crop. A hefty percentage of Japanese tofu is now made with soybeans grown in the American Midwest, and the Japanese had an American partner in this venture. It was the partner who came up with the idea of the fast-food fish joint when the subject of dinner arose. It was late and at any hour, fine dining is not among the varied blandishments of central Illinois. So there they were, and the Japanese businessman looked at the menu behind the counter and noted a fish platter special. "What," he asked innocently, "kind of fish is it?"

The kid behind the counter reacted as if he'd just been asked the atomic weight of plutonium. To his credit, he said, "The fried kind." To the credit of the chain, the manager came out and took the question and called the corporate headquarters, and before the two soybean partners left the place that night, they'd gotten a reply. The typical Japanese, you see, does not think of "fish" as a generic term when it comes to meals, any more than the average American thinks of "meat" as much of an adequate description. Some details are necessary. That isn't to say, though, that the Japanese are always unfailingly exact in describing the fish they eat. *Hata* is a good example.

"Hata," like its closest English equivalent of "grouper," is a term that can cover more than three dozen different fish. Just narrowing it down to the genus *Epinephelus* alone still leaves about eight different fish that are all sold and eaten in Japan as "hata." So if you're in a Japanese market and looking for fresh hata for dinner, you are, for our purposes here, taxonomically out there on your own, baby. On the other hand, if you are ordering hata in a sushi-ya, we can focus much more precisely. Chances are very good that you will get a tane from *ma-hata*, the "true grouper." Up to yardstick size when full-grown, it is known as well as the "seven-band grouper," since it has seven darkish bands running vertically along its length, giving a ma-hata the raffish air of Papillon in his Devil's Island prison outfit. Home for the ma-hata are the waters of Tokyo Bay—where they were once common and are slowly making a comeback—all the way down south to the equator. *Konbu-hata*, or kelp grouper, is very closely related. But the kelp grouper has stripes running diagonally rather than vertically, and a lot of sushi snobs and connoisseurs of fish in general in Japan insist that it is superior in taste, cooked or raw, to the ma-hata.

The urge to merge, spawning-wise, hits the ma-hata around March, and they keep at it until May. So ma-hata is a late-winter tane. A shiromi-dane tane to be exact; the meat is pearly white, very much like sea bass, though slightly denser. It is cut from fillets, a trifle thinner than is typical for white-meat tane. Some sushi tsu in Japan will not eat hata unless the tane is cut so finely that the grains of rice in the shari underneath can be seen through the fish, though others insist too much flavor is lost that way. That flavor is fresh and lean and slightly salty. It is the aftertaste of hata, however, that attracts many sushi snobs. They describe it as a pleasant finish of seaweed that lingers on the tongue. For this reason, hata is among the best choices for sashimi, particularly when you are ignoring my advice about what to drink (see page 211) and are having sake with your meal. The combination of the grouper's lingering aftertaste and the flavor of sake do go very well together.

The hata on American sushi-ya menus is usually one of several groupers with names that read like a paint store color chart. In addition to red, white, black, and yellow-edge, you will find dusky, snowy, marbled, mottled, and misty grouper all prepared as sushi tane. Though they are different species and their taste isn't quite as complex, they're all in the same genus as ma-hata and they all work nicely as tane.

≋ **By Any Other Name:** *Hoki-hata* is a good name to drop if the subject of hata comes up. It is a subspecies found around Ise, where some of Japan's oldest and most important Shinto shrines are located. Hoki-hata is a specialty of fish restaurants there, including sushi-ya. The typical tourist will get off the bus at the city of Ise, clutching guidebooks that lead him to the Grand Shrine and the complex of lesser shrines that dominate Ise. The sushi snob will be recognized as the one looking for a good sushi place that has hoki-hata.

≋ **Ask the Itamae:** Sometimes, when hata is served, itamae will dress it up with the usual condiments of grated fresh ginger or chopped green onions. Ask him to serve it without any of these if you haven't had it before, so that you can savor it unadulterated. Or try it as we mentioned, as sashimi, with a bottle of chilled sake.

≋ **Trivia:** "Hata" is written with two kanji that mean "a large wing," since the colorful fish looks like the bright plumage of a bird's wing.

HIRAMASA 〜 AMBERJACK

Most forms of snobbery, at some level, are all about discrimination. Discrimination is not always bad. For example, it figures in La Rochefoucauld's definition of an educated person: one who prefers the best not only to the worst but also to the second best. It's impossible to be a sushi tsu without discriminating. *Hiramasa* affords you an excellent opportunity to do just that.

For the average sushi enthusiast, it will be enough to assume that hiramasa on the menu, translated as "jack" or "amberjack," is simply another name for yellowtail, or hamachi. Easy to do since, if you've read the section on that fish, you know it collects names the way the phone company tacks on charges to your monthly bill. Even many, if not most, Japanese sushi fans make this error. It doesn't help when itamae, perhaps lacking the linguistic skill to make the distinction, tell their customers that "hiramasa" is just another word for yellowtail, indistinguishable from hamachi. They're wrong. It is true that hiramasa is very closely related to hamachi, so close it has the same distinctive yellow streak along its side. It is a different species, though. If you have a chance to see the whole fish and compare it side by side to a hamachi yellowtail, you can see the yellow line is brighter and more clearly delineated on the former.

Except for a brief period in early summer when they spawn, hiramasa do not run in schools like other species of yellowtail. They're hooked or netted more by accident than design. Consequently, hiramasa isn't always available in Japanese sushi-ya. It is even rarer outside that country, though it is offered from time to time in sushi-ya in larger cities. The meat of hiramasa is leaner than hamachi and more densely textured. It's also more delicate. The best meat is taken from fish around three feet long; they grow a couple of feet larger when fully mature, but their flavor declines noticeably. The itamae also has to be careful to slice this fish a little more thinly than for most shiromi-dane, so don't mistake his thin cuts for those of a cheapskate. Hiramasa has to be sliced nearly transparently fine to bring out the flavor. It is also not a tane that benefits much from wasabi or even shoyu. It is best presented with just a few grains of rough sea salt and a drop or two of lemon juice.

Partly because of its scarcity and partly because it has long been in the shadows of the much more popular hamachi, it has always been tough to build a following for hiramasa among sushi fans. Devotees are small in number. Don't be surprised if you run into Japanese sushi aficionados who know little or nothing about it. Still, it goes without saying that if you're serious in the quest for sushi snobbery, you ought to try this *tane* when the opportunity arises. Keeping in mind what you have learned here, you will at least have mastered the gastronomic equivalent of this clique's secret handshake.

≋ **Watch For:** Hiramasa is frequently offered in sushi-ya along the Gulf Coast, from Florida to Texas. Be sure to ask, however, if this isn't really a completely unrelated fish that tastes a lot like hiramasa, called cobia, cabio, crabeater, or lemonfish. Any sushi tsu in a sushi place in this region ought to be skeptical, since this is a common substitution.

≋ **Ask the Itamae:** Aside from the salt and lemon juice, hiramasa can be served with *momiji oroshi*. It's a standard side dish for tempura and other fried foods that goes well with some milder shiromi-dane sushi like hiramasa. A fresh daikon is pierced all over with the sharp end of a chopstick, then small red chilies are stuffed in the small holes. The daikon is then finely grated (*oroshi*); the resulting pulpy condiment has a faint reddish hue. *Momiji* is the word for "maples," and calls to mind their scarlet autumn hue.

HIRAME 🐟 FLOUNDER

When Commodore Perry's armada arrived in Tokyo in 1853, the welcome *tatami* wasn't exactly rolled out for him. For more than three centuries under a succession of shogun of the Tokugawa family, the country had maintained a strict members-only policy. In hopes of placating the Japanese, Perry brought gifts, including a complete narrow-gauge railroad and track. He also hedged his bets, steaming into the bay with all his ship's cannons in plain view, just in case the look-what-nice-things-we-brought-you-natives approach didn't work out. When the anchors of his frigates and steamships plopped onto the soft sand of the bay, chances are they disturbed a hirame. What's now called Tokyo Bay was once lousy with these bottom-feeding flatfish, which swam in with the tides, gorging on small shellfish. Reasonably cheap, plentiful, and delicious, flounder have long been considered the very tastiest of the shiromi-dane used in sushi. However, the waters of Tokyo Bay today, despite considerable progress in cleaning them, are a tough place for any aquatic species not capable of surviving in a 30-weight-viscosity environment. So hirame are no longer quite so plentiful there. Tokyo sushi-ya import virtually all of it from other waters in Japan and elsewhere. Still, when Japanese sushi snobs think of Edomae shiromi-dane, the white-fleshed fish of traditional sushi, this is very often the fish that has their mouths watering.

The appellation is confusing, both in English and Japanese. "Flounder" refers to nearly 600 species of flatfish. The closest Japanese equivalent, *hirame*, isn't much more specific. What may end up topping your nigiri sushi or tucked into a corner of chirashi sushi could be any one of more than a dozen flatfish, from brill, to witch flounder, to fourspot, to halibut. The flesh is more or less indistinguishable and it is always prepared in the sushi-ya the same way. Normally, two pairs of fillets taken from right around the fins are the only part of the hirame used in sushi; they are called the *engawa*, or porch. These can be the only real clue you might have about exactly which flatfish you're eating. Smaller types yield much smaller engawa, sometimes so small that a couple of pieces will overlap one another atop one piece of nigiri sushi. (Doubled up is the most common way hirame is served in Japan, where most of the native species of flatfish are comparatively puny. If your nigiri sushi has a large single piece of hirame, you might want to wager it came from a halibut, the largest of the flatfish, common in the Atlantic.)

What most of these flatfish have in common is that they are dextral, a good word to add to your vocabulary. It means "inclined to the right side," and you should be able to work it into a political discussion soon, as in "I'm fascinated by Bob's recent dextral inclinations on military spending." Among hirame, it means that as adolescents they look like normal fish, but as they age, and perhaps cynicism and ennui set in, they begin to rotate themselves over to the right. That is, both eyes rotate around until they're on "top," or on the right side of the flounder. They spend the rest of their lives on sandy ocean bottoms, camouflaging themselves when necessary by changing color to match their surroundings. Their natural hues can range from a mottled russet to deep olive green, but their bottom, ventral sides are without exception very white. What shows up on your sushi is a filet that is pearly translucent, with maybe just a faint line of pink running through it.

Hirame is served plain in sushi, but it can be dressed up a bit. A dash of lemon juice or ponzu brings out the clean taste of the meat. Some sushi-ya use the mirin and shoyu nikiri reduction sauce to marinate hirame briefly before serving. The key to good hirame sushi is almost entirely in the thickness of the cut. Too thin and it loses an important aspect of texture. Too thick a cut, however, has a decidedly unpleasant feel in your mouth; the taste is even less appetizing. Prevailing wisdom is that a proper thickness of hirame for nigiri or chirashi sushi should be one *bu*. A bu is about ¹/₄ inch or so, give or take a *mo*. (Japan's traditional measurement system is sort of metric. Ten mo make a bu.)

≋ **Watch For:** The sushi tsu orders hirame only during the colder months of the year—never after February—when it has the least amount of fat. The lean, clean taste of winter hirame is the epitome of a white-meat sushi. Hirame harvested in the warmer months has a noticeably flabbier, mushier texture and flavor. However, if the sushi-ya has *soge* on hand during the spring, say from March through April, give it a try. *Soge* is a colloquial fisherman's expression for hirame that are about a foot and a half in length and keep their flavor well past winter's last snow.

≡ **Ask the Itamae:** If he can serve hirame that's bathed in a *momiji oroshi-zui.* It's a marinade of green onions, momiji oroshi (see page 88 in the section on hiramasa), and ponzu. It has just a slight kick to it that accentuates the basic flavor of the fish.

HOKKIGAI 〜 SURF CLAM

The sushi snob will do well to stock a few archaisms in a well-supplied vocabulary. Instead of *doressingu*, for instance, refer to dressings for salads as *koromo*, even though to any home cook in Japan or anyone under the age of 75 or so, "koromo" is used only to describe tempura batter. Call side dishes of pickled vegetables *o-hashi yasumi*—"chopstick rests"—another word that hasn't been commonly used for decades. The occasional and carefully spontaneous use of these old-fashioned terms will endear you to any elderly Japanese within earshot. They will establish you among younger Japanese as something of a *henna-gaijin*, an "odd foreigner." (They need to be reminded gently, if they use this expression in front of you, that in this country *they* are the gaijin.) And if such antiquated speech does not advance you to the status of the sushi tsu, it at least confers the mantle of eccentricity. And being an eccentric can be almost as much fun as being a snob.

To this end, sometime when you're in the mood for it and you see *hokkigai* on the menu, ask for it as *ubagai* instead. If the itamae looks puzzled, quickly say, "Oops. Sorry; sometimes I forget you younger Japanese are so informal. I guess you all say 'hokkigai' now, right? Such a shame to see proper spoken

Japanese decline so." An *uba* is a fairly archaic word for an older woman. Don't use it in conversation; the word is confined almost entirely to literature these days. The name of the clam comes from its wrinkled shell, like the skin of an elderly woman. *Ubagai* is still the proper Japanese name for the shellfish and most Japanese will still recognize it, though it may take a minute. But it's been almost entirely replaced, especially in the lexicon of the sushi-ya, by "hokkigai." It is most often referred to as a "surf clam" in English. A rough translation of "hokkigai" is "clam from the north," a geographical nod to where most are harvested, in Hokkaido and on the Sanriku coast, a region along Japan's far north Atlantic shore. The Sanriku coast is otherwise famous as the site of one of the most destructive tsunami in history, which occurred in the 1890s. The hokkigai is common as a tane in sushi-ya there and in most of northern Japan. Most sushi-ya in other parts of Japan and the rest of the world often include this clam in their menu as well.

Hokkigai are a wintertime tane, when the meat tastes best. The texture is chewy almost to the point of crunchiness. Those Japanese who don't like it say the texture is *kori-kori*, or unpleasantly rubbery. Its admirers insist that as the fibers break down with chewing, more and more of the flavor is released onto the palate.

The color of the meat ranges from a dull white to a darker beige, with a purplish black tip at one end. The "foot" of the hokkigai is the part you're eating; it's long and curved and pointed and is split with a knife down the middle, resulting in a pair of tane shaped like hooks. It is the tip of that hook that is clearly darker than the rest of the meat. When hokkigai is served raw, the tip is black or nearly so. More commonly, the clam is quickly dipped in boiling water, a process called *yu-buri* or *yu-furi* in the sushi kitchen. The treatment turns the blackish tip a lush crimson. That's probably the way you've had it in sushi. The hot-water dipping treatment is as much for hygiene as anything else, since hokkigai go bad quickly. Still, if they are very fresh, raw hokkigai are definitely superior in taste, the meat a luxurious sensation that carries a faint tang of sea salt.

≋ **Ask the Itamae:** Hokkigai have the same pair of adductor muscles as many other clams and bivalves. They are delicious, though rarely available. Ask for them as *hokkigai kobashira*, which, if he has them, the itamae may serve to you gunkan style, with a spritz of lemon or a sprinkle of *shichimi togarashi*, dried pepper flakes.

≋ **Trivia:** Since the late '80s, Canadian fisheries have been experimenting successfully with cultivating hokkigai on aquaculture farms. The hokkigai sold frozen in Japanese-style grocery stores here and meant for sushi making at home almost all come from these farms. As a sushi-dane, it does not seem to suffer much in taste or quality from a Canadian upbringing.

HOTATE-GAI 〜 SCALLOP

The comparison, for history teachers, is inevitable. Japan and England: Both are small island nations, sharing a similar form of feudalism for centuries. Both are in proximity to powerful neighbors, yet they maintain unique civilizations, languages, and cultures. The parallels are obvious, which makes their differences all the more striking. England, for instance, became the world's greatest seapower, sending its ships all over the world. The Japanese finally got around to building a navy in time to kick the borscht-flavored stuffing out of Russia in the early 20th century, but for most of its history, Japan's ships never progressed much past the technological stage of the *Kon-Tiki*. Aside from coastal fishing, there is little of a seafaring tradition in Japan. The Japanese term for "scallop" is one of the few examples of the cultural influences of ships. "Hotate-gai" means "sail-raising clam." When scallops flap their shells open and shut, propelling themselves through the water, it looks like a sail being hoisted.

Scallops are among the best-known shellfish to seafood lovers; rare is the sushi-ya that does not offer hotate-gai. There are several species worldwide. They range in circumference from the size of a contraceptive diaphragm to a Little League catcher's mitt. In Japan, hotate-gai thrive in colder northern waters. Hokkaido and Aomori Prefecture are famous for their scallops. Nearly all scallops on the market anywhere in Japan, though, are commercially farmed. The same goes for at least half of the scallops used in sushi-ya in the United States. The other half are still regularly dredged directly from the open ocean, all along the northern latitudes of both coasts. Commercially raised or wild, they might be different species, depending on how close you are to the Atlantic or Pacific and your sushi-ya's seafood supplier. As a general rule, the firmer and sweeter the meat, the farther north the scallop's home address. Unlike other shellfish, scallops don't lie about as inert as a first-timer on a cruise on a Dramamine overdose, waiting for the current to bring them dinner. They cavort. They frolic. Hotate-gai actually scamper about, flapping their shells to jet hither and thither so happily that if you see them in their natural environment, you almost hate to eat them. Almost.

Along with its presumably upbeat attitude about life, an adductor muscle that constitutes more than three-fourths of the entire body mass accounts for all that activity in the scallop. While the adductor is a tasty tidbit in some other bivalves destined for sushi, in the hotate-gai the big adductor *is* the tane. It's called a *kaibashira* (clam pillar) or just *bashira*, as are the adductors of all shellfish, so you'll have to specify, if you're not ordering off the menu, *hotate-gai-bashira*. The viscera surrounding it are cut away—but not thrown away—and after a rinsing, it is ready to use once it's been sliced across the grain into a disk. Hotate-gai is arguably at its best served this way.

More often, however, you'll see scallops presented in nigiri sushi as a nimono-dane. You may hear them called *ni-hotate*. The meat is quickly parboiled—*yuderu*—and then sliced. As anyone who's been the least tardy in tending the skillet or pot in preparing any kind of scallops knows, too much heat of any kind causes them to toughen worse than a Marine drill sergeant, so this is a critical stage. After boiling, they're sliced and the nimono sauce is brushed on.

As with all nimono-dane, wasabi is a no-no for scallops. Even if hotate are eaten raw as sushi, most sushi tsu will pass on adding the wasabi to it. The skilled itamae won't add any in the first place. The sweet, clean taste of hotate-gai doesn't need any accompaniment. Sometimes hotate-gai are coarsely chopped and served gunkan style. One variation of the basic gunkan presentation for scallops is adding the trimmed filaments with the rest of the scallop meat and topping the meat with a sprinkle of the roe of either flying fish or smelt. Another is to incorporate the sex organs of the hotate-gai. Male scallops have a beige testis gland; females a reddish roe sac. In some Japanese sushi-ya, these are served with the hotate-gai, a treat sadly unavailable here, though some Canadian shellfish suppliers sell "rims and roe," a combination of the filaments and roe meant for use in chowder, and some enterprising itamae there may eventually make use of this.

≋ **Watch For:** Fake scallops are the stuff of epicurean legends. Stories abound about factories turning out ersatz scallops that are actually plugs of shark or skate or some other fish. If you have any doubts, look for the muscle striation in the hotate-gai flesh. In the real thing it'll run vertically. Scallop-looking plugs made with substitute fish would have horizontally running muscle tissue. But the sushi tsu is far more likely to encounter "wet" hotate-gai. These scallops have been treated with tripolyphosphate. Who the hell knows what this stuff is? Sounds like something used to power a Klingon warship. At any rate, it somehow works to keep scallops and other shellfish edible longer, but it also gives them an artificially shiny appearance and a distinctly soapy taste. No good sushi-ya should ever use these treated scallops.

Pencil eraser–size nubbins of bay scallops may be used for gunkan sushi; they're markedly sweeter than the larger variety. The meat of calico scallops are smaller than bays, with a brownish fringe. Their taste is fine in dishes where they're sautéed or fried, but they're not suitable for sushi.

≋ **Ask the Itamae:** There isn't much to the insides of the scallop aside from the massive adductor muscle, but the rest of its viscera, along with the filaments that connect the body to the shell, are all edible. In Japanese sushi-ya, the itamae will present the whole shebang. That is less common here for two reasons: One, the scallop with all its guts and connective tissue attached doesn't look all that great and doesn't look much better after it's been brushed with nitsume sauce, and itamae are conscious of the squeamish factor in presenting sushi to Western customers. And two, when the viscera are left on, they add a distinct new dimension in taste. *Horotto* is a word used to describe an enjoyable and palatable bitterness. Small fish grilled whole are a good example; the sweetness of their flesh contrasts with the pungent bitterness of their intestines. Whole scallops have some of this horotto. If you want to try it, you'll need a sushi-ya that caters to a large Japanese population, and you'll have to explain to the itamae that you want *zentai no hotate-gai*, "the whole thing."

≋ **Trivia:** Scallops can have up to 50 eyes. All of them are situated along the edge of the shell, which means the hotate-gai has a splendid view of where he's been, but not the foggiest of what's ahead.

IKA ⤳ SQUID

S quid lead fairly interesting lives for undersea creatures. Thanks to chromatophores in their skin, depending on their moods, their entire bodies can flash with an electric iridescence, like miniature Goodyear blimps over a nighttime football game. Some deepwater species can even generate their own headlights. Their intestinal tracts pass directly through their brains, giving them something in common with many sushi snobs. The female squirts her eggs out through an internal siphon, then collects them with her tentacles to deposit them in a safe place—assuming she survives the love thing. Squid are cannibalistic; males can switch, midembrace, from an amatory to a gustatory mode. And here's the cool part: No one knows how big they can grow. Fifty-foot squid have been captured, and the sucker scars found on sperm whales indicate squid four times as big might be swimming the ocean depths.

A squid large enough to clog the Holland Tunnel whets the appetite of the imaginative sushi tsu. Disappointingly, perhaps, *ika*, or squid destined for sushi, are small enough to fit comfortably in a Saturn's glove compartment. (Don't try this.) The most common species of squid used is the yari-ika. Fishermen, fishmongers, itamae, and other chefs all have their own terms for the many species of squid. Local names vary as well, so you'll hear of *maika, koika, surume-ika*, and more. In terms of sushi cuisine, though, ika varieties are categorized by the density of their meat. Some are as solid as a rib-eye steak, while others have flesh as flimsy as a soap opera plot. The yari-ika is just right for eating raw (a *yari* is a Japanese spear; the body of this squid ends in a sharp point with a couple of flaring, blade-like fins on either side). So it, or one of its close cousins, is the natural choice for sushi. It's thick enough to provide a pleasantly chewy consistency, but not so dense that it's like a slice of bicycle tire in your mouth.

In the days before modern refrigeration, ika was about as popular a tane as capri pants for overweight men, largely because it spoiled and began reeking so very quickly. (See the admonition on the previous page about putting one in your glove compartment.) When it did appear on the sushi-ya menu, it was boiled, then brushed with nitsume sauce. The best ika for this preparation is the *aori-ika*. Back a car over a Frisbee a couple of times to stretch it out, and add eight tentacles, and you'd have the approximate aori-ika shape. This variety is called an ika in Japanese even though it's actually another, related cephalopod, known in the West as a cuttlefish. Aori-ika is popular in Japan; you might see it in sushi-ya in the United States from time to time, though you probably won't find it specifically mentioned on the menu.

Yari-ika, served raw without any sauce, appeared after World War II; it is a standard now. Ika's popularity is partly because of its texture, which is tacky enough to form a nice bond with the rice, with a smear of wasabi to seal the deal. A freightload of amino acids in the meat add a distinct sweetness. This is a good tane to try dipped in shoyu without any additional wasabi, to get the full effect of texture and taste.

We don't think of any squid as being among nature's towering intellectuals. Truth is, they're even dumber than you'd guess, dumb enough that they succumb to a kind of lunacy— literally. On moonlit nights, huge schools of squid, sometimes *miles* in length, will swim toward the light until they reach the ocean's surface. They mill about there, addled as a septuagenarian senator, scooped up by the dragnet-full by squid fishermen. It's too bad for the ika, great for the sushi tsu. It's even better if it is wintertime, when yari-ika tend to be at their prime taste-wise. Some sushi tsu in Japan insist they can tell how close to spring the ika they're eating was harvested, and they'll insist on examining the pen, the cartilaginous "bone." The pen is softer during the spawning season. Maybe so, but nearly all ika are frozen now, so just because you're eating it in January doesn't mean it wasn't caught last July, or vice versa.

Ika eaten raw in sushi is just gutted and cleaned, the surface membrane scrubbed off, and it's ready. (That membrane is what can make squid taste odd when you grill it at home.) If the ika's being served with nitsume, it is boiled until just tender. Either way, what's critical is how it's sliced. Squid muscles are concentric, spiraling like rings around its body. It has to be sliced against the grain of the muscle fiber or it will be gummy and decidedly unpleasant to chew. For the same reason, your ika sushi might be scored lightly. When it is served with nitsume, the scored slices create more surface area for the sauce to stick to. If you've had a less than tasty experience with ika, try it at another sushi-ya or two to make sure it has been properly sliced as a tane.

≋ **Watch For:** *Geso* are the squid's tentacles, usually boiled, wrapped around nigiri sushi with a band of nori, and brushed with nitsume. There's little about sucker-lined strands of rubber band that speaks fondly to the average Western palate. They have their fans, though, and the sushi tsu will not pass on the chance to sample them if it arises. Note: *gesoku* is Japanese for "footwear." The idea of shoes, or at least talking about them in polite company in Japan, is still considered just a trifle common. So old ladies and other fussy types might be hesitant to order geso, just for this reason. Just thought you'd like to know.

Occasionally, the itamae will also stuff the tubular body of the ika with sushi rice, sesame seeds, little chopped bits of tentacle, and cucumbers, and then slice it into rings. This is *ika no sugata sushi*, a kind of squid sushi sausage that is even rarer than geso and is never to be missed. Another squidly sushi variation is "pine cone," or *matsukasa sushi*. Flat fillets of squid are scored in a cross-hatch pattern, then rolled around a mixture of sushi rice, white fish meat, kanpyo, shiitake mushrooms, snow peas, or other ingredients, and cut into bite-size pieces. The hatching on the outer side of the squid makes it look like a pine cone.

≋ **Ask the Itamae:** Inquire if he can make *tora maki*, or tiger eye, sushi with ika. It's a fillet of squid fat enough to be sliced through the middle, creating a pocket that is opened wide enough to stuff with a roll of salmon or another fish, usually wrapped in nori. The effect, when the fillet is sliced into cross sections, is like an eye, the white of the squid surrounding an iris of fish. It's nouveau, to be sure. No one in Edo ever had it. But a lot of young itamae like to make tiger eye sushi to show off their skill, and if they do and you appreciate it, you'll definitely gain some points with them.

IKURA ⇨ SALMON ROE

The "sushi as fish bait" shtick is a standard for stand-up comics from the Catskills to Vegas. Of course, in the case of salmon eggs, or *ikura*, used in sushi, it isn't entirely a joke. They *are* fish bait. That isn't to say they aren't delicious. It's just that a wide range of fishes, most noticeably trout and— if you don't think nature has an occasionally sick sense of humor, consider this—salmon, share your culinary enthusiasm.

Early Japanese did not eat ikura per se. They ate *sujiko*, also called *suzuko*, which is the same thing as ikura except that the eggs have not been separated and strained, and are still in a loose sac, the ovarian membrane, just as they came out of the mother salmon. Sujiko are best when they are soaked in sake lees (*sakekasu*) and eaten as a side dish for sake. They are occasionally employed for sushi in Japan; sujiko in a U.S. sushi-ya would be quite a find. Don't let it pass untasted if you encounter it.

In the 1930s, Japan set up a network of spies in Russia, some funded by the government, others financed by shady terrorist organizations like the Black Dragon Society. They had a war with Russia in mind for the near future, along with similar ideas for the United States, Europe, China, and the rest of Southeast Asia. The '30s were a feisty time for the Japanese. Intelligence agents brought back from Russia gallons of strategic military information. More important, they also brought back caviar. Japan doesn't have the sturgeon needed for first-class caviar. Nonetheless, their salmon sujiko, separated and salted, made an approximate and delightful delicacy. It wasn't until after the 1940s (the Japanese had most of their excessive expansionist energies worked out by the end of that decade) that ikura—an obviously borrowed word from the Russian *ikra*—was presented as a topping for sushi.

There are two products called *ikura*; one cured with salt, and the other with shoyu and a little borax. It is the salt-cured ikura that's used in sushi, either in a heap in chirashi sushi or as a topping for gunkan sushi. Given its delicate appearance and fragility, ikura would seem to be extremely perishable. Actually, it keeps well after it's been salted correctly, and it is common in sushi-ya everywhere now. The bulging, translucent red eggs burst in your mouth in a satisfying way, and the salty taste goes well with the slight sweetness of the rice and the crispy nori wrapping. Ikura past its prime shrinks and shows wrinkles. It has a slimy taste that lingers on the palate, and definitely not in a good way. A well-known trick in the sushi biz is to spray a mist of sake over ikura that is starting to get old and tough. It restores the luster and much of the moisture to the eggs, but you can, if you tilt your sushi in front of a light, see where the inside has become milky. The eggs may still taste fine and certainly shouldn't be harmful; just know that what you're eating isn't as completely fresh as it should be.

The majority of the world's supply of ikura, even the roe eaten in Japan, comes from Alaska. Alaskan fisheries export it to factories, most of them in Hokkaido, where the eggs are

ALAMEDA FREE LIBRARY

processed and sent out to distributors, who ship it anywhere there is sushi. Ikura comes from chum salmon (also called keta or dog salmon) that are in a family way, a species that has almost no commercial value otherwise. Alaskan fishermen sardonically have referred to chum as "floating ikura manufacturers." They're enjoying a healthy profit on fish they once pitched overboard when they were accidentally netted.

About 20 years ago, a few people, mostly children, got food poisoning after eating ikura, and markets all over Japan pulled ikura from the shelves. The fishermen, sensing a tremendous loss in revenue, were having an industry-wide pants wetting until the source of the poisoning was revealed to have been at the processing plant and not the fish themselves.

You're wondering, of course, what the difference is between the ikura in a sushi-ya and the stuff sold in bottles in bait shops, and whether next trout season, you might, if nothing's nibbling, have a nibble yourself. Don't do it. The salmon eggs for bait have been heavily treated with preservatives sufficient to give them a shelf life longer than a Tom Clancy novel, and with fluorescent dyes to make them more attractive on the shelf in bait shops and putatively more visible to the fish. It's fine enough fare for trout, but not for the sushi snob.

≋ **Watch For:** *Tobiuonoko*, or flying-fish roe, is sometimes served on gunkan sushi like ikura. That's fine so long as there isn't any attempt to pass it off as ikura. The difference is obvious; tobiuonoko are much, much smaller and more of a reddish brown, or, if they have been dyed, a fake-looking clown-hair orange. See page 185 for more about these eggs.

≋ **Ask the Itamae:** The idea of ikura as a topping for sushi is so new that some creative itamae feel they can experiment with it without clog dancing on any of the hallowed traditions of sushi-dom. Consequently, you can find ikura sushi with a sprinkle of poppy seeds, slivers of yuzu (Japanese citron), bits of hard-boiled egg yolk, and all kinds of additions that may or may not be welcome in your mouth. One sushi-ya in Tokyo piles ikura atop a toasted cracker flavored with shoyu, and another in Osaka serves it on a slice of *shishi-togarashi*, a kind of mild green pepper. Unless he goes completely overboard and starts adding stuff like peanut butter or Vegemite, indulge your itamae in this opportunity for him to walk on the wild side. Such tolerance becomes the sushi snob, in part because it provides an opportunity to meditate on matters that, however tangentially related, may concern sushi. In this case, it is the contrasting subjects of *sakui* and *sakui no medatsu*.

"Sakui" refers to sense of creativity or originality. "Sakui no medatsu" is sakui gone over the line and stumbling awkwardly into realm of the kitsch and self-consciously artificial. Georges Seurat's pointillism was sakui, while Jackson Pollock's pigment experiments were sakui no medatsu. *The Flintstones* were sakui, but *Scooby-Doo* was profoundly sakui no medatsu. Get it? Okay, ikura with a dab of grilled miso paste is sakui. Blackened Cajun ikura on polenta sushi is sakui no medatsu. To recognize the difference between these two when it comes to sushi is a responsibility of the sushi tsu; the various incarnations of ikura are a good place to begin one's study.

≋ **Trivia:** In magazine and newspaper surveys taken in Japan, ikura is dependably among the favorite sushi for Japanese women, though just as reliably further down the list for men.

≋ **More Trivia:** Japanese who supposedly know sushi may confide in you, as though it were a great secret, their foolproof method for detecting fake ikura. They will drop an egg in their hot tea and, if it turns cloudy, that's a sign it is real. The truth is that all eggs, including hen's eggs, will cloud when they're heated. It's called *cooking*. Your Japanese friend will probably also be at a loss to explain just exactly how one might manufacture fake ikura, anyway.

IWASHI ⇨ SARDINES

There are those who seriously believe in psychics, alien abductions, and that water bottled in France and sold for ridiculous prices is something more than, um, water. They are charitably described as gullible. Among their number would not be those who believe in sardines. Sardines are, after all, a canned staple as well as a perennial, useful metaphor for describing seating arrangements for coach-class air travel. But the truth is, there's no such creature. Sardines are, by international law, whatever a country says they are. Really. If, say, Uzbekistan wanted to market shark and call it sardine, they'd have (a) difficulty procuring the product since, lacking a coast, they have very few sharks, and (b) trouble with name recognition since not many consumers are familiar with Uzbek comestibles, but (c) smooth sailing as far as legally advertising it as "Select Uzbek Sardines."

Humor at the expense of our Uzbek friends aside, most of what are called sardines worldwide come from the same three genera, though that includes 300 different fish. In Japan, the *iwashi* used in sushi and many other preparations are a few species of the *Sardinella* family. It is, next to cod, the most commercially exploited fish in the world. Hundreds of thousands of them are eaten daily in Japan all kinds of ways, from grilled whole to chopped into a paste-like pâté to make *dango*, a kind of seafood dumpling for stews. Air-dried iwashi were a staple before refrigeration. Strings of sardines drying under the eaves of houses are, for the Japanese, an evocative picture of yesteryear, one perhaps best enjoyed upwind. Sushi lore has it that iwashi were not formerly presented on menus because itamae wanted to keep them as a secret tane, enjoyed only by themselves. For whatever reason, they have become popular as sushi only in the modern era.

Iwashi are a handsome fish, sleek and silvery, with a row of black blobs running down their lateral lines. (A market name in this country is "black-spotted sardine.") Technically speaking, it is the *ma-iwashi* species, though the slang for it is nearly as widely used: *aki-iwashi*, or "autumn iwashi," since that's when this tane is best. September through October finds the iwashi primping to spawn, and they are fat and oily, not the most favored attributes in humans lookin' for love, but irresistible to other sardines. After iwashi spawn, in late March, you'll detect a marked decline in their flavor.

Pencil-length or shorter iwashi are called *koba-iwashi*. *Chuba-iwashi* are those up to around eight inches. A couple of inches longer than that and they are as big as sardines get: *oba-iwashi*. While any of these sizes will work as a tane for nigiri sushi, itamae will, if they can get them, always opt for oba-iwashi, since they're meaty enough to make a nice-size tane. They are served raw, simply filleted and laid on the rice, though iwashi aren't often available that way. More often, they've been filleted and frozen and, after thawing, they are soaked in rice vinegar, then salted and allowed to sit for at least a couple of hours. After that, they're rinsed with fresh vinegar and thoroughly drained. A trick of the sushi trade is to recycle the vinegar used for marinating other hikari-mono (see page 35) and use it for iwashi or mackerel. Having absorbed other flavors, the vinegar provides a richness to the meat of these oily fishes that elevates them considerably. Raw or marinated, iwashi are always filleted so that the cut results in twin slices, both the right size for tane. These are nicked or crosshatched so they'll conform to the shape of the nugget of rice. To skin or not to skin is a personal choice of the itamae when preparing sardines. The skin is soft and thin and can be left on for eating, but it adds a slightly fishy flavor, and if he removes it it's probably to make this tane more palatable to the majority of his clientele.

Iwashi can have that pronounced fishy taste, given the high content of oil in their meat. They are apt to be too strong for the occasional sushi diner. The tiny, nearly hair-like bones that are left in the fillet may also put off those unaccustomed to it.

They've been softened by the vinegar soaking and provide an interesting texture, but given the hysteria some have about swallowing fish bones, don't recommend this one to any friends who aren't completely enthusiastic about sushi to begin with.

Iwashi served as nigiri sushi is often presented with a dab of grated ginger or a sprinkle of chopped chives. Go sparingly on the shoyu with this tane. Just a touch is enough to mellow out the sharpness of the vinegar. The itamae should have added a little more wasabi when he prepared it as well, since that works to cut through the oiliness of the fish and adds another element of flavor.

≋ **By Any Other Name:** In the United Kingdom, a larger or adult sardine is called a pilchard; a small or young pilchard is a sardine. Americans use the names interchangeably, though sardine is far more common. There are dozens of regional names in Japanese. A few you might hear are *karakuchi-iwashi*, *urume-iwashi*, and *seiguro-iwashi*.

≋ **Ask the Itamae:** Given that iwashi are so central to the diet of the Japanese, it follows there would be a plethora of ways to prepare it. A lot of the tastiest preparations involve grilling. If you're in a sushi-ya that also serves other Japanese food, consider a side of grilled iwashi to go with your sushi. Sometimes served with a dash of ponzu, it can satisfy that longing for the taste of something warm that can afflict even the most fervent sushi snob.

≋ **Trivia:** Little dried fish, collectively called *niboshi*, are a staple in the Japanese kitchen and are often eaten as snack foods. Sardine fry figure in some kinds of niboshi, including *almond kozakana*, made from baby iwashi soaked in sugar, then dried and mixed with almonds. This is a popular side dish for children's school lunches.

KAJIKI 🐟 SWORDFISH

Not many potential sushi tane have a sporting chance of taking out the fisherman who's trying to take them. *Kajiki* are an exception. We call them swordfish. The ancient Hawaiians called them *a'u*, which probably by no coincidence isn't all that different phonologically from their expression for "hurt" or "pain," *auwe*. At more than 12 feet in length, with a lot of that an ice pick–shaped, viciously sharp bill, and much of the rest muscle, a swordfish could stab through the side of a wooden boat while in the process of being hauled over the side, and could stab through a fisherman just as easily once aboard.

When the Hawaiians went fishing for swordfish in centuries past, they used live humans from the lower, and therefore expendable, classes as bait. It would make a great show if it were revived for the tourist trade there. Alas, few swordfish would actually be attracted. They go for smaller fish swimming in schools, which they attack by thrashing about with their bills, then making a meal of the resultant devastation. Less imaginative fishermen today in Hawaii and in most parts of the temperate oceans go after kajiki with hooks or catch them in nets set for tuna.

Japan does not have a large population of kajiki. It has been eaten in various ways there, but it wasn't on the menu at all during the Edo era. Then, in the 1930s, fishermen ranging far afield in the South Pacific began taking some monsters and packing them on ice to deliver them to markets in Japan. It wasn't long before sushi itamae were experimenting with them as tane. There was a period, just before the Second World War, when kajiki were to the sushi tane of Tokyo what Tevas are to Cape Cod. The craze lasted for several years. Old-timer sushi tsu in Tokyo still reminisce about the golden age of kajiki like Chicago Cubs fans getting teary about that period in the ancient past when their team was not an embarrassment to the sport of baseball.

Kajiki lost much of their popularity as a tane for a couple of reasons: First, the big ones became harder and harder to catch as kajiki became more and more popular as a food fish. Second, the relatively strong flavor of kajiki went out of vogue. When you consider that a major explanation many diners have for not liking fish of any kind is that it smells "fishy," kajiki's fall from sushi grace isn't hard to understand. It is not a subtle fish, neither in odor nor taste. Raw swordfish has a distinctive flavor, and with the introduction of so many lighter tane for sushi, this one lost favor. It's still around, though, and the educated sushi snob will recognize kajiki and know something about it.

While your local fish dealer or market is most likely to have swordfish cut into steaks with their distinctive whorls of muscle, suitable for grilling (swordfish may be the best fish to grill with teriyaki sauce), in Japanese markets the fish is often sold in cubes that look like giant dice. Cut from the flanks of the fish and frozen or shipped fresh, they are easily sliced into tane for nigiri sushi. If kajiki appears at a sushi-ya, it is because a good fresh or quick-frozen specimen has become available to the itamae and he wants to take advantage of it. If so, it'll be mostly older Japanese who will order this as a nigiri sushi tane—and, of course, you, the consummate sushi snob, who would not miss an opportunity to try a taste of sushi's past.

Since few swordfish are taken from Japanese waters, terminology for kajiki isn't substantial in Japanese. There is frequently some confusion between a true swordfish and the closely related marlin. Names can be used interchangeably. If the fish is to be cooked in some way, the variations in flavor aren't quite as obvious. Eat raw swordfish or one of its relatives in the sushi-ya, however, and you can see and taste a significant difference.

The true swordfish is most often called *mekajiki*. It is instantly distinguishable at sea, lolling about at the surface as it often does unless it's feeding, because the forward dorsal fin is blunt and rounded. It prefers the warmer waters of the South Pacific. Good to know if you're fishing for your meal, but assuming your quest for sushi does not include chartering a boat, look instead at the tane in the sushi counter case. If the meat is pearl white or very light beige, that's mekajiki, and it is the top-of-the-line in terms of texture and taste. There isn't any season when mekajiki are that much better, but to the minds of most Japanese sushi tsu, they are a tane associated with summer.

What's most commonly called *makajiki* in Japanese is not a swordfish proper but a Pacific marlin. It is much more common in Japanese fish markets since it likes the comparatively cooler ocean currents from northern Japan down to the central part of Honshu. The front dorsal fin of the marlin comes to a sharp tip. The tane looks almost exactly like lean tuna: a pale red, with much the same meaty consistency. Its flavor is clearly inferior to mekajiki, though some sushi tsu prefer it, particularly those who like a lot of shoyu with their sushi. If you want to really slosh a lot of shoyu, this is a fine tane to order. Marlin tastes best with the salty tang of soy sauce and it benefits as well from a liberal dose of wasabi. Again, though there isn't a season where it is any better, it is associated with summer.

Here are some linguistic hijinks: *Shirokajiki* means "white marlin" in Japanese; the rest of the world calls it a black marlin. What the rest of the world calls a blue marlin is, in Japanese, a *kurokajiki*, or black marlin. The sushi tsu doesn't give a damn because while both are fine grilled or prepared in other ways, neither is suitable for sushi. If you see them listed on a menu in a sushi place, assume it's either a serious breakdown in communication or that the establishment is trying to slip some kind of weird tane past you.

≋ **By Any Other Name:** Makajiki can also be called *kaji-maguro*, or swordfish-tuna, because of the color of the meat and its consistency, which is so much like that of a tuna. In English, it might be sold or translated as a "striped marlin" or a "Pacific marlin." A *basho-kajiki* is what American fishermen call a sailfish, a marlin with a blunter bill than the swordfish and a huge dorsal fin. While it makes a fabulous wall hanging for your den, it isn't eaten as sushi.

KANI ⟿ CRAB

Writing with ancient characters in a flowing script, a woman creates and sends invitations to a traditional tea ceremony. Dressed in formal kimono, she greets her guests, then leads them through a garden to a rustic hut specifically designed for the ceremony. She begins to boil the water for tea in a magnificent old charcoal-fueled brazier. What could be more essentially Japanese? Well, aside from Pocky, the chocolate-covered breadstick snack, and glove-wearing cab drivers, not much. But look behind the outer appearance. You'll find that while traditional Japan has managed to stay upright and is still taking nourishment quite nicely into the 21st century, it has, along the way, neatly incorporated a lot of modern shortcuts that make the traditions a heck of a lot easier. Those characters on the invitation, for example, weren't done with ink ground in a stone inkwell and mixed with water. They came from a pen with a soft rubber nose that looks just like a brush tip, complete with its own supply of ink in the shaft. It's 2nd-century A.D. technology updated courtesy of Magic Marker. The kimono she's wearing is formal. But the *obi*, the wide belt that once consisted of yards and yards of brocaded silk and needed at least one assistant to wrap and knot, is a fake. It goes around once and is fastened with cleverly concealed Velcro strips hidden under the big knot. And look closely into the brazier heating the water and you'll see, instead of charcoal, an electric heating element doing the work.

Kani, or crab, is still easily found in higher-quality Japanese sushi-ya, both as a tane topping for nigiri sushi and as a gu in maki sushi. And it is not uncommon in sushi-ya in the West as well. But in many establishments kamaboko kani, the ersatz fish-paste product we'll discuss under the heading of *Surimi* (page 168), has replaced real kani. It is a lot easier to spot fake crab in sushi than it is to pick up on the calligraphy that's been done with brush-shaped pens, or a Velcro obi, or a Westinghouse tea ceremony brazier, of course. The fake stuff has no striations of muscle running along it. The color of the fake is a disturbing shade of red, a post–nuclear holocaust fluorescence instead of a mottled reddish pink, like the real thing. The taste of kamaboko kani isn't bad at all; it's perfectly acceptable as long as everyone's up-front about what it is. But the flavor of real kani is more subtle, and the grain of the muscle is detectable as you chew it.

That the kani on or in your sushi is as inauthentic as the hue of Wayne Newton's hair is not, in and of itself, cause for renting of garments, teeth gnashing, or the sort of ululation favored by Middle Eastern women at funerals. The sushi snob checks the price of what's listed as kani. If it's cheap, he assumes it is the processed fish paste, molded to look like the section of meat from inside a crab's leg, then inserted in maki sushi or split and wrapped in a slice of nori atop nigiri sushi. If the cost is what he would expect to pay for, say, a weekend in Paris, he asks the itamae or waitress, *"Nan no gani desu ga?"* or "Which kind of crab is this?" He will elicit at least two related responses in addition to the answer: (a) the itamae or waitress will wonder why a non-Japanese is using a form of question preferred, for the most part, by a native speaker, and (b) he or she will be even more surprised that someone knows there are different kinds of crab used in sushi. Either way, the answer itself should be an honest one. If they are using fake crab, they won't hesitate to say so—it is immediately obvious as soon as it goes in your mouth—and they'll have to explain why it is so expensive. If the answer is taraba-gani or kobako-gani, the snob understands he isn't dealing with an imitation but with real crab.

Taraba-gani is the word for king crab or sometimes the related snow crab; casual Japanese terminology doesn't recognize the distinction, though if it has to be made, the snow crab is *suwai-gani* or *zuwai-gani*. The crabs are taken from the oceans of northern Japan, especially from around Wakkanai in Hokkaido or from Kushiro in the eastern part of that prefecture. The name *taraba-gani* means "crab from the cod place," since these waters are also rich in that fish. Enormous amounts of crab are also imported from Alaska and Canada. American crab fishermen rely on big square wire traps, while Japanese crab ships use nets designed to intercept the crabs when they are migrating to deeper waters to breed. Either way, the season is short, from around November to March. Bomb squad members lead placid lives compared with the lot of crab fishermen. Often hauling Porta Potti–size crab traps with one hand while using the other to crack shrouds of ice off the ship's rigging, they risk frostbite, exhaustion, and the occasional capsizing to bring home the goods. Probably no other sushi tane is bought more dearly.

The bodies of king and snow crab aren't much bigger than dinner plates and don't have much commercial use. As any devotee of the All the Crab You Can Stuff Down Your Throat dinner buffets can tell you, the attraction is their legs, which are Elle MacPherson long and filled with snowy, succulent flesh. They're either steamed or boiled, the shells cracked, and the meat extracted. If it comes from the upper leg, the sections of meat can be split. If it is from the smaller joints and is meant for nigiri sushi, two or more pieces can be lined up side by side. With nigiri sushi, these pieces are almost always attached to the shari with a strip of nori. Since taraba-gani come from the wilds of northern Japan, kani does not have a long history as a tane in Edomae sushi. Only since the 1950s has it become readily available in Japanese sushi-ya. It is far more popular in U.S. sushi places because of its taste, familiar to many Americans, and the fact that it isn't quite so overtly fishy or raw, which adds to its appeal in some quarters.

≋ **By Any Other Name:** The name for snow crab, "suwai-gani," is from the eastern half of Japan. The best come from around Fukui, Kyoto, and Ishikawa Prefectures, which surround a big bay on the Inland Sea. In the west, the same crab is called *matsuba-gani*. It can also be called *kobako-gani*, *echizen-gani*, and *mappa-gani*, depending on the locale. Hanasaki-gani is a blue king crab that's sometimes used for sushi, a slightly smaller version of the taraba-gani that is found primarily off the Nemuro peninsula in northeast Hokkaido. (Don't confuse this with another hanasaki-gani. There is a famous dish in Japan called *kani-shabu*. Chunks of crab-claw meat are dipped in hot broth, and the meat expands as it briefly cooks in the broth, like a flower blossoming. That's what *hanasaki* means in this latter context.)

≋ **Watch For:** *Watari-gani*, the blue swimmer crab, is found all around Tokyo Bay and in other coastal waters through much of the southern half of Japan. The watari-gani from the Ariake Sea is justly famous. This crab has a lot of meat, which is sometimes shredded for a kind of crab salad that's presented atop gunkan-style sushi. It isn't found much in American sushi-ya, though an itamae might substitute one of our native crabs in the same kind of salad. If so, the sushi tsu can enjoy it but sagaciously observe that it isn't quite up to the Ariake Sea crab salad, of course.

≋ **Ask the Itamae:** *Kani-miso*, the guts of any one of several species of crab, is used as a topping for nigiri sushi or in chirashi sushi, though rarely in this country. *Seiko-gani* are crab roe, used the same way. Both are tough ingredients to get outside Japan. Still, if you know an itamae well, ask him if he knows of them, and he might surprise you. And if you are with anyone who isn't a sushi snob and you order a plate of nigiri with crab guts and eggs, you will sure as hell surprise them.

KANPACHI 🐟 YELLOWTAIL

K*anpachi* is a lot like professional-level soccer. While neither has caught on with widespread enthusiasm in the United States, both have their stalwart fans and you can get both if you know where to look. Nomenclature can be trying for both as well. In soccer it is players with names consisting entirely of consonants and symbols. "Kanpachi" is easy to pronounce; it is the translations that can perplex. It doesn't help that most of the few sushi-ya carrying it outside Japan translate "kanpachi" on their menus as "amberjack" or "young yellowtail." That's kind of sort of true, but seriously misleading. Kanpachi are young. And they are, technically speaking, yellowtail, which are also called amberjacks. They are not, however, the same yellowtail as the hamachi yellowtail, also likely to be on the menu. True kanpachi are one of two fish, both in the same family as other yellowtails, though different species.

Kanpachi are fished in the waters of the China Sea and all around southern Japan. Sakurajima, once an island and now a peninsula in Kyushu, is famous for its kanpachi catch and for having one of the most active volcanoes in the world, one spewing ash on a regular basis and that's less than a long lava spurt away from Kagoshima City. Kanpachi are also extensively farmed, not only in Japan, but in China and Taiwan as well. Their name means "eight between the eyes," probably a reference to an upside-down V shape on their foreheads. (It resembles the way the numeral 8 is written in Japanese.) They are a deep, dark, purplish blue on top, pale along their bellies, with the distinctive yellow stripe running laterally down their sides, like other yellowtails. Kanpachi grow to more than twice the length of those other yellowtails, up to about seven feet. The meat from a fish that size would be excellent for grilling, or even the whole fish if you had a really big grill. It is far too bland for a good tane, though. Few sushi fish decline so obviously in taste when they reach full size as do kanpachi. When it's about two feet long and around two years old, it's prime for sushi.

Distinguishing kanpachi from other yellowtail is tricky. It is not so challenging in the fish market, where you can see the whole fish. Kanpachi are much darker in color than other yellowtail, and they are "wider." That is, the distance between their ventral and dorsal fins is greater than on other yellowtail, giving them a flatter shape. A dead giveaway is the mouth. Other yellowtail have that smiley face, with an upward-curving lip. Kanpachi lips form a blunt right angle. Assuming you don't know your itamae well enough to be tagging along when he goes to the fish market, and do not have an intense and vaguely disturbing interest in comparing fish lips, you will encounter kanpachi already filleted and paired with rice on a plate in front of you. At this point, making the call is for the expert. Here's how: If both are offered, order hamachi and kanpachi together so you can make a side-by-side comparison. You'll see that hamachi looks decidedly pinkish next to the paler kanpachi. If they've both been sliced to the same, proper thickness, about three bu or $3/16$ inch, the kanpachi will seem almost translucent; the hamachi won't. Kanpachi is not as dense as other yellowtail, and it doesn't have their rich, buttery taste. Despite this, some Japanese sushi tsu insist kanpachi is far superior to hamachi. That's debatable. Kanpachi *is* much leaner, with less than half the fat of hamachi. So it makes a nice palate cleanser if you've been gorging on a lot of fatty tane.

In Japan, kanpachi is a standard early summer tane. At its peak, especially in southern Japan, it's sometimes called *tsuyu-kanpachi*, or rainy season kanpachi, since the soggy rainy season there, from late May through the first part of June, is when kanpachi tastes best. Note, though, that by mid- to late summer, the flavor of this tane takes a dramatic nosedive. When the first back-to-school sales are going on, the kanpachi have spawned and their meat reeks worse than a '70s-supergroup reunion concert.

≋ **By Any Other Name:** Be leery of any kind of qualifying terminology connected with kanpachi. It either is or it isn't, yet given its reputation and scarcity and the looseness in terminology for all yellowtail, you might see one of them being passed off as *hirenaga kanpachi* or some other fill-in-the-blank kanpachi. If the itamae can't readily confirm the difference between this kanpachi and hamachi, pass on it. In Kyushu, kanpachi is sometimes called *akabana* (red nose). In the United States, you might see it called a rudderfish.

≋ **Watch For:** Kanpachi that is really a related yellowtail species called almaco jack. Almaco lives in warmer waters all over the southern Pacific, and it is heavily fished on the Pacific Coast of Mexico. The flavor of this fish is not in the same league with kanpachi. The same can be said for the Atlantic's lesser amberjack, which is also passed off for kanpachi from time to time. If it is real kanpachi, the price will be as high as that of any other tane on the menu, or higher. Even though commercially farmed kanpachi is making this fish more affordable, it's still rare and eagerly sought by itamae in good sushi-ya. Assume that bargain-basement "kanpachi" is almaco if you're in the western part of the United States, and lesser amberjack if you are in the East.

≋ **Ask the Itamae:** Kanpachi is much more popular in Japan than elsewhere. Ordering it if it is on the menu will do much to enhance your reputation as a sushi tsu.

KASUGO ⇝ YOUNG SEA BREAM

Cultural expressions of sexuality are diverse, varied, and complex, and the sophisticated and worldly cosmopolitan would never be judgmental or insensitive about them—except in the case of the Japanese, who are, to be perfectly frank, pretty weird on the subject. Take the word *kawaii*. It means "cute." It connotes an ideal of a young woman, from her gawky pigeon toes to her cutesy-poo T-shirts and knee-high socks to her breathy, babyish lisp, who may be in her twenties, may have a college degree, may have a career, and who is nevertheless trying hard to pass herself off as a barely pubescent Lolita. Kawaii, also called *burikko* (pretend kids), are as Japanese as Mt. Fuji and squid-flavored snack chips. Any current list of popular actresses and pop singers will include several women who appear and behave as if adolescence is still a couple of semesters away. In the rest of the world, girls try to look grown up to attract men. In Japan, women try to look like they're 12 to accomplish the same thing. Barbie dolls were a flop in Japan until a special kawaii version came out, with flattened breasts and hips. Now, by any standard, youngsters in Japan are safer than anywhere else in the world, and child sexual abuse is certainly no worse and probably not as bad as in any other country, so who knows? Maybe the Japanese are on to something. Youth has its attractions, arguably, and in sushi it is celebrated in the case of the preadolescent sea bream, or *kasugo*.

"Kasugo" is a Tokyo word; in much of the rest of Japan it's called a *kodai*, or little tai. By the definition of Japanese cuisine, a tai enters adulthood once it has spawned. So kodai are virgins, under a year old, and about the length of a Cross pen. For reasons known only to themselves, tai prefer the Inland Sea and western side of Japan; they're harder to find on the Pacific coast and command higher prices there. Toyama Bay claims the best kasugo, though nearly every region of the country that borders the ocean has its own locally celebrated populations of young bream. There are dozens of methods of preparation for it in addition to kasugo's inclusion in sushi. Kasugo as an adolescent or an adult doesn't travel outside Japan, neither under its own power nor frozen. There might be an exception now and then, but this is one tane for which you'll almost certainly need a passport in order to enjoy.

Since kasugo by definition haven't spawned, they really do not have a season. They are, however, to the Japanese imagination and appetite, a fish of springtime. They are about the right size for sushi when the cherry trees blossom and, having a similar light pink color, they are associated with that time of year. Kasugo sushi in Japan is sometimes presented with a sprig of cherry blossoms decorating the plate, just to reinforce the image. In less classy sushi-ya, presentations of chirashi sushi with kasugo can be startlingly gaudy, with white and pink CD-size paper cherry blossom "petals" arranged around the sushi.

The meat of the kasugo is prepared as a hikari-mono with salt and vinegar, just like kohada (see page 132). Since it is extremely delicate, though, special care has to be taken by the itamae. He handles kasugo only with his fingertips. When they are steeped in vinegar to "cook," the fillets have to be carefully folded over so the skin sides touch, allowing the vinegar to more fully penetrate the soft meat. If your order of kasugo tastes muddy or mushy, the fault is almost certainly due to poor processing by the itamae. Back in the 1940s and '50s, kasugo was probably the most popular hikari-mono used for sushi. Though it is likely just a coincidence, kasugo's popularity declined at about the time *Sputnik* went up, and today the majority of Japanese list kohada as their favorite hikari-mono. That's one reason younger itamae may not be as expert in preparing it, particularly in a sushi-ya that is less than top class.

≋ **By Any Other Name:** Kasugo are called young porgy in English translations. *Chidai* and *kodai*, both of which mean "small tai," are alternative names used in some parts of Japan for kasugo. They're *makodai* in Kagoshima Prefecture, and out on the Kansai, they are sometimes *chariko kasugo* or, more commonly, *suzume-dai*, or "sparrow tai." We'll get to that below.

≣ **Watch For:** Kasugo is filleted so that the fish's spine is snipped off with the tail left on the meat. Then the fillet is sliced in half, meaning half a tail is left attached to the tane. Yes, the tail is meant to be eaten. It adds texture, if not much taste, and since you'll have come all the way to Japan to try it, you may as well go, so to speak, whole hog. Kasugo is also a classic ingredient in chirashi sushi and in pressed oshi sushi. If the tail isn't on the fish, though, assume you are getting a fillet of the adult fish being passed off as the younger kasugo. The difference in taste, unless you have a lot of experience, requires a side-by-side comparison. Kasugo will be lighter and more delicate on your palate than the older tai. In sushi-ya all over Osaka, you will see *suzume kodai* advertised. Today, the term is loosely used and can refer to any kind of pressed sushi that includes kasugo as an ingredient. In more correct parlance, "suzume kodai" means "pressed triangles of sushi that look like a straight-on view of a plump, perched sparrow."

≣ **Ask the Itamae:** To reiterate for those who may have been skimming or drifting off, this fish is almost completely unavailable anywhere but Japan, either as an adult tai or as kasugo, its younger version. Invest in high-tech stocks from Paraguay before you buy into a sushi-ya advertising kasugo outside Japan. And remember: If the tail's not there, don't you dare. You may, however, see something listed as kasugo on the sushi menu. Ask about it. If you pursue the subject, you may be told it is "an American kind of kasugo." Nope, and while the itamae might be perfectly well-meaning and not consciously trying to be dishonest, this is wrong. It will probably be a young red snapper or something like ocean perch or rockfish, which are known as *hatsume* and *mebaru*. These are adequate tane for sushi, though they are not anywhere close to the real thing and should not really be advertised as such.

KATSUO ⇌ BONITO

Want to see what Tokyo looked like back before everyone above the age of three there was talking on a postage stamp–size phone and ferro-cement structures were metastasizing like mutant insects in a bad science fiction movie? Head southeast from Shinjuku Station, toward the mouth of the Sumida River. Take the Tsukuda Bridge, which in 1964 replaced the ferry that had been operating perfectly well since 1645 (the Japanese can never leave well enough alone) out to Tsukuda-jima. It's an island at the mouth of the Sumida River where it empties into Tokyo Bay. The neighborhoods of Tsukudajima are a jumble of old shops and tenement houses, laid out haphazardly along narrow lanes. Every month or so, a Quikie-Mart or some such thing replaces another ancient wooden house; the charming old places continue to shrink year after year, giving way to modern buildings. Even so, there's still enough left to get a feel for what much of urban Japan looked like before World War II. While you're there, you will want to visit Sumiyoshi-jinja, the local Shinto shrine. If you take the A tour at the Sumiyoshi shrine, you will go past a dirt-brown stone obelisk on the shrine's property, marking Katsuozuka, the "Bonito Mound." It is dedicated to all the katsuo, or bonito, that have been harvested by local fishermen. Once a year the priests gather at the mound for a ceremony to honor the katsuo that have given their lives in the gastronomic service of mankind. It's the sort of formal occasion the sushi tsu can really appreciate.

The existence of a plot sacred to the memory of digested bonito gives some suggestion of their importance in the Japanese diet. They are roasted whole or filleted, or grilled teriyaki style. Dried and scraped into shavings, their flesh is used to make soup stock or garnishes for hundreds of dishes. To be sure, bonito is eaten raw as sashimi or sushi. While all kinds of fishes are important to the cuisine of Japan, it is safe to say that should katsuo disappear, Japan's food would change in a very fundamental way.

Katsuo is an example of a *kudari sakana*, a "descending fish," which means it migrates throughout the year and is caught in different parts of Japan at different times. At the beginning of the year, they appear in nets in the islands far south of Japan, the Ogasawara and Ryukyu archipelagos. By March, bonito have reached Aomori Prefecture, cruising along on the Black Current as the waters warm. It isn't until September that they make it as far north as the south coast of Hokkaido, where, like irritating Canadian retirees who never use their turn signals, the katsuo promptly turn tail and head back south with the first frosts. So each region of Japan celebrates the coming of the first bonito of the season. In Tokyo, that happens around May, just as spring arrives. The *hatsuo-gatsu*, or first bonito of the season, are heralded with as much folderol as the popping of the first Beaujolais Nouveau cork in France. It is a very big deal and has been for a long time. A well-known haiku from the Edo era sums it up:

> *Me niwa aoba*
> *Yama hototogisu*
> *Hatsu-gatsuo*
> Green leaves appear before one's eyes,
> Cuckoos call from the mountain—
> The season's first bonito.

In the United States, while its first seasonal appearance is met with about as much enthusiasm as the next Yanni album, katsuo is a descending fish as well, caught off Long Island beginning in early May. By mid-July, the majority of the harvest is taken from the coast of California. In late summer, when the popularity of katsuo drops off significantly, itamae in the United States will always check the tail of a fish they're considering buying. It should be firm; if it droops, he's looking at a less than optimally fresh fish, and while he might buy it earlier in the summer, he'll probably pass on any katsuo not perfectly fresh after mid-August. The itamae in the United States and in Japan is pickier about katsuo as Labor Day approaches because he knows demand for it slackens and he has to present the best. He and the sushi snob also know, though, that this can be a mistake. (See "Ask the Itamae," page 125.)

Bonito grow to more than three feet in length, but such hefty specimens come from the oceans of Australia. In Japan, katsuo are about half that size; the same is true for most of the bonito caught in American waters, which are most likely to be the katsuo served in U.S. sushi-ya. They are classy-looking fish; gunmetal blue on top with slanted, darker blue racing stripes down the side, and silvery white on their bellies. They look a lot like their tuna cousins, and they swim nearly as swiftly. When katsuo put it into overdrive, pursuing smaller fish or squid, they can actually come out of the water in arcing leaps.

Katsuo, unfortunately, has a shelf life shorter than the average celebrity marriage, and unless it is served within hours after it is killed and filleted, a noticeable aroma begins to come off the fish that's distinctly unpalatable. It doesn't reek, but it isn't appetizing. And it signals a bacterial happy hour that is all too soon underway. Katsuo was once considered a meal for the upper classes, simply because they were the only ones who could afford to eat it fresh enough to be safe. Even so, more than one aficionado of katsuo died of ptomaine poisoning. But katsuo was as irresistible as it was perishable. Consequently, it was almost always cooked before it was eaten.

Once katsuo became safe to eat raw as sushi or sashimi, thanks to modern refrigeration and freezing methods, it became fairly common in Japanese sushi-ya. It is readily available at many places outside Japan. If it is eaten this way, it has to be very, very fresh, either taken that day or skillfully quick-frozen. Otherwise the off odor is too distinct. It will have been skinned too, since the hide of the katsuo cannot be eaten uncooked. Even so, at least as much, if not more, bonito is prepared *tataki* style as a nigiri sushi. The sushi snob should be completely conversant in the tataki process.

Tataki is a method of cookery from the feudal province of Tosa, now a part of Kochi Prefecture, on Japan's southern Shikoku Island. Another word for the tataki style of preparation, in fact, is *Tosa-mi*. Tosa was the home of Sakamoto Ryoma, a kind of early 19th-century Japanese Luke Skywalker who was fighting against the Evil Empire of the Tokugawa shogunate. Ryoma spent a lot of time in Nagasaki around the large contingent of foreigners there, and he picked up the European preferences for grilling meat. Lore has it that he is the one who brought the tataki method of quick-searing katsuo back to Tosa. (Ryoma met his end not by a light saber but by an assassin's knife, while he was hiding in a shoyu factory in Kyoto. The Kyoto National Museum still has a scroll that was hanging on the factory wall at the time, spattered with Ryoma's blood.) That's all "tataki" implies: a fast, searing grill atop high heat that gives a crispness to the skin of the katsuo and barely cooks just a few centimeters of the flesh right below the skin. If it is done right, the surface of the meat will turn white, contrasting with the pink and red underneath. Once the flame has kissed it, the katsuo meat goes into a bath of rice vinegar for just a few moments. Then it's done.

There are all sorts of variations on this technique. Sometimes the raw katsuo fillets are marinated in rice vinegar, along with other ingredients like mirin, before grilling. They are sometimes plunged into ice water as soon as they come off the flame to set the flavor and draw off excess fat. A smidgen of garlic can be added to the grill for additional flavor. No matter how it is done, the smells of tataki cooking, with pungent smoke as the skin crackles, and savory meat roasting, are mouthwatering to any fan of open-pit barbecue or grilling. Once the katsuo's been grilled, it is cooled—again, ice water might play a part in that—then sliced thinly enough to make a tane. Note that "tataki" means "pounded" or "hit into pieces." It's misleading. The meat is not pounded. It is the ginger that's ground or pounded into a paste. A dab of the ginger, along with slivers of green onion stems that usually go on top the tane, gives tataki its name.

Whether raw or tataki style, katsuo is one of the best examples of *shun no aji*, the "taste of the season," which once dominated Japanese cuisine. It tastes different at different times of the year, as different as a fresh garden tomato will taste in June from a hothouse version eaten in February. The sushi tsu must appreciate the seasonal fluctuations in katsuo in order to plumb the depths of the art.

By Any Other Name: *Ma-katsuo* and *hon-katsuo* are a couple of alternative names for bonito in Japanese. Don't be confused if you happen to see *mana-katsuo* on a menu. Despite the name, it is really a very distant relative of the katsuo called a pomfret, and it's much better grilled or roasted than as a tane for sushi. In English, besides bonito, katsuo goes by the names skipjack or skipjack tuna. If a place is advertising "Oriental bonito," it should be the true Japanese katsuo. To be exact, the bonito taken from American waters is not the same fish as the Japanese version. It is in the same family, but a different species. The Indo-Pacific or Japanese katsuo is found in the western Pacific, out to Hawaii and down to the west coast of Central America. Another species is common along the coasts of North and South America. Still another, the Atlantic bonito, is found all over that ocean. Most likely, your order of katsuo sushi came from the species that swam in waters nearest you. The difference in taste among these individual species is not nearly so marked as the variations in taste throughout the year. On the whole, however, Japanese katsuo has the best flavor.

Katsuo is the other akami, the only tane correctly called "red meat" in the sushi lexicon, aside from maguro, or tuna. The freshly caught fish is cut up and filleted exactly the same way as tuna (see page 136). If it is raw, katsuo looks exactly like lean tuna. It is presented similarly, on nigiri or in chirashi sushi as a tane. Cuts of bonito in spring and summer will—or should be—a little thicker than those prepared in the autumn, because there's less oil in the flesh during spring and summer, and the palate can appreciate the texture of the fish more then.

If the sushi-ya serves katsuo tataki style, the garnishes of ground ginger, chives, or onions will be heaped on top. Go very lightly on the shoyu with katsuo served raw; forego it altogether when you're eating it tataki style.

≡ **Watch For:** As we've mentioned, katsuo is one of the essential fish of spring and the hatsu-gatsuo, the first taste of bonito, is Christmas, New Year's, and Super Bowl Sunday all rolled into one for the gourmet. In addition, there's a folk saying in Japan that eating the first product of anything coming into season will add 75 days to your life. So between hatsu-gatsuo in March and a couple of bottles of Beaujolais Nouveau in November, you could still be vertical and mobile until the decade Bill and Hillary finally pay off all their legal bills. Truth be told, though, it is autumn's katsuo that are the choicest in terms of flavor. The fish have had an entire summer to fatten up, and their oil content is highest in September and October. This is when a lot of sushi tsu and other serious eaters will enjoy katsuo. It is called *modori-katsuo. Modori* means "to go back," a reference to the bonito's return migration when they head back and follow the warmer currents that recede to the south for the winter. Modori-katsuo are pumping oil through their systems like a '73 Dodge with leaky valves, and no matter how much publicity the first bonito of the year get, if you have a chance to try modori-katsuo, you'll taste this fish at its absolute best. It is equally worthy raw or as tataki.

≡ **Ask the Itamae:** There is another method of preparing katsuo for sushi that a good itamae should know. Ask him if he can fix you *katsuo-zuke.* The "zuke" here is the same character used to write "tsuke," as in *tsukemono*, the generic word for vegetables pickled in various brines that are a staple at a Japanese meal. Once again, tuna is the only other sushi tane prepared this way. In the zuke process, the katsuo is drizzled liberally with ginger juice and shoyu. The exact amounts and mixture are a secret of the individual itamae, but it is usually done in a tightly meshed bamboo basket so the meat is slowly basted in the liquid. The strong acidity of the ginger juice does a number on the katsuo, not unlike what lime juice does for fish in ceviche. After a few hours, the liquid is gently washed away and the tane is placed on the sushi, which is then brushed with a nikiri sauce. Wasabi never goes anywhere near katsuo-zuke; the only proper condiment for it is a thin paste of *karashi*, or Japanese mustard.

Trivia: The sushi fan will know, of course, that the dried shavings of bonito used for stock are called *katsuobushi*. The sushi tsu, naturally, will be aware of a finer distinction: the wider shavings for stock are more properly called *hana-katsuobushi*; *ito-kezuri-katsuobushi* are the finer, thread-like shavings of katsuo that are used as a garnish.

More Trivia: Bonito was a favorite dish of the samurai (katsuo sounds a lot like *katsu uo*, "victorious fish"). Presumably, were there a fish with a name that sounds like "losing badly and forced to commit suicide along with all my family," it would have been less attractive to the Japanese warrior set.

KAZUNOKO ⇨ HERRING ROE

The Japanese word for herring is *nishin*. There's no reason for the sushi tsu to know that; herring is a delicious fish prepared in a variety of ways in Japan, but it isn't suitable as sushi tane. When herring are in their adolescent years, they are canned as sardines. When they are *very* young, as in embryonic young, that's when you become interested. Kazunoko, or herring roe, is used atop gunkan sushi. The name, incidentally, is a bit of a mystery. It probably derives from an archaic term for herring, *kado*. *Kado-no-ko* are the "eggs" or "young" of the kado. Where does *kazunoko* come from? Well, from herring, obviously. It's harvested from female herring in ships that go out each year after the herring have spawned, in places like the sea off northern Japan and British Columbia; the latter has become something of a mother lode, so to speak, for herring roe production. Commercial fishermen are able to estimate within a week or so when the females' eggs will be ripe. They hang around, catching a few each day or two, so they will know when the moment is exactly right. Then they go into a frenzy, netting the fish by the millions and cleaning the females of their roe. Each female herring ovary can contain up to 100,000 eggs, so it is tedious work, though time well spent. Kazunoko is one of the most expensive sushi toppings around. It is also eaten by itself in Japan as an accompaniment to sake. Kazunoko is a fundamental element in *osechi-ryori*, the symbolic (but pretty tasty, nonetheless) cooking associated with the traditional Japanese New Year. Kazunoko is always on the menu for these meals, since the thousands and thousands of tiny eggs are a subtle hint of fecundity and prosperity.

Kazunoko is salted to preserve it. Before it can be used in sushi, the egg sacs are gently washed clean of the salt and often soaked in sake for a time. Their membranes absorb the sake and are firmed by the salt, and then they are cut into pieces to go onto the gunkan sushi. The taste is creamy and buttery; the color a pale lemon. Each individual egg is about the size of a pinhead. If they are dark or overly salty, you've got kazunoko that hasn't been handled correctly or has been allowed to sit around too long. Kazunoko was once as rare as a fluently English-speaking cabbie in Manhattan is today. In the past few years, it has continued to show up as a gunkan sushi in more and more higher-end sushi-ya.

Watch For: *Kazunoko wakame*, a rarity worth searching out. The way it is made is one of sushi's more entertaining tales. Whether it's the backseat of a Volkswagen or Monte Carlo in the spring, everyone's got a favorite place for doing the reproduction rumba. For herring in the waters around Japan, that place is amidst filmy, gossamer sheets of seaweed that undulate with the currents. Specifically, herring are fond of *wakame*. Those are the thin sheets of green floating in your bowl when you order miso soup. Herring spawn at the same time down amid all that wakame. That means a *lot* of eggs, which are all deposited on the leaves of wakame floating all around. To the ordinary person, this would be little more than a few moments from a *National Geographic* special. To the sushi tsu, however, it means that dinner is served. The wakame is collected, very briefly dried, then packaged so it all stays moist. It is sold to sushi-ya in sheets the size of notebook paper as kazunoko-wakame, also called *komochi-wakame*. *Kazunoko-konbu* is the same thing, but with konbu kelp instead of wakame. Apparently, some herring either can't get into the best wakame beds or are just so promiscuous that they can't wait for an opening and settle for laying their eggs on the kelp instead. Either of these are cut into rectangles to fit atop shari for nigiri sushi, usually tied into place with a strip of nori. They will often have a very thin layer of katsuobushi, or bonito shavings, in between the rice and the topping, which works deliciously to bring together the salty fishiness of the eggs with the taste of the seaweed.

Trivia: Kazunoko, because of the iridescent nature of the tiny eggs, shimmers and sparkles under a light, and so the slang term for it in the sushi-ya is "diamond."

KISU ⌁ SILLAGO

A bout the length of a Taco Bell Burrito Supreme, the *kisu* is known colloquially outside Japan as a sandborer and a Japanese whiting. The first name comes from the kisu's propensity for burrowing into the sand when in danger. The second is because some people aren't very precise or perceptive. Kisu aren't related at all to whiting. They're in a different family; various species of them are caught all over the world. If the name "sillago" doesn't sound familiar, you should not be surprised. Don't bet on it being in the frozen-fish section of your local grocery. While it is an early summertime favorite in Japanese sushi-ya, it is among the most unusual of tane in the United States. If you find kisu, it was most likely harvested in Thailand and processed in Japan, then shipped here frozen. While it would be odd to think of anything sushi-related as aristocratic, kisu has a reputation in Japanese sushi circles as an upper-crust tane, a preferred choice not only for the sushi con-noisseur but also for the Japanese gourmet of every persuasion.

Two species of kisu are eaten in Japan. The blue sillago (*aogisu*) is fried in tempura; its meat is too strong for sushi. It is the white sillago (*shirogisu*) that's a delectable shiromi-dane topping. They are easy to distinguish. Aogisu have a bluish-green sheen in their scales. Shirogisu are a luminescent golden yellow, with snowy white bellies.

Some sushi tsu consider kisu the lightest of all tane, for good reason. While they might not be in the same category as rice cakes, with only one gram of fat for every 100 grams of kisu, nobody's going to become obese eating this fish. Unfortunately, that lean meat means a "Vacancy" sign read by every itinerant bacteria around goes up in kisu flesh almost as soon as the fish stops twitching. Most won't hurt you (Feelin' lucky?), but they give the kisu a decidedly fishy taste. Kisu so fresh that its pals haven't noticed it missing from the old swimming hole is good served raw as a tane. Otherwise, the meat is soaked in vinegar briefly after it has been filleted, whacking the evil germs and contributing to the flavor. That filleting is not an easy job; kisu are extremely bony. The itamae's dissection leaves two fillets, both cut in half, and these are what go on your sushi, provided you are fortunate enough to frequent a place that offers this tane.

≡ **By Any Other Name:** Sometimes kisu are called "Japanese smelts." That's okay. But what are very often sold in Asian fish stores as kisu are actually American smelts. That's not okay, since kisu are not at all related to the smelt family. No matter what it is called, assume that unless it came from Japan, what you're buying as kisu is probably smelt. Kisu may also be called sardine, or kiss fish. The latter derivation is obvious: "kisu" is the Japanese pronunciation of "kiss." The itamae might be using it to sound cute. If so, come back with *kuchizuke*, the literary Japanese term for kissing (mouth touching) that can also be a slang term for a vinegared tane like kisu, since "kuchizuke" can also mean "mouth pickle."

≡ **Watch For:** Tane-size fillets of kisu don't fit well on rice, so the itamae slits them lengthwise not quite all the way through, or *han-giri* (halfway cut), so they fold over the rice more neatly. If he's good, these cuts will be absolutely uniform, never completely through the flesh. If the kisu is cut this way, it came from the forward part of the fish's body. Pieces toward the rear are served whole.

≡ **Ask the Itamae:** Even though the taste of kisu doesn't vary much at all with the seasons or during its spawning period in late August, it is considered a summertime tane. That's when you might see it offered. If so, have the itamae serve it with finely chopped green onion, or fresh-grated ginger, or with just a touch of garlic. All three of these sprinkled atop kisu are traditional; all bring out the flavor of the fish.

≋ **Trivia:** Kisu have been used for lots of research programs involving reproduction. Turns out they're amorous little buggers, perhaps burrowing into the sand not to escape a threat but just to find a quiet place to fool around. Their breeding season lasts from May all the way to October, making their preternaturally active gonads a plentiful source for those looking into the biomechanics of romance.

KOCHI ⇨ DRAGONET OR FLATHEAD

The Elephant Man of the fish world, *kochi* has never been offered at sushi-ya outside Japan other than maybe as an occasional oddity if a fresh specimen came on the market. Despite its startlingly ugly appearance—it's even uglier than catfish—kochi has a light, sweet flavor. It's a shiromi-dane; the flesh is nearly transparent and is usually found as a topping for nigiri sushi. It is also popular as sashimi and batter-fried in tempura.

Kochi has a certain fan base among Japanese sushi tsu because it stays fresh for a long time. It is most popular in the summer, although the sushi connoisseur prefers to eat it in March and April, since early spring fish of the species have less fat and taste cleaner. Many itamae go heavy on the wasabi on kochi, since the sweetness of the flesh needs a little kick to avoid becoming cloying on the palate.

≋ **By Any Other Name:** Kochi is also called *magochi*, or true kochi, although it is hard to believe any other fish would want to try to claim the name, given its appearance. In English, it is called dragonet, flathead, and sand scraper.

KOHADA 🐟 SHAD

Japanese have tended to be somewhat fluid in terms of personal names. Children's names are not infrequently changed. The author Yukio Mishima was called Kimitake until he was fifteen. Even though he adopted a *geimei*, or art name, as a writer, name changes occur for many reasons, and not just among teenagers. Sometimes it is after consultation with an *ekisha*, or fortuneteller, or to celebrate some accomplishment that an adult will change his name, which involves filling out a simple form at a local government office. Also, because of the homonymic nature of kanji, there can be different ways to pronounce a written name. So Chikuma can be written to mean "bamboo horse" or "1,000 bears," both pronounced the same way. It is a neat way of allowing a kid to experiment with his adolescent persona a little, without resorting to tattoos or piercings or joining cults that encourage drinking specially prepared Kool-Aid and worshipping the moons of Jupiter.

Similarly, several fish go through name changes as they mature. They are known as *shusse-uo*. Kohada is a shusse-uo. Kohada just beyond the fry stage are *shinko*. When they are around five inches long and at their best for sushi, they're kohada. A couple of inches longer and they become *nakatsumi* (or *nakazumi* in some dialects), and when they're fully mature, a little shy of a foot long, they are *konoshiro*, which is really the proper name for the fish. *Tsunashi* is a regional term for konoshiro, used more in Kyushu. "Kohada" is a Tokyo word, though it has spread to much of the rest of Japan and is heard mostly in fish markets and sushi-ya. And there it is heard a lot. That's because kohada are to hikari-mono tane what the 1968 VW Microbus was to premarital sex.

The kohada looks like a herring that has been squashed a little. It is slimmer and trimmer and it has a long, supple

filament that extends from the very back of its dorsal fin, looking like the antennae whipping out behind a roadster with a
CB radio on board. Kohada are bright and silvery, with a row
of black dots decorating each side. A fish unique to the western
Pacific right around Japan, it commonly swims in large schools
very deep in the waters along the southern half of the Japanese
islands. There is a shad in Atlantic waters called a gizzard shad
or a hickory shad. But it is not even in the same genus as the
Japanese shad. So kohada must be imported for sushi, and
more and more it is.

Kohada starts showing up in Japanese fish markets in the
first part of autumn, when it is still technically a shinko. The
taste is too bland for sushi; there isn't enough fat content.
When the fish has had a couple of months longer to pack on
something around the middle and grows to five to six inches
long, the meat gains considerably in flavor. So kohada is a traditional favorite wintertime tane, retaining its peak all through
the colder months until it has reached full size and becomes a
konoshiro in the spring. Konoshiro, incidentally, are popular as
a grilled fish, but many Japanese will politely wrinkle their
noses if you mention it. That's mostly because if the shad isn't
extremely fresh, it gives off a rank aroma.

When you run into kohada at the sushi-ya, it will have been
put through the basic vinegar treatment, as are most hikari-
mono. The word "pickling" comes to mind. But that's not
entirely accurate and conveys a fish pickle, which isn't entirely
appetizing. Maybe "curing" is a better word. It is the same
process, no matter what the fish. Kohada are cleaned and
gutted and filleted, then salted on both sides. Most itamae will
use a dampened bamboo strainer for this, spreading salt on the
strainer, then laying the fillets on top, then adding another
layer of salt so it cures both sides of the fish. Seems simple, but
this is another place where the itamae who really knows what
he's doing gets separated from the rest of the pack. Kohada, to
taste best, have to be left in this salt for varying lengths of time,

depending on the weather. If it is warm, they don't need much time. If it is cold, they have to sit a while longer. So it's anywhere from an hour in late September to three or four hours by midwinter. A good itamae can judge this perfectly, varying the amount of salt as well. He'll take the fillets out of the strainer just as the last of the salt is dissolving. Then he puts them into a wash with lots of fresh water, washing off the salt and the excess fat and oil that were drawn out.

After *furishio*, or salt scattering, comes *suarai*, or "vinegar washing." Each fillet is dipped into a solution of rice vinegar, and top-level sushi-ya will reuse vinegar that's been used for this part of the process before. The recycled vinegar acquires a richness that adds to the flavor of the fish. It will have lost some of its acidity, though, so the fish doesn't "cook" like ceviche. Lesser-quality sushi places may not use recycled vinegar, and you'll taste the inferior consequences. The kohada will taste slightly bitter or harsh and have an unpleasant fishy aroma. Finally, fresh, full-strength vinegar is used for *tsukekomi*, a last bath that will, in half an hour or so, start to turn the inner flesh of the fillets a very pale white, like frost settling. Again, some sushi-ya will use kohada right after it has been drained from this bath. The best, though, allow the fish to sit for several more hours so its flavor develops, a period that ages the hikari-mono to perfection.

The itamae might have spread a touch of wasabi on the underside of a kohada tane; don't use any, though, when you eat it. Kohada prepared as a hikari-mono is about as complex on the tongue as sushi flavors can get. There's the fish itself, fairly strong and full, with just a slight tang of salt and the piquant smack of rice vinegar, all working together. Don't gum up the works with any additional seasoning if you want to get the full effect of the itamae's mastery. It's a long-standing tradition in the *Edokko* style of eating sushi to order kohada as a first course. If you want to do this as they do in Tokyo, you say, with just a touch of sophisticated world-weariness after perusing the menu or signboard, *"Saa. Mazu, kohada."* (Well, let's see. . . . I'll start with the kohada.")

≋ **By Any Other Name:** Translating "kohada" is a tough proposition. In addition to the misleading term of "gizzard shad" and the slightly less so but still misleading "herring," it is sometimes called a "young punctatus," which sounds like something a senior senator might call a junior colleague, as in "I was bringin' home the pork to my state while that young punctatus was still bribing his first election judge." Actually, it refers to the Latin name of the kohada. On the sushi menu it might also be called Japanese shad or spotted shad.

≋ **Watch For:** Kohada's flavor is hidden. That's why this is a favorite opening order for the sushi tsu, to test the itamae's ability to draw it out. The quality of the final product all has to do with his skill, assuming the fish is fresh, in working with the salt and vinegar to prepare a good hikari-mono. Even with all the modernizations in factory preparations of sushi tane, this is one area where the itamae's prowess is essential. If kohada is available at a sushi-ya, consider making it your first choice. Be on the lookout too for "kohada" that seems too large. Kohada fillets are about the same size you'd have if you filleted minnows. If larger than that, or, especially, if cut into pieces that clearly aren't an entire side of the small fish, then you need to ask if what you're being served is konoshiro, the adult version. Its taste can range from bland to excellent, and some sushi tsu in Japan prefer it to kohada. But it should not be nearly so expensive. Shinko, the babies, are also marinated hikari-mono style and served as a sushi tane.

≋ **Ask the Itamae:** Often in Japan, and only occasionally in America, kohada will be served as a sushi tane in the *maruzuke* style. It is marinated the same way, but the body of the fish is left whole after it has been cleaned and gutted. The flavor is more pronounced and there's a meaty heft to the fish that will have a different feel on your palate from the way kohada is usually presented.

≋ **Trivia:** Kohada are harvested by the untold millions yearly in Japan, and they're always available in Japanese fish markets, whether for sushi or for grilling or for some other method of preparation. But kohada are wimps when it comes to falling temperatures, and they are susceptible to massive die-offs if the water where they live gets too cold. That's one reason kohada prices may jump unexpectedly at sushi-ya.

≋ **More Trivia:** One of the dumbest mistakes an itamae can make is to clean kohada and then fail to thoroughly wipe the knife before moving on to another fish. Kohada, before they are marinated, are quite strong; their scent sticks to the knife and it is immediately detectable if other fish have been contaminated.

MAGURO ⟶ TUNA

The dreams of the alpinist are of Himalayan peaks. Surfers long for those big curls that break to the left at Waimea. Class-action-lawsuit shysters salivate at the thought of a toxic waste dump. For the sushi tsu? It is tuna. The Everest, the Banzai Pipeline of sushi, tuna, or maguro is to the sushi world what Bordeaux is to the wine snob. It is the apogee, the sine qua non, the kissed-for-the-first-time-on-New-Year's-Eve-in-Times-Square of the sushi experience. The history and allure of Edomae sushi would be entirely different without it. Learn the lore of the tuna, and if you know nothing else about the way of vinegared rice, you will have earned your reputation as a sushi tsu. That's the good news, that your expertise can hang reliably on an erudite knowledge of this single fish. The bad news is, just like memorizing Latin verb conjugations you swore you'd master before the end of your junior year, or learning to ballroom dance, it is complicated. The ships laden with Latin conjugations and sparkly balls have rather long since left port, I think we'd agree; let's turn our energies to learning all about tuna while there is still time.

For starters, tuna are in the same family as mackerel, among the high-octane members of the fish world. Tuna are built like seagoing Ferraris. They travel faster and farther than next year's most pernicious influenza strain, which means they can be found in nearly all the world's oceans. There are more than 50 species in the family. Relax. Only about 10 are worth filleting for dinner in one form or another, and only half of those are good for sushi. Let's review some of those you are most likely to be meeting and eating in the sushi-ya.

Hon-maguro, or real tuna, is the top of the line in traditional sushi circles in Japan. They're the *sumotori* of the seas, up to nearly 1,000 pounds of streamlined herring- and squid-eating machines and longer than your Uncle Lester's Bonneville. You'd think that since *hon* here means "real" or "true," there would be one specific species. You could learn it, ask for it by name at a sushi-ya, and be graduated from Maguro 101 before the end of the first semester. Sorry. "Hon-maguro" applies to any of several species of tuna given that general name in Japan; since there are also different common and local names for the same fish, it gets even more confusing. So "hon-maguro," *shibi-maguro*, and *miyakijima-maguro* could all, depending on who's doing the talking in Japanese, refer to the same tuna. Fishermen from Japan's northeast Miyagi Prefecture call a certain tuna *sanriku-maguro*, named for the region of the ocean right off the coast there. But over on the southwest corner, in Shimane Prefecture, that name won't ever be used. The only way to conclusively, scientifically identify some of the tribe of tuna going under the "hon-maguro" moniker is to examine the lobes on their livers or the distinctive patterns of their gill rakers. Since neither of those parts is edible, the sushi tsu will leave it up to the ichthyologist to make specific taxonomic calls of this nature.

Generally speaking, most versions of hon-maguro toddlers are called *meji*; their flesh is not quite dense and muscular enough for good sushi. Sofa-size adolescents, or *nakaboushi*, coming in around 400 pounds, are the most popular choice; less oily than adults, firmer and meatier than their younger siblings, and small enough to be cut into manageable hunks at fish markets like Tokyo's famous Tsukiji.

When you see news of a huge tuna selling in Japan for Palm Beach real estate prices (it is the most expensive wild animal on the planet), it is almost always a hon-maguro. Most of the time it will be the legendary species, the bluefin, or *kuro-maguro* (black tuna). Here in the United States, you will most likely be eating those bluefin caught somewhere in the North Atlantic. Like a lot of East Coast elite, these piscine patricians are most comfortable in well-established havens like the Narragansett Bay in Rhode Island, or off Cape Cod. Nearly all tuna species run in schools. Bluefins, though, as they get bigger, tend toward less socializing, with the monsters often running nearly alone, which makes them even harder to catch. In Japan, the sushi tsu prefers all cuts of hon-maguro in the winter. Yet for some reason, in the Atlantic the meat reaches its peak in flavor and texture during the summer. That's why tuna fishermen on the East Coast go into overdrive once spring is past and why, if you want to try hon-maguro at its absolute best in the United States, you should forego the hot dogs and chips and make reservations at your favorite sushi-ya next Fourth of July.

Minami-maguro is the Japanese name for what we call the southern Atlantic bluefin. *Minami* means "south"; most of these fish that end up in Japan are caught in the southern or Indian oceans. Recently discovered by those who have time for such matters is the fact that southern bluefin taken from waters 30 to 50 degrees south latitude consistently have both a lot of fat and good taste, rather like a couple of restaurant critics currently writing for—nope, not going to go there. Southern bluefin are punier than their northern relatives. They reach their top weight somewhere around 200 pounds. There is some nit-picking terminology for subspecies among them, so you may hear alternative terms for southern bluefin like *indo-* or *goshu-* or *bachi-maguro*. One problem with southern bluefin is that the quality of the meat varies so widely from place to place. It's undependable. Without eating a lot of it, you cannot be sure whether you dislike minami-maguro or just ran into some inferior fish. To make matters worse, minami-maguro is often frozen and shipped to various places all over the world and, of all species of tuna, the southern bluefin travels worst. Its flavor, once frozen, declines dramatically. If you see it mentioned specifically on a menu, minami-maguro is worth a try. Be reserved in your judgment, however, until you've had it in a few different places and at different times of the year to give yourself a broader perspective.

Yellowfin tuna, most tropical of all the tuna species, also hang out in the warmer water of the oceans, in tropical climes. They're *kihada* in Japanese (yellow skin), or *kiwade maguro*. Their flesh runs from a deep rose to a light pink. Next to hon-maguro, yellowfin is the tuna most often served in sushi-ya in this country, and in some places, especially along the East Coast, it is a better-than-fair bet that you are eating yellowfin, particularly in the winter and into early spring. The flavor is outstanding, rich and meaty. Sometimes yellowfin will be faintly webbed with veins of darkish blue that don't affect the meat at all. It shouldn't be necessary to say this, by the way, but don't confuse yellowfin with yellowtail hamachi.

Mebachi or *mebuto* are known in the West as bigeye tuna. They tend to hang out in warmer parts of the Atlantic and Pacific and they reach peak flavor in the spring, when they are most likely to be served as sushi. This is the fish, along with yellowfin tuna, known as *ahi* in Hawaiian (even though bigeye is often sold at seafood restaurants that refer to it with irritating redundancy as "ahi tuna"). The sushi tsu often complains that the mebachi meat is flabby and soft and unpleasantly sticky. This is always an indication that it isn't fresh enough. The bigeye is a pain for itamae because it has a foul-tasting layer of oil right under its skin that starts leaking into the fibers of the meat when the fish is killed. The offensive layer, about half an inch deep, has to be trimmed away completely. If you eat maguro that has any kind of disagreeable kerosene after-taste, that's poorly prepared mebachi. A less-than-excellent ita-mae will sometimes sear a chunk of mebachi in the method of cooking called tataki—we'll discuss it below—as a way of hid-ing the poor taste. That's not to say any seared tuna you get as sushi is mebachi or even inferior tuna. It's just a clue to watch for if the meat seems less than ideal.

Taiseiyo (Pacific Ocean tuna) or blackfin are the runts of the tuna litter, barely tipping the scales past 30 pounds. At one time, the sushi tsu outside Japan or Asia would never have seen this species. Now, however, it is sometimes preserved with a flavorless smoke at factories in different parts of Southeast Asia, vacuum-packed or frozen, and imported here as maguro. Tech-nically it is maguro, though the taste is clearly not up to the standards of the sushi tsu. You'll know it when you take a mouthful, if you have any experience with maguro at all. Watch for maguro that has a neon-red color that just doesn't look natural. The color is a result of the smoking process.

Shiro-maguro, "white tuna," hit American sushi-ya a few years ago like free kegs of cheap beer at a fraternity party. Would-be sushi experts raved authoritatively about it. When they got it in stock, itamae saved it for the most valued cus-tomers. The hype has since subsided somewhat. Still, in the minds of many, a professed adoration of shiro-maguro consti-tutes inclusion in a sushi cult. The real story is that shiro-maguro is albacore, the same fish better known at the grocery store as the stuff of tuna fish sandwiches. It is a tuna, one of the smallest species, usually harvested when it's around 50 pounds. The best season for shiro-maguro served as sushi is from late June to late October. The raw meat is a healthy, peaches-and-cream color similar to that of the canned variety.

Shiro-maguro, kept unprocessed, tends to lose its creamy attractive color over time, although the taste doesn't change much, if at all. It is milder than other tuna, with less of a heavy, rich taste. While much of its popularity comes from its scarcity and from the hoopla surrounding it, some sushi tsu find it an interesting contrast to other maguro. To hide the dull look of the meat once it has sat for a while or been frozen, itamae often sear shiro-maguro tataki style. It's a telltale sign, and while it does nothing to alter the taste, the shiro-maguro should be less expensive than fresh. Shiro-maguro is also called *binnaga*. Don't confuse it, in any case, with escolar, a completely unrelated fish sometimes sold in fish markets as "white tuna."

Now that you know the players in these big leagues of sushi, the next step is to know how they're hacked into pieces small enough for lunch. Here's how it's done:

Lay Charlie out on the counter, so the head's hanging over the sink, the tail flopped over the dishwasher. Whack both off. If you draw a line along the length of the carcass that remains, the meat above the line is the *se-itcho*; below is the *hara-itcho*. In the fish market, these are separated, then sliced vertically, about three *take* thick. (A "take" is a fish peddler's term meaning "the width of four fingers.") These hunks, called *cho*, must be cleaned of bones, membranes, skin, and especially the *chiai*, a dark purple streak running the whole lateral length of the tuna. The cho are then cut about an inch thick and one take wide; these smaller pieces are what you'll then slice to make a series of single servings of sushi tane. Assuming you're sane enough not to do it yourself with a whole tuna, you can buy these manageably sized cho in fresh-fish markets. You will, however, lose the opportunity to cross-section a maguro, which would give you the best view for seeing the different cuts used for sushi. You will, in any case, need to know each of these cuts, and know them well.

Starting from the upper, dorsal section, here's what you'll find:

Akami, or red meat, is the thick, dark burgundy center section of a tuna and is a nearly solid muscle mass that propels the fish. You should remember the word from our discussion of the different forms of tane. Typically it refers to this part of the tuna specifically. If you're eating prepackaged sushi like those sold in groceries and there is tuna, it will certainly be akami; it is the cheapest cut on the fish. Even in a good sushi-ya, this will always be the least expensive offering of tuna on the menu. Akami is nearly always the center filling in tekka-maki. How times have changed. A century ago the red meat was the *only* cut of maguro eaten as sushi. (Don't get too conceited; our forefathers used lobster as feed for their hogs and servants. The former never complained, but the servants demanded they be limited to lobster meals no more than twice a month.) Even then, the akami wasn't presented raw, but with nitsume sauce.

For all its ordinariness, there's no need for the sushi snob to relegate akami to the status of that cup of raspberry-lemon yogurt crowded into the back of the fridge. It isn't something you're reduced to eating only when there's nothing else in sight or within price range. In maki sushi, where the flavor of the fish must blend with other ingredients, or in tekka-maki, where the consistency of the tightly packed rice complements the texture of the meat, the lean flavor of akami is perfect. Even on top of nigiri sushi, akami has a clean, simple taste that's welcome in between sushi choices of richer or more complex flavors. And if you do have the chance to slaughter your own, remember that the better akami is toward the front of the fish. (If you have access to a fish market where they *habla* Nihongo, ask for *nakaochi*. Nakaochi are the scrapings and odds and ends taken from around the spine of the tuna that don't look all that great as nigiri sushi but that are wonderfully suited for stuffing in maki sushi.)

Chu-toro is a layer of fat-marbled meat that wraps around the inner musculature of the tuna. It insulates as well as an expedition-weight down parka and tastes, by all accounts, much, much better, especially served raw. *Toro* means "to melt." It is a not altogether fanciful description of what this cut does in your mouth. Filigreed with spidery fingers of fat, chu-toro is the most affordable of the fatty cuts of tuna. Want to know something interesting about tuna fat? You wouldn't have made it this far into the book unless you're the sort who'd answer that with "You bet!" So here it is: Even though tuna are true fish and therefore cold-blooded, they have a remarkable ability to raise their body temperature up to 18 degrees above the temperature of the water in which they're swimming. If scientists know how tuna do this, they're keeping it a secret so far. They do know it has something to do with the unique distribution of fat on the tuna. Maguro fat is not like your ordinary angioplasty-inducing beef fat. Nor is it like the fat on nearly all other fish, which is concentrated in one place. Instead, maguro fat marbles the whole section of the tuna where it is found. That is the key factor in tuna's taste and its popularity as a sushi ingredient.

Halfway down the fish is the *chiai*, the longitudinal streak of bloody, dark meat that's extremely strong flavored and never served as sushi. Below that is another layer of chu-toro. Farther down below the chu-toro, right about where the tuna's beer belly would start if he were given to popping the occasional cool one, lies the "falling frost," or *shimofuri*, section. The meat here is the same shade of pink you would see on a Scandinavian tour group 10 minutes or so after hitting the sands of Waikiki. Most noticeable, though, is that this part of the tuna is finely webbed with a mesh of white fat. The texture is distinctly buttery smooth, and the meat holds the fat together and gives it an additional succulence. Shimofuri as a topping for nigiri sushi requires a deft touch with the chef's knife. Sliced too thick, and it will be gummy; too thin, and you'll taste only the rice underneath. When it's just right, Goldilocks would trade her entire portfolio of porridge futures and wrestle all three bears for a couple of bites. Never pass on the opportunity to enjoy shimofuri. The tides of sushi will flux and Lord knows what flotsam will wash up on the beaches of sushi-ya in the future, from grits 'n' sushi to mutton maki rolls. But rest assured that shimofuri, when it is available, will always be a criterion by which the meal is measured.

Some sushi tsu insist that shimofuri is the height of maguro sushi. There is another cut you might encounter, however, that can give shimofuri a run for the money. *O-toro* is a layer of meat and fat running along the ventral side of the tuna. It looks a lot like uncooked bacon, with wide strips of fat and lean running side by side. Italians call this part of the tuna *ventresca*; it figures in a lot of their seafood recipes. A slang expression in the Japanese kitchen for o-toro is *suna-zuri*, or sand rubbing, since it is the bottom part of the fish. Grilled or sautéed, it's great. In sushi, the taste of o-toro can be a little overwhelming. It is so expensive it would be hard to gorge on it anyway.

Okay, having had a round-the-world tour to meet relevant members of the tuna family, and an introduction to dismembering them, we arrive at what's arriving on your plate. Few other sushi tane are so exquisitely matched with shoyu as tuna. Shoyu does for tuna what Champagne does for oysters; it brings out all the complexities of flavor. Without overdoing it, allow a liberal dip in the shoyu plate to put a glossy brown sheen on your maguro. If you have not tried it, do so, and you will be surprised at what it does for the fish. A caveat: the fattier the cut of tuna, the less shoyu it will need. Chu-toro benefits from just the lightest touch. As you taste the tuna, be aware as well of the texture. It is a critical aspect of sushi appreciation often overlooked by the amateur. Tuna is a splendid tane to refine the sense of texture, from the coarse meatiness of lean maguro to the buttery fattiness of shimofuri.

≡ **Watch For:** You should, with some practice and experience, be able to instantly identify all the cuts of maguro while they're still sitting in the counter case. Color is key for distinguishing good akami. Not-so-fresh akami becomes markedly paler. Fatty cuts of tuna tane have distinctive patterns of fat. On a cross section of chu-toro, the distribution of fat and lean looks like the stripes on a candy cane, with the red much wider than the white.

≋ **Sushi Well Done:** That's more than a little overstated, but maguro is sometimes, as mentioned earlier, introduced to a frying pan before it becomes sushi. The process is tataki. See page 123, in the section on katsuo, for an explanation of the process, one that works just as well for tuna.

≋ **Ask the Itamae:** On a slow night at the sushi-ya, ask the itamae if he'll make you a roll of *suzi*, also called *maguro suji-yaki*. It is a scrap of tuna meat, fatty and stringy with silver connective tissue, suitable for making stock, unless the itamae knows how to fry it with just a bit of garlic. Along with a bowl of rice and some pickled vegetables, suzi is a great late-night snack, with a generous splattering of ponzu sauce on top. Another side dish featuring tuna that has been a sushi-ya favorite since they were still carrying swords in Japan is *yamakake* or *yamaimo-kake*. A *yamaimo* is a Japanese yam. It is grated to a rough paste, then ladled atop cubes of tuna and seasoned with wasabi and shoyu. Yamakake is about as authentic as it gets for sushi accompaniments; no one can really be called a sushi tsu without at least giving it a try.

≋ **Interesting Trivia:** At Tsukiji and other fish markets, a small plug is cut about two-thirds of the way down the tuna's body. Buyers routinely stick their fingers in this hole and rub around a little, to get a feel for the firmness of the flesh.

≋ **Slightly Less Appetizing Trivia:** A choice part of the tuna that can only be found at fish markets in Japan is the eyeballs. They are eaten raw, almost always dressed with a sauce of some sort. The taste—not to spoil the surprise for you— is really sort of bland. The texture is much tougher than you might expect. It is almost like a soft piece of beef jerky. It is a custom, in those households where tuna eyeballs are eaten (many Japanese would be as put off by them as the average Westerner), that the eyes go to the host, who may enjoy them or dispense them to guests as a sign of favor.

≋ **Noticeably Less Appetizing Trivia:** In police argot, a maguro is a victim struck fatally by a train.

MIRUGAI ⇨ HORSE CLAM

If you have reached the age of 61, or *kanreki*, in Japan, then you have completed one full cycle of the zodiacal calendar and lived through all the possible permutations of the 12 years of the different animals. In the old days, when you'd passed this mark, you were allowed to begin a life of *rakuinkyo*, or "enjoyable retirement." Nowadays, 61 is not much past middle age in Japan.

If you are getting closer to kanreki, you may wish to soften the blow by a meal with a tane that might well have been celebrating its *second* full go-round on the zodiacal carousel. *Mirugai*, or horse clams, have been clocked in at close to 150 years old, remarkably looking not a day over four, when they are considered adults. After a short larval period, mirugai begin house hunting by digging down into the sand and mud of the subtidal zone, the place just deep enough offshore where fluctuations in tides don't expose the bottom. They're not in any hurry; they go down a foot or so a year until they are three feet under. That's where they stay for the next century or so, extending a thick, rubbery siphon up to the surface of the ocean floor and sucking in most anything edible. Mirugai can grow to be up to seven pounds. Most are a little less than half that, still a fairly good-size clam. Harvesting is done commercially by dredging in some parts of Japan. A lot of mirugai is imported from the coasts of Oregon and Washington, and nearly all mirugai used in American sushi-ya comes from there.

Mirugai, for the Japanese sushi tsu, is often thought of as the late-winter and spring complement to abalone, since the latter comes into season just about the time mirugai goes out of season. Despite its origins down in the sandy muck of the ocean bottom and its nearly R-rated appearance, a mottled brown shell with a thick, flaccid tube flopping out that practically shouts "phallic," mirugai has always been considered a high-class tane. It is a choice of the sushi connoisseur and one of *the* choices among shellfish tane.

The entrails and adductor muscles of the mirugai are edible, but only the long siphon is used for sushi in most circumstances, particularly in the United States. The itamae buying mirugai gives the siphon a yank. We do not have to be an itamae to know that if it's firm, it's good. In the kitchen, the siphon is cut away from the body of the clam, then the leathery dark skin and a translucent membrane underneath it is sliced away. (Baths of alternating hot and cold water make the skin easier to remove.) What's left is a yellowish-white meat that is split open, the sand thoroughly washed out, the black tip of the mouth cut away, and the remaining meat sliced into portions for tane. As with many other shellfish, the itamae will often make shallow crosscuts on both sides of a tane of mirugai to make it easier to eat as well as to sit more securely on the rice.

The flavor of mirugai is among the strongest of the shellfish used for sushi. It is briny and tastes distinctly of the sea, and it has a rubbery resistance against the teeth that many fans enjoy. Probably not a good tane to present to an amateur, mirugai should be reserved for those who appreciate it or who are at least intrigued with the concept of eating something older than the average greeter at Wal-Mart.

≋ **By Any Other Name:** "Horse clam" is the most common term for mirugai when it is translated for the sushi-ya menu, although the Native American name geoduck is often used as well, especially on the West Coast, where mirugai are a popular dish. Note, though, that while "mirugai" is the standard word for this clam, it is actually a misnomer. The correct word is *mirukui*. You might run across some itamae who know it; it's always interesting to order mirukui and see if they do. "Mirugai" is a corruption of the correct term, a corruption that has led to some fanciful explanations for it. *Miru* in Japanese can mean "to look." (Kai or gai is "shell.") So some Japanese food dictionaries have flailed about and suggested the "miru" of "mirugai" came about because the long siphon is poking up out of the seabed, "looking around." The sushi tsu and all connoisseurs of Japanese food know the truth. It is—or was, originally— "mirukui," or "miru mouth." The "miru" here is a kind of seaweed. Mirugai often have their siphon mouths protruding around beds of the miru seaweed. That's where the name comes from.

≋ **Watch For:** When an itamae takes a big piece of mirugai out of the case to cut it up, he may slam it on the counter hard enough to get the attention of everyone in the place. He may do the same thing with other clams as well. It is something of a tradition in some sushi-ya, akin to those who shout *"Opa!"* when flaming dishes are presented in Greek restaurants. The wannabe sushi authority will enthusiastically explain to anyone who'll listen that this is the itamae's way of graphically demonstrating how fresh the product is, because look and you can see how the clam responds to the treatment, constricting there on the cutting board. Or he'll explain that this is a way of tightening the meat of the clam to make it easier to cut. Itamae themselves might tell similar tales, if you ask them. Crapola. Itamae like to liven things up in the sushi-ya, and slapping the clam, if you'll forgive the expression, makes a big loud sound and gets everyone laughing and talking. If your order of mirugai or another clam doesn't get whacked around, don't worry. It'll taste the same, abused or not.

≡ **Ask the Itamae:** This is a tane that stands up to a little extra kick of wasabi, so if you're the type who enjoys the bite, ask the itamae to go a little heavy with the green stuff. Another excellent condiment for this tane is a couple of drops of lemon juice. If you are on the West Coast or in some other place that has access to fresh mirugai, ask the itamae if he will make sushi with its adductor muscles and entrails. It is eaten this way in Japan, mostly gunkan style, heaped on top of the rice and nori cone. The taste is something like squid, though much more powerful, which is why it is almost never included on regular sushi menus outside Japan.

SABA ⌐⊃ MACKEREL

J apanese dogs do not go "bow-wow" or even "woof-woof." They go *wan-wan*. Chicks say *piyo-piyo* instead of "cheep-cheep." Kittens in Japan mew *nya-nya*; frogs croak *kero-kero*. By now, a lot of you are thinking, "Wan-wan? Nya-nya? Are these people all hard of hearing or something?"

Now, now. We can all celebrate our common humanity despite our differences. And we may take comfort in knowing that even though several million of our Japanese friends apparently cannot hear that cats are plainly saying "meow," we do have some things in common. For instance, when our maritime ancestors looked up and saw a sky filled with cirrocumulus clouds, they called it a mackerel sky. The striations of clouds looked to them like the shimmery skin of that fish. Early Japanese saw the same; those clouds are *uroko-gumo* in Japanese, or fish-scale clouds.

Not surprisingly, the French (who cannot hear cats properly either, by the way) saw something sexual about the mackerel. *Maquereau* is a word for "pimp," since the flashy skin looks like the slick, shiny appearance of a Marseilles procurer. That skin is important to the sushi tsu, not because of any venereal connotations but because it provides probably the only reliable clue as to exactly which kind of saba or mackerel he's being served in the sushi-ya. Look at the skin (always left on) on the fillets in the itamae's case or on your sushi. Is it streaked with long, thick lines that look like they've been drawn with a black marker? If so, you're going to be eating either the Atlantic or Pacific mackerel, or perhaps one of the intimately related subspecies that swim all over both oceans but are much more plentiful in the Pacific. This is *hon-saba*, also called *ma-saba*. If that skin has small, darkish spots on it, it's Spanish mackerel, called *goma-saba* in Japanese, since those spots look like black sesame seeds, or goma. You might also hear native Japanese refer to hon-saba as *hira-saba*—"flat mackerel"—since its body shape is noticeably trimmer and flatter than goma-saba. Goma-saba is, conversely, also known as *maru-saba*, or round mackerel, since it is markedly chubbier in cross section.

Of course, the sushi tsu would like to depend on his extraordinarily refined taste buds to make these kinds of distinctions. Trouble is, saba is presented in sushi raw only about half the time, and even less than that at average-quality sushi-ya. Mackerel flesh secretes an enzyme that starts dissolving the meat as soon as the fish dies. Those enzymes, even if they do not create an environment for some nasty bacterial growth, cause a rash-like allergic reaction in some who eat mackerel. Others will be unable to digest it. An itamae's trick of the trade in judging a mackerel's freshness is to look at the tail. A droopy tail is a warning sign the fish isn't as fresh as it should be. Still another secret is to sniff the entrails. That's where bacterial nasties set in first.

Before modern refrigeration, virtually the only enthusiasts of saba in the raw were the fishermen who were hauling it into the boats. Saba is served raw now; it is just as common, though, to have it slightly pickled, as with other kinds of hikari-mono. That means even the dedicated sushi connoisseur won't have a lot of opportunity to learn to discern the various species or varieties of saba by its raw, unadulterated taste alone. (If you're on the spot, guess that the saba you're eating is Japanese; the majority of the mackerel served in American sushi-ya is honsaba, caught and frozen in Japan.)

Mackerel do more traveling than an international drug courier. They can cover 50 miles in a day, looking for the smaller fish on which they dine. So the best cut of the fish is from the big swimming muscles along the backbone. Look closely at a saba tane and you will probably see variegated bands of light and dark. That's two kinds of muscle. They work to propel the fish when it's alive. As soon as the mackerel is filleted, the meat is salted, then marinated in rice vinegar. The fresher the fish, the less time it needs in the marinating bath. However, some itamae prefer the stronger taste of saba marinated for a couple of days. If you've had the marinated version before, there won't be any question when you put a piece of raw saba in your mouth. The flavor is much more intense; the texture is meatier. The oiliness of mackerel is considerable. It is dripping with the stuff. This is definitely not a sushi tane for the inexperienced. For the sushi tsu, exposure to saba marinated and raw is mandatory. If, having tried it both ways, you don't like it, you can always cite mackerel's declining popularity in Japanese sushi circles. Once a favorite in that country, saba as a nigiri sushi tane has not been nearly in as much demand as it was before World War II.

≋ **By Any Other Name:** *Seki-saba* is a smaller version of mackerel; you can recognize it because the darker V shape of the muscle is nearly red. *Me-saba* and *toki-saba* are two other smaller species, both found in Japan, that may appear in American sushi-ya. There is no way to recognize them by their appearance; their taste is slightly inferior to honsaba. You should not confuse—and, more important, your itamae shouldn't either—true saba with *sawara*, a subspecies of mackerel that is, like the goma-saba, also translated as "Spanish mackerel." Sawara is indigenous to Japan; it's abundant in the Inland Sea, and it is eaten cooked lots of ways there. But it is susceptible to certain parasites and is never eaten raw.

≋ **Watch For:** See the section on pressed sushi (page 27) for an explanation of Kyoto's battera sushi. Saba is a classic topping for this variety of sushi. It is also a favorite ingredient for bo sushi, also mentioned in that section. Since Kyoto is inland, mackerel could be eaten there only after it was preserved by the the hikari-mono vinegar process. Pressing it into cakes of rice aided in the preservation, and so Kyoto and its environs developed pressed marinated mackerel sushi to a delicious degree. Both these versions present saba at its finest, and the sushi tsu should learn to appreciate them and indulge whenever the opportunity presents itself.

Saba no sugata sushi is a specialty of Kochi Prefecture on the little island of Shikoku. It's mackerel that's gutted, then stuffed with sushi-meshi, and it is very probably worth the trip to Shikoku if you're in Japan and are serious, as every sushi tsu should be, about getting a good meal.

≋ **Ask the Itamae:** The season is particularly critical for getting the best saba. In autumn, they're packing on calories like Olympic athletes; the taste is luxuriantly rich and oily. The fat content of a mackerel in its prime can be about 20 percent of its total body weight. Spring and summer find mackerel exhausted from the exertions of spawning, and their body fat percentage drops to around 5 percent. The taste is flabby and insipid then. Consequently, summer is when some fish shops turn to goma saba. Its taste declines too during that part of the year, but less dramatically. So you need to ask what kind of saba you're being served so that you can develop a palate for the best this fish has to offer.

≋ **Trivia:** The unique taste of saba comes from histadine, an amino acid also found in its cousins the tuna and some other fish with red meat. These fish are also high in eicos-apentaenoic acid, which, in addition to being a word that is a near surefire winner on the Scrabble board, promotes good cholesterol while lowering its evil twin.

≋ **More Trivia:** *Saba o yomu* means "to read the saba" and is an expression used to describe those who manipulate numbers to their advantage in accounting. Since saba spoils so quickly, fishmongers historically were always eager to get rid of it as soon as possible, and so would inflate the number of fish in a pile of mackerel to make it seem as if the buyer was getting a better deal.

SAKE ⟶ SALMON

There probably isn't a sushi place in the United States that doesn't serve salmon as a tane. Again and again, sushi enthusiasts cite it as among their favorites. The majority of those trying sushi for the first time have doubtless taken the plunge with an order of salmon nigiri. So many a sushi tsu is surprised to learn that salmon isn't all that popular in Japanese sushi-ya. Neither is it a part of the tradition of Edomae sushi. Here's why:

Hokkaido, the northernmost island of Japan, is, historically speaking, to the rest of Japan what Appalachia is to the United States. The indigenous population of ancient northern Japan, the Ainu, were forced there by invaders, and Hokkaido was, according to popular political thought in the 2nd century A.D., just the right place for them. It is cold and wild and has always been, in the imagination of many Japanese, a sort of far-flung hillbilly heaven where the tattooed aborigines worshipped bears and practiced polygamy and ate who knew what. Not coincidentally, the only salmon native to Japanese waters are found up in Hokkaido. Even if the rest of Japan had wanted to eat salmon, it would have been impossible to have had it trans- ported fresh any distance at all. So that, combined with the backwoods reputation of Hokkaido, meant that for the rest of the Japanese population, *sake* was the equivalent of sow belly or squirrel brains: rustic country fare best left to the natives, who could truly enjoy it. Even up through the 1950s, a dinner of fresh salmon might have been fine vittles for some Jethro-*san* out in the boonies of Tokachi, but no sophisticated Tokyo urbanite wanted any part of the fish.

The attitude about sake has changed slowly. It can now be found in most markets throughout Japan. Salmon is still best eaten there, though, in *Hokkaido-ryori*, restaurants that special- ize in far-northern cuisine. Dishes like *ishikari-nabe*, a thick, rich stew of salmon, miso paste, and vegetables, are extremely popular everywhere in the country now. And while salmon is now used in Japanese sushi, it is still fairly common to find sushi-ya in Japan that do not have it on the menu. So the non- Japanese sushi snob is apt to know a great deal more about it than his counterpart in Japan.

What fishermen call dog salmon or chum salmon are the native Japanese sake species. They are not among the best grades of salmon, and the sake served in U.S. sushi-ya is rarely, if ever, Japanese salmon, for that reason. Why would we import a third-string version when we have prime salmon in our own oceans? The majority of sushi-grade sake comes from farm- raised salmon on the Atlantic coast. Unlike their rough, wild cousins, commercially reared salmon don't end up hanging out in the wrong side of town, which for salmon is places where they pick up bad habits and worse parasites. Harvested, they are easily cut into steaks or long fillets; that's what the sushi shop buys. In most cases, it will have been frozen, which knocks the parasites afflicting salmon out completely. Don't think, though, that you can do this trick at home. Sake has to be frozen at 0 degrees for at least 72 hours. Typical home refrig- erators won't quite cut that. In the old days, before refrigeration, parasites were controlled to some extent by salting the skin of the salmon until the salt melted into the flesh. It may not have killed all parasites, but it weakened them considerably so that a healthy person wouldn't be harmed.

There is arguably not much difference in taste between wild and farmed salmon, except that commercially grown sake has more fat than the wild variety. Salmon fat is chock-full of the omega acids that help prevent heart disease, so eating it may play a role in keeping you alive long enough for disco to come back into vogue again.

Salmon, as anyone who's ever watched a Discovery Channel documentary on them should know, are born in freshwater streams and rivers and migrate to the open sea after they hatch. When it comes time for them to spawn, they make the return trip, completing it if brown bears or environmentalists, squashing them while wading into a stream to protest some new dam, don't kill them. Once they start back toward freshwater, they stop eating. By the time they make it back to the old home place, they're anorexic and have just enough energy to mate, and then they die. A skinny salmon is not a tasty salmon. Sake taken from the wild after the end of August wouldn't be good for sushi or anything else comestible. A sushi-ya will serve wild sake that was harvested in spring, when they're fattest. Of course, commercial farms can fool around with the natural cycles of the fish and so they can have fat and sassy sake for much longer periods of the year. Even so, you will note a difference in the quality of this tane. Assuming it has been handled and presented properly, the difference is in the time of year the fish was taken.

Good sake looks fake because its color is so vibrant, so neon. Depending on the exact species and the time of year it was taken, sake ranges from a shocking pink to a nearly obscene carmine hue. It appears to have been dyed with some chemical soon to be proven to cause pancreatic cancer in mice. Most farm-raised salmon is, in fact, dyed in an attempt to imitate this vibrancy. In general, what you're looking for in good sake, however, is not the color of the lean meat, but the stripes of pale white fat that are banded in between the muscles. The more fat, the better the sake is going to taste.

Salmon shows up in nearly every form of sushi. When it is cut for nigiri or chirashi sushi, the slices will be slightly thicker than for most other tane; the flavor is better exploited that way. Sake also benefits from a healthy dab of wasabi, which the itamae should handle. If he doesn't, use a little of the glob on your plate. Few sushi tane go better with shoyu as well. So even if you normally forego soy sauce, try it with sake.

Those in the know about sushi will tell you that salmon is never served raw and is always, even in the sushi-ya, preserved in some way to get rid of possible parasites. Even some itamae in the United States insist on this. It was probably true a decade or so ago. It is not, however, the case today. Fresh, raw, unpreserved salmon is being eaten in a sushi-ya right now somewhere. You can eat it that way as well. After the freezing process, there is still some very slight chance a parasitic infection could remain in the meat. It is far more likely you're going to get sick from eating undercooked hamburger, however, than from raw sake.

Salmon skin is a standard ingredient in temaki, or ice cream cone–shaped rolls of wrapped sushi. The skin, with some meat left on, is grilled with a spritz of shoyu, then wrapped in sushi-meshi, perhaps with some vegetables like daikon sprouts (kaiware), and then in a sheet of nori. The Japanese term for salmon skin is *sake hada*.

≡ **By Any Other Name:** Sake is often pronounced "sha-kay," especially in Tokyo, but also in the north and other parts of Japan as well. It is also called *shirozake* (white sake), and there are some regional names in Japanese for salmon. *Benizake, beni-mazu* (sockeye or red salmon), *kenzake*, and *keiji* are some you might hear. Do not, by the way, confuse shirozake with *shiozake*. The latter, "salt sake," is salmon that has been cured with salt. It is kind of a Japanese version of lox and can be found in any grocery store. Shiozake is eaten grilled by a lot of Japanese for breakfast. It isn't used for sushi.

Smoked salmon and lox, not incidentally, have become very popular in U.S. sushi-ya. It doesn't require a rocket surgeon to figure out why. The meat isn't raw, making it more palatable to the "I'd prefer my meal not pulsing" crowd. The taste is also more familiar. Salmon preserved with smoke or salt means it is a far cheaper product, of course; another significant factor. The down side is just as obvious. The smoke flavor in salmon preserved that way obliterates much of anything else on your tongue. The salty taste overpowers the delicate flavor of the rice that is so essential to sushi. So you're not getting the flavor of the sake; you're getting the salt or smoke in which it was preserved. If you insist on eating salmon sushi prepared with either of these, make it the last tane of the meal.

≋ **Watch For:** *Harasu* is the belly section of the salmon that has the most fat, much like the same cut on tuna and some other fish used for sushi. *Sake harasu* on a sushi menu is a signal that should never be ignored by the sushi tsu. It is nearly as rich as hamachi or chu-toro and will almost certainly be much, much cheaper.

Sooner or later, Hokkaido-style Japanese cuisine will be introduced to the West and when it is, be ready for *ruibe*. A reasonable translation would be "salmon-cicle." It is a simple, remarkably good dish inspired by the cooking of the Ainu. Shreds of fresh salmon are frozen, then served before they thaw. Diners dip the meat into shoyu and eat it. It sounds weird, but as the slivers of salmon thaw in your mouth, their flavor continues to grow, and the shoyu adds to the effect. It's a spectacular form of sashimi. Hokkaido chefs who prepare it are such sticklers for preserving the flavor of the fish that they refuse to use steel knives to cut up the fillets, fearing the taste of the metal will be transferred to the meat. Instead, ruibe is chopped into pieces using a sharpened abalone shell.

≡ **Ask the Itamae:** When you're ordering sake as a nigiri sushi or as sashimi, ask for benitade, also called *murasaki-tade*. It is a small, dark purple flower from the water pepper plant that is a garnish for salmon and other fish served raw. Benitade is available in the United States now, and some better sushi-ya might have it on hand. The sharp, peppery taste goes well with sake.

≡ **Trivia:** Is sake a shiromi-dane or akami-dane? White or red? From the color of its meat, it's not a tough call, true. Even so, salmon is almost never listed among the "red-meat" tane in Japanese sushi texts. That's simply because it is not a traditional part of sushi, and so it exists outside the rigid Japanese nomenclature for the cuisine.

SAYORI 🐟 HALFBEAK

Japanese folk wisdom is replete with all sorts of nostrums regarding a person's physiognomy. A long philtrum, the space between the bottom of the nose and the top of the lip, means the person is sexually enthusiastic. Long earlobes indicate a person who is, or will be, rich. And a lower jaw that protrudes more than three times farther than the upper one? That, especially if you also have scales, indicates a better-than-average chance you're going to end up as sushi.

The *sayori*, or Japanese halfbeak, is a thin black-and-sliver fish about the length of a windshield wiper. The sayori's lower jaw sticks out several inches beyond the upper. It looks dangerous. Sayori, though, are a threat to nothing much beyond the plankton and algae on which they feed. There are several closely related species of sayori in oceans throughout the world and, in many places, their primary use is as a bait. The Japanese sayori is the only one eaten as a sushi tane. Sayori swim in schools just below the surface of the water, and they have an ability to levitate when they're being chased by predators, skimming along the wave tops with just their lower fins still in the water. It is a relatively effective ploy against tuna and bonito, which often dine on sayori, but less so against nets that round these fish up by the millions in waters off northern Japan. A lot of sayori destined for Japanese sushi-ya are now being taken off the Pacific coast of Russia. It is appearing more and more often in sushi places outside Japan; if you have it, the fish was almost certainly imported from there as well since virtually the entire Japanese harvest gets eaten at home.

Sayori have a pattern of large, thick scales that have to be cleaned, even though their skin will usually be left on for sushi. They are one of the three most famous hikari-mono, which are salted and soaked in vinegar. In Japan, the sushi tsu begins spring with kisu, then segues into sayori just as the weather starts to warm (March through April), then, when summer's in full bloom, goes on to kohada. Of the three, sayori is the lightest and leanest. It develops a strong fishy aroma very quickly, so it is prepared fresh the morning of the day it will be served. Its intestinal cavity has a very thin membrane separating the innards from the flesh; consequently, if the cleaning is sloppy, the meat can be contaminated with a darkish sludge that tastes worse than it sounds. When selecting sayori, the itamae looks for a couple of signs of freshness. First, if the silver-white skin of the sayori's belly is dull or brownish, it is past its prime. Second, the brighter the red jaw on the males, the fresher the sayori catch.

Sayori has a thin dark streak, or bloodline, like a tuna's chiai running down its flank that has to be cut out; otherwise, the meat's treated just like any other hikari-mono. One exception: The vinegar solution used to marinate sayori sometimes has *konbu*, or kelp, added to the concoction. This *kombu-jime* imparts a slightly salty, seaweedy flavor to the meat that is popular with many sushi tsu. Sayori is served as a nigiri tane with the skin left on, though in some cases, especially with larger fish, it can be skinned. The meat is white; the taste is rather complex. Fresh on the palate, it seems almost as delicate as sea bass or some of the other pale-fleshed tane. But the taste develops in your mouth. If it seems lacking in flavor, drink some tea and try another piece, and you might detect a subtle multilayered sensation on your tongue the second time around.

Sayori is often served with grated ginger or finely chopped *wakanegi* onion stems atop it. It is also common to serve it with a mound of oboro, ground fish usually dyed a bright pink, which adds another taste.

≡ **By Any Other Name:** Sayori goes by several different names in Japan, depending on the region or dialect, including *saero*, *saeri*, *sukubi*, *suzu*, and *yodo*, but it is always called sayori in a sushi-ya.

≡ **Watch For:** Sayori is, by reputation, a spring and summer tane. If the chance arises to try the autumn version, give it a go. Autumn sayori tend to be smaller—they've worn themselves to a frazzle after a midsummer's spawning revelry—but their taste is very light, perhaps the most delicate texture and taste of any sushi tane.

≡ **Ask the Itamae:** One delicious variation on sayori likely to show up in a sushi-ya is sayori *ponzu-yaki*. Sayori fillets are briefly grilled with a spritz of lemony citrus ponzu sauce, then served as a nigiri tane.

≡ **Trivia:** The halfbeak figures in several Chinese herbal medicines as a cure for arthritis and other inflammatory ailments.

SAZAE ⌦ TURBINATE SHELL

Not very long ago you were more likely to meet one of Elton John's ex-girlfriends than to come across *sazae* outside Japan. In just the past few years, some high-end sushi-ya have imported this shellfish. It has a small following among some sushi tsu. The price will still be commensurate with silver by the ounce. That being said, you should recognize the little fellows and be prepared to dig in.

Sazae are baseball-size sea snails that feed in seaweed beds all around Japan. They have an unusual method of locomotion for a snail. Their foot is split and they move first one side, then the other, "walking," in a way, as they feed. It is the foot that is typically used for sushi. Sazae are turban shaped, hence their English name. Their color varies according to their diet. Those feeding on lighter-colored seaweeds and grasses have light beige shells; darker shells are a sign they've been dining on a diet of black or green seaweed. Two versions of the species exist as well. Sazae living in relatively placid waters have smooth shells; those from beaches where there's a lot of wave action have spiky protuberances, making them look like the punk rockers of the shellfish world.

Turbinate shells call the intertidal zone home, a place where the shore's rocks and beaches are exposed as the tide goes out, leaving sazae available for picking. All spring and summer Japanese do just that. Sazae are eaten more often than any other sea snail in Japan. The most common way of preparing them is *tsubo-yaki* style, tossed on the grill while still in the shell. The *tsubo* here is Japanese for "pot," and *yaki*, of course, means "grilled." They cook quickly, then are cooled and the meat is pulled out with a toothpick, a lot like a Japanese version of escargot. They are in such demand that a few years ago, importers tried to pass off some look-alikes. The Japanese government intervened and issued stern warnings that any fraudulent sazae schemes would be met with serious consequences.

Sazae were not used as sushi tane in sushi until about 25 years ago. They were probably added to the repertoire of the sushi-ya through their inclusion as a *sake no sakana*, snacks eaten while drinking sake. They are best thought of as an equivalent of Spanish *tapas*. Sazae has always been a fixture in sake bars, grilled and nibbled while drinking. Doubtless, some itamae got the inspiration to add them to sushi. Sazae appear on nigiri sushi and sometimes on gunkan-style sushi. The foot is grilled or, more typically, boiled briefly in a broth with konbu kelp added. Either way, the meat is very, very chewy and the taste, given the sazae's diet, is definitely that of the sea.

≋ **Watch for:** *Tsubu-gai* is a kind of whelk, used much the same way as sazae. It comes from Hokkaido and often is called *Ezo-sazae*, *Ezo* being an archaic term for Hokkaido. Don't let anyone tell you tsubu-gai is the same as sazae, however. Sazae have a crunchier texture and a much more pronounced flavor.

≋ **Ask the Itamae:** The true sushi tsu is always willing to travel where ordinary souls dare not go. In the case of sazae, that journey will take you farther up into the shell of the sazae, past the foot and into the entrails and reproductive organs of the creature. They're called *wata*, a generic name for entrails, so you'll have to specify you want *sazae wata*. They are spread on top of gunkan sushi and are excellent with a dash of togarashi, or crushed red pepper flakes.

≋ **Trivia:** *Sazae-san* is the name of one of the most enduringly popular cartoon strips in Japan, begun in 1946. It was originated by a woman, Machiko Hasegawa, and details the adventures of Sazae-san, a housewife who lives with her family in Tokyo. In the late 1960s, it was made into a TV program that was an equally a big hit all over Japan. In the cartoon, Sazae-san is always getting into adventures that are not even mildly dangerous or unique. One episode has her getting lost in a department store. In another, the family cat steals the fish meant for the evening's dinner. It's wild.

SHAKO 〰 MANTIS SHRIMP

At first glance (and second, and third), it seems unlikely that something so small could be so ugly. In that sense, though, the mantis shrimp, or *shako* as it is known in the sushi-ya, is the ocean's version of the Volvo. Small, about a finger's length long, and breathtakingly unattractive, shako are some vicious little bastards. They aren't shrimp at all but stomatopods, surly thugs who lurk along coral reefs and rock ledges, mugging any prey that comes close. Take a rock lobster tail and fit it with a head from a Romanian science-fictional movie prop and you'd have a fair approximation of one of these foul-tempered beasts. Shako are divided into those that spear their prey with needle-edged claws and those that bash dinner to death with club-like claws. The former are called "thumb splitters" by divers dumb enough to fool around with them. The latter have claws capable of shattering $1/4$-inch-thick aquarium glass, as has been proven in captivity. They are aggressive hunters, have binocular vision, and come in trendy shades of bright green, blue, and red. And they taste great.

Some of the 400 species of shako live alone in warm-water oceans all over the world; others mate for life. The sushi connoisseur's interest in the mantis shrimp's domestic arrangements has to do with the animal's breeding season in the spring. Both sexes are tops in taste during this period; more important, females carry huge numbers of eggs for about a month afterward. Shako loaded with roe offer one of sushi-dom's rarest treats. The connoisseur who takes the opportunity to try it can spend many years working the feat into conversation with an envious cohort. Even without the eggs on the side, shako have an exceptional flavor and texture that is somewhere between eel and shrimp. Their freshness declines fast, so they are usually boiled almost immediately after harvesting. In the sushi-ya, they're brushed with nitsume and presented as a nigiri.

Until after World War II, sushi tsu had the good sense to avoid eating a creature that could, during the harvest, either slice the fisherman's fingers open or bash them into jelly. In the 1950s, it began appearing at sushi-ya. Shako for sushi were originally boiled in a sugar syrup. Later it became a nimono-dane, but the price has always limited its popularity in Japan and elsewhere.

≋ **Watch For:** The kid at the drive-through window gets your burger order right more often than shako appears on the average sushi-ya's menu. It is even rarer that you'll have the chance to try mantis shrimp raw. It is occasionally available, though, and if it is, look carefully at the meat. Good fresh raw shako looks as if it were quickly dipped in blue ink, with just a slight tinge of color. More important, it has a glossy sheen and looks plump. Many itamae will add a more liberal dose of wasabi to raw shako that overwhelms its delicate flavor.

≋ **Trivia:** "Shako" was once used in Japanese to describe a building where any kind of vehicle is kept; it's pronounced the same as the mantis shrimp shako but written with different characters. The English loan word "garage," or *gareji*, though, has largely replaced the word in modern Japanese. That's why the pun-happy Japanese will sometimes call the shako mantis shrimp a "gareji."

SHIMA-AJI ⫘ STRIPED JACK

Back in the 1950s, when the federal government began investigating organized crime in a big way, trials featured billboard-size charts with the family and business ties of the Mafia clans diagrammed. They went on and on, with names connected by arrows and lines, which must have been hard for juries to follow. (The assumption was that anybody anywhere on those diagrams who was even close to being indicted was going to become part of a bridge abutment on a Pennsylvania highway project.) It's just as hard to get a perspective on the "jack" family of fishes. There are more than 200 species that can be considered jacks, or aji. The majority of those used for sushi are covered in the section on aji. *Shima-aji* gets special mention because it is usually treated as a separate tane in the sushi-ya.

Looking a little like swimming silver serving platters, shima-aji are bright and attractive, with a narrow yellow band running crookedly down their flanks. (*Shima* means "striped.") They differ from most other jacks in that while they have large, Mick Jagger–ish lips ("thick-lipped jack" is one name for them), the lower one doesn't protrude as it does in other aji.

Shima-aji reach their full size at three feet. When they're that big, though, the quality of the meat declines and they end up grilled or prepared some other way. The itamae looking for good sushi tane selects those around a foot long. He prepares it the same way as any other kind of aji, but he will use special care when he fillets, peeling away the skin so that the shiny, glossy surface of the meat underneath is preserved. That shininess is one sure sign you're looking at shima-aji. It will also probably have a sliver of pale red flesh along one side of the tane. While it doesn't add anything to the taste, it looks nice and serves as another indicator it's shima-aji. The flavor and texture of shima-aji are pleasant, enjoyable, and inoffensive. The fish doesn't inspire a lot of poetry among sushi tsu, but it is dependable, and most sushi enthusiasts at all levels of connoisseurship tend to like it.

Shima-aji is caught all over Japan south of Hokkaido and throughout the Pacific. It is regularly available in sushi-ya in the United States. In Japan, shima-aji is a summertime tane since it spawns in July. It is often thought of as a *tsuyu-dane*, a sushi tane for *tsuyu*, the rainy season that occurs in Japan then. Sometimes shima-aji will be passed off as kanpachi, since it's cheaper and has a similar color. Even minimal exposure to kanpachi will give the sushi snob the ability to discern the difference: Kanpachi's musculature is much firmer and meatier than shima-aji's. The muscle striations in kanpachi are compact and close together compared to those in shima-aji. On the other hand, in sushi-ya outside Japan, pompano has been passed off as shima-aji. This substitution is easy to spot as well. Only real shima-aji will have that glossy surface, and pompano doesn't have the red streak along the side that's usually found in shima-aji. The taste of pompano is flabbier and more watery than shima-aji.

≡ **By Any Other Name:** Shima-aji is called *buta-guchi*, or pig mouth, particularly among fishermen in southern Japan. *Mabuta shima-aji*, despite the similar name, is not related to shima-aji. It is a different fish, not normally used for sushi.

≡ **Watch For:** *Shima-aji no kuzu uchi* is a summertime delight that appears as a side dish in sushi-ya. Slices of shima-aji (other fish like sea bass are also used) are dusted with *kuzu*. In English that's "kudzu"—yes, the leafy vine indigenous to Japan and transplanted here to wreak more environmental havoc in the American South than the Union Army, boll weevils, and monster truck rallies combined. It is used in Japanese cooking. Prepared kuzu is a fine cornstarch-like powder. The kuzu-doused slices of fish are dunked briefly in boiling water, then piled on ice. They're served immediately, with all sorts of garnishes like shiso leaves, grated wasabi, and chopped preserved apricots. The fish takes on all the flavors of the garnishes, making it a delicious refresher between courses of sushi.

SHIRAUO ⤜ WHITEBAIT

Odorigui, or dancing mouth, is one of those fabulous tales that intrepid travelers like to bring back from exotic places, and no discussion of wacky Japanese eating customs and foods is complete without it. The dish consists of small fish, swallowed live, either alone or after having been dumped in a glass of sake or other alcohol, wriggling as it goes down. If the adventurous diner asks what kind of fish it is swimming down his gullet, he's often told it is *shirauo*. Sometimes it might be, but it probably isn't and shouldn't be. Real odorigui came from the coastal area of Fukuoka, on the northern side of Kyushu, where a fish in abundance is the shirouo. True, the names are similar. But they are two completely different fish. *Shirouo* are slightly smaller than shirauo, and the former are eaten live because they taste better alive and start to deteriorate as soon as they die. That's the reason, and not to give tourists a great story to tell, the custom of odorigui got started. Even many Japanese don't make this distinction between the two fish.

Having cleared that up, we turn to the shirauo itself. It is usually translated as "whitebait," but also as "icefish," perhaps a better description. About the length of your middle finger, shirauo at full maturity are nearly transparent. They look, swimming in schools, like slivers of ice. When they die, they immediately turn white.

Shirauo have a long history in connection with sushi. They were once prolific in Tokyo Bay, around Tsukuda-jima, the island that is very near to where the first outdoor sushi stall opened for business. Fishermen used torches to draw shirauo up to the surface of the bay at night, and nets to haul them in. Shirauo was used in stews like *chirinabe* and other dishes. It has always been one of the classic fishes for tempura, battered and deep-fried whole. Since it was so common in Tokyo Bay, it was one of the first tane used in the sushi of old Edo. By the beginning of the 20th century, it went out of favor to a considerable extent. Shirauo will still be on the menus of many Japanese sushi-ya and it may, from time to time, show up in places outside Japan. It is a tane to watch for, both because of its long association with the cuisine and because the taste and texture of the tiny fishes, eaten whole, is different from any other tane, even if the shirauo aren't still wriggling.

Shirauo is usually served on top of gunkan-style maki. They may be split in half if they're bigger, with four or five of the smaller ones lined up or bunched together to make a good mouthful. Snippets of green onion may be added, and this is another tane that's good with a couple of drops of ponzu.

≋ **By Any Other Name:** *Shirasu, katakuchi-iwashi, seiguro-iwashi,* and *shiko-iwashi* are all variant names for shirauo. Those with the *–iwashi* (sardine) suffix are misleading. Whitebait isn't even distantly related to sardines. By the way, just as Japanese often mistake shirauo for shirouo, there's a lot of confusion about whitebait in the West. In England, where "whitebait" has been consumed since at least the beginning of the 17th century, the word refers to the fry of herrings and sprats and other little fish. In the United States, "whitebait" is usually used to describe silversides or sand eels. None of these are in any way substitutes for true shirauo.

≋ **Ask the Itamae:** A fine side dish for sushi is *shioi-mushi*, or steamed shirauo. It is one any good itamae trained in Japan will know how to prepare.

≋ **Trivia:** Shirauo and everything related to it are deeply associated with the advent of spring in Japanese haiku and other literature. A haiku poet in times past using the expression *shirauo-kaji*, or whitebait fire, knew that his reader would immediately picture the torchlight of fishing boats out hauling in shirauo in the last chilly days as winter gave way to spring.

SURIMI ⌦ FISH PASTE

A h, yes, the elusive and legendary *surimi*. Rare is the sport fisherman who will forget the first time his hook met the maw of this sleek beauty, feared and prized for the ferocious battles it wages. Given the esteem with which the

surimi is held by discriminating anglers worldwide, it's curious
how few trophy specimens are mounted and hung on den or
library walls.

Surimi—a "rheologically gelatinized processed fish product"
as it is known in the food industry—is one of those modern
marvels that would either have fascinated our ancestors or
turned their stomachs. Truth is, though, surimi was being
turned out as early as the 7th century. The *Nihon Shoki*, an
early, semibelievable chronicle of ancient Japan, credits the
Empress Shinko with the first surimi. While involved in an
altercation with three other kingdoms along the Korean Peninsula, during a break in the action the empress ground up some
fish, wrapped it around her spear point, and roasted it. Spear
points being difficult to procure currently, manufacturers
today make do with extruders that spew out various shapes
of compacted fish paste. (*Suru* means "grind, process, smash";
mi is "meat.") It is probably nothing more than a myth that
certain chain seafood restaurants, which shall go unnamed
here, have conspired with surimi manufacturers to produce
everything on the menu from cleverly shaped surimi. Even so,
lobster tails, scallops, king crab legs . . . if it swims, crawls, or
slithers in an ocean somewhere, there's probably a surimi
doppelgänger available.

Surimi does begin as fish. Before being reduced to the consistency of fresh window caulking, surimi was almost always
pollock or a combination of hake and whiting, white-fleshed
species common in most of the planet's cold oceans. What gives
surimi its taste are artificial flavorings; its specific shapes come
from chemical gels that harden the stuff. Even though making
it is a pretty simple process, the battle for surimi supremacy is
every bit as vicious as those campaigns Empress Shinko waged.
Manufacturers constantly search for less perishable, tastier, and
more cost-efficient ways to fake fish.

Until only about a decade or so ago, the most common
form of surimi were the long semicylinders mounted on
boards, shrink-wrapped, and sold as *kamaboko*. These are the

half-moon slices of fish paste, tinged pink on the outer rim, that you'll find in soups and other Japanese dishes. The word "kamaboko" has an interesting origin, by the way. It was originally *gama-no-ho*, meaning the top part of the *gama*, or cattail, which it resembles. Surimi pressed into *chikuwa* look even more like cattail heads, sausage shaped with a hole lengthwise through the center. You'll find them sliced in *oden* and other Japanese-style stews and casseroles.

You shouldn't encounter surimi often in a high-quality sushi-ya, either in America or Japan, but it's ubiquitous in both countries. Sooner or later you'll run across it, and knowing the story of its imperial roots is a good one for the sushi tsu to have handy, proving you're not so narrow-minded about cuisines as to be uninformed on other Japanese foods. And it occasionally appears as a filling in low-end maki sushi, where it substitutes for crab leg. You can tell the difference three feet away, of course. Surimi's texture is consistent; it doesn't have the fibrous muscle strata of the flesh in a real crab leg. It is acceptable for inexpensive sushi purchased at a grocery store, or maybe in some of the goofier creations turned out by sushi places that like to experiment and figure that Westerners will be more or less up for anything that's cooked. If, however, you are presented with leg-shaped sections of surimi atop nigiri sushi, or passed off as a real fish or crustacean appendage in any other form, you should hit the road faster than you can say "rheologically gelatinized processed fish product."

SUZUKI 🐟 SEA BASS

This is not the bigmouth or smallmouth, not the kind of bass that's the beloved subject of late-night cable programs on the outdoors, the quarry of fishing tournaments won by portly men steering boats with outboard motors that could power a Caribbean cruise liner. Sushi's bass, or *suzuki*, are sea bass, the kinds that swim mostly into freshwater rivers and estuaries only to reproduce, spending the rest of their time in the ocean. They're euryhaline, which sounds like some kind of toxic waste that's discovered in your neighborhood but actually refers to fish that can survive in brackish freshwater as well as the ocean. There are three related species of Japanese bass served as sushi, though you should, if you're eating in better sushi-ya, only encounter one.

The true suzuki is the Japanese sea bass, found in warmer waters off southern Japan. It is as common in these regions of Japan as the last name Suzuki (kind of the Japanese version of Smith). That Suzuki, by the way, like the motorcycle, is written with different kanji than the one used for the fish. The itamae buying bass is looking for a specimen about two feet long. He wants it taken sometime in the early summer, just before the species gets the urge to spawn. Suzuki at that time are as fat as they are going to get, which isn't that fat. Some sushi connoisseurs regard their flesh as the epitome of shiromi-dane, light and delicate. Broiling the meat, as is often done with suzuki, turns it flaky white. Filleted raw as a tane for sushi, it is pearly and almost translucent, with perhaps just a tinge of pink along the edge. By the end of November, the quality of fresh suzuki falls off sharply, once they've burned up all their fat looking for a mate the way a lowrider goes through a tank of gas when its driver is looking for the same thing.

Blackfin sea bass (*hira-suzuki*) is fished from waters off central and south Japan, from around Chiba down to Nagasaki. The flavor isn't quite up to that of Japanese sea bass. You can say the same about *kokuchi ishinagi*, also called *ishinagi-zoku*, or giant sea bass. Before you think about staging a scene if you suspect you have encountered either of these in a sushi-ya being advertised as suzuki, reconsider. Neither is common in U.S. markets. They are not likely to be shipped here. All suzuki in sushi restaurants outside Japan has been imported and frozen, and it is going to cost, considerably. Suzuki caught at the height of its season and shipped here can be among the most expensive items on the menu. However, in sushi-ya in the United States you might see "suzuki" translated as "striped bass." If so, heads up: There's nothing wrong with this species of sea bass, but the quality of the flesh is not nearly what you'd get in a Japanese sea bass, and you shouldn't be paying the same price for it. You should also ask if the striped bass is wild or farmed. The ones from the wild have a noticeably superior flavor. Note, too, that suzuki is now farmed in Japan. Without a lot of practice, it is hard to tell the difference. Wild suzuki has a more pronounced flavor and a distinct saltiness that's evident when compared with its tame brethren.

Suzuki is often served as a tane with a dash of ponzu, or with the tiniest sprinkle of togarashi (red pepper flakes), both of which work to bring out the flavor of the fish.

≋ **Watch For:** *Suzuki usu zukuri* is a form of sea bass sashimi; the slices are cut transparently thin, then arranged in a radial pattern on the plate. Sometimes it will be laid out to look like a flower, hence the slang expression for it: *hana-zukuri*, or flower styles. You may see hirame sashimi presented the same way. See page 166, in the section on shima-aji, for a description of kuzu uchi, a dish that is also frequently prepared with suzuki.

≋ **Ask the Itamae:** Whenever the subject of suzuki comes up with an itamae, ask if he can prepare it *arai* style. He may not show it, but he will likely be impressed. *Arai* means "to wash." Thin fillets of suzuki or some other delicate, white-meat tane are soaked in ice water until they pucker. The process leaches some of what little fat there is in the meat and it becomes pale as a Goth kid. The fillets are cut to fit atop nigiri sushi and dressed with *sumiso*, a combination of rice vinegar and miso bean paste. The preparation brings out a lot of the subtle flavor of the bass. The arai method of preparing suzuki is a culinary relic from the days when refrigeration wasn't around to keep bass as fresh as it must be to be enjoyed.

≡ **Trivia**: Japanese people, as I've noted in the section on kohada, have long practiced changing their given names to commemorate some milestone in their lives, or just for the heck of it. The idea of recognizing this sort of advancement through life is called *shusse*. *Shusse-uo* are fish (*uo*) that change names as they mature. A fingerling suzuki is called a *koppa* (only around the Tokyo area). At about a foot long or so, it's a *fukko*. Then it's a *suzuki* and, if it grows beyond three feet or thereabouts, it's a *seigo*.

TAI ⌁ BREAM

Annually in Aichi Prefecture, a procession of young men winds through the city streets of Toyohama, behind a Mardi Gras–scarlet, bungalow-size tai (sea bream) made of paper and bamboo. The parade ends when the fish float, along with the men, drunk on sake and buck naked, go careening right off the dock and into the waters of the harbor. The ceremony has to do with ensuring a good catch for the season or propitiating local deities or something like that. But really, it sounds like just a hell of a good time. The Toyohama Tai Festival also illustrates the importance of tai, one of the most popular fish in Japanese cuisine.

The praises of tai are sung lyrically by introductory texts on sushi. It is the King Kong Daddy of shiromi-dane, the white meat equivalent, for the sushi tsu, of tuna—exquisite in taste. Tai often gets the honorific *o* attached to it, and the *t* becomes a *d*: *odai*. Here's what they don't tell you, though: "tai" is used to describe more than 100 varieties of what are labeled variously in the West as sea beam and snapper and porgy, and probably Bess as well. Consider, if you will, *amadai*, a common tai. Just around Tokyo alone, it's also known as *aka-amadai*, *shiroamadai*, *Shirakawa-dai*, and *akakuzuna*. And guess what? What the Japanese call amadai isn't even a true tai at all; it's a guji, or snapper. And even that is problematic, and switching to English isn't going to help. The FDA lists more than three dozen varieties of snapper.

Even at its narrowest definition, "tai" can refer to a dozen fish of the Sparidae family. If you want to be sure, and you happen to have access to the carcass, file this away: All true tai have between 11 and 13 spines on their dorsal fins. They also have, for all you readers who are fish dentists, large molars. Chances are, though, you will have to rely on the itamae to clarify just what kind of tai he's serving. If you are eating in the sort of sushi-ya you should frequent in Japan, he will usually tell you that it is *madai*, by far the best-tasting and most popular tai. Madai are briefcase-length, alcoholic schnoz–pink fish with a black line running down their back fin and indigo spots above each of their huge black eyes, which makes them look sort of like Bette Davis with gills. A little pudge around the bottom of their bellies is a sign of freshness that the itamae looks for. He often finds it. Of all sushi fish, tai keeps its just-out-of-the-ocean taste longest. Its flesh doesn't have a lot of the enzymes that start the flavor of other fishes sliding off peak faster than a 73-year-old novice snowboarder.

Smallish, younger tai may be served with their skin on. If so, the fillets are *yuderu*, "blanched." The fish are wrapped in coarse cloth and hot water is poured over them; then they're plunged into ice. (Using ice *water* is a no-no; it breaks down the meat fibers.) They are patted dry and stored cold in the case until served. Another colloquialism for the blanching process sometimes used in the sushi-ya is *matsukawa-zukuri*, or pine bark style, because the treatment causes the fish's skin to pucker and resemble the rough bark of the tree.

Larger tai are skinned and served raw. Note that tai fillets tend to be skimpier than those of other fish because a stringy, fibrous connective tissue has to be cut away. So tai served as nigiri will have a little more rice underneath to even out its appearance next to other nigiri. Note too that if the flavor of tai you order on Tuesday is not quite up to the standards of the one you had on Friday, it may be an indication that (a) you're not eating sushi often enough, since what were you doing all weekend? and (b) the tane on Tuesday may have come from a bigger fish than the one on Friday. Tai has an ideal size of about a foot and a half; much beyond that and there is a marked decrease in taste.

Even though madai is the ne plus ultra of the tai family as a tane, here's a delightful chance for you to engage in a bit of one-upmanship so dear to the heart of the sushi tsu: It's July, and you and some sushi enthusiast acquaintances are contemplating the menu. You opt for tai. Tai? Your friends react if you'd just suggested at a gathering of the Beacon Hill Gourmet Club, "Hey, let's try some tomatoes in the chowder." They all know tai is at its best in the winter. Some will "educate" you with a slice of trivia they have long been hoarding for just such an occasion. Tai—madai, that is—spawn in April and June, and the flavor falls off considerably right after, they'll inform you. Summer tai are called *mugiwara-dai*, or barley straw tai, they will add to demonstrate their knowledge, because the coloration of their skin turns a pale, reddish yellow at that time. You nod indulgently as they explain all this with relish at the thought of instructing a tsu like yourself. You understand. They are, after all, sushi *enthusiasts*. Big difference, as you are about to illustrate for them by explaining patiently that you will be ordering *chidai*. Chidai is known in English as a crimson sea bream. It spawns in the fall; it is at its best in the summer, and it ranks second only to madai as a tane for sushi. Of course madai is a winter fish, you tell them. Chidai, you explain, is what the sushi tsu enjoys in summer. They are properly humbled. Your legend grows.

A couple of other kinds of true tai species you should recognize are kichinu (black sea bream) and kurodai (also called a black sea bream in English, but lacking the yellow-tipped fins of the kichinu; it is also called a *chinu* on the west coast of Japan). These are common substitutes for madai when it's out of season. There are also several species passed off as tai, as we said, that aren't. *Ishidai* is a Japanese parrot fish. *Hedai* is the flat sea bream. There is nothing wrong with the flavor of these or many others, but you need to develop a taste for madai to make informed comparisons.

≋ **The Bad News:** You've learned a lot about tai in our little interlude here, which should serve you well in your quest to become a sushi tsu. You probably know at least as much as the average Japanese. He has just one advantage over you. He has tai available and you probably don't. Tai is so popular in Japan that it is very rarely exported. There may be some exceptions. But the odds are better that the United States wins soccer's next World Cup than what is advertised as tai in sushi-ya outside Japan is really tai. More likely, it is red snapper or porgy. We'll get to that in a minute.

≋ **Watch For:** Sushi tsu distinguish a couple of kinds of madai that deserve special consideration. Taken from the Kurushima Straits around the Seto Inland Sea off Kyushu, the akashidai and narutodai are generally regarded as the best of all madai. Since we don't have any kind of madai in Western waters, you will be eating some tai frozen and imported from around Japan. It is reasonable to ask exactly what kind of tai you're eating, and if you hear either of these names, *akashidai* or *narutodai*, know that you're enjoying a rare treat for the sushi snob outside Japan.

Watch, too, for exactly what is being advertised as tai outside Japan. It is common for sushi-ya to serve a couple of pretenders from the Atlantic that are passed off as tai. Porgy, or scup, is closely related to bream but it doesn't taste the same at all. Red snapper isn't related closely to tai at all but it does taste a lot like it. Until or unless you gain a lot of gastronomic experience with real tai, you'll be depending on the honesty of your sushi-ya here. If they are the least bit evasive or tell you "it's very much like tai" or "it's American tai," give a pass to whatever they're peddling.

≋ **Ask the Itamae:** Osaka natives are to tai what Chicagoans are to pizza; utterly confident that they are the final and only important arbiters in the cuisine. They have a number of sushi-related ways of preparing it; there's more on this in the section on pressed sushi (page 27). If you are ever in Osaka, not to exploit the possible expertise of a local itamae would border on the criminally negligent. At the very least, an Osaka-trained itamae, and most other good itamae, should know how to prepare *tai no sugata sushi*. It is an entire bream, cleaned and stuffed with sushi rice. The presentation is beautiful, the taste is unforgettable, the cost is apt to be stratospheric. But this is a summit to be bagged in the climbing experiences of the sushi snob. And if matrimony is in the foreseeable future for you or any sushi tsu you know, consider that whole sushi rice–stuffed bream may be at the center of an ultimate wedding banquet.

≋ **Trivia:** *Medetai* is a catchall word in Japanese that can mean "happiness," a "festivity," "joyous," "felicitous," or "lucky." So whole tai is often broiled or otherwise prepared with bamboo skewers run through the fish to make it hold its original shape, and served at holiday meals or other gatherings of a celebratory nature all over Japan. "Medetai." Get it?

≋ **More Trivia:** If you were ever tempted to have a snack of fish eyeballs, well, tai peepers are an excellent choice. They are high in vitamin B_1 and ranked by connoisseurs of ocular fish cuisine as the tastiest of orbs. Keep it in mind.

TAIRAGAI ⌒ PEN SHELL

The *tairagai* exists, in part, as a reminder that no matter how prolix the palate of the sushi tsu, there are always new vistas to visit and explore, culinary corners and nooks wherein lurk sensations to tempt us further and further from the ordinary and mundane. At least, that's the way it seems in the case of the tairagai, or pen shell. The Western sushi tsu, confronted with a tairagai's fat, pillowy adductor muscle, looking like a cream-colored marshmallow strapped onto a nugget of rice with a cinch of nori, is particularly impressed with it, even more so after taking a bite. How come, you may reflect, we don't eat more of these sorts of things? Indeed. Aside from a few species of clams, oysters, and mussels, Americans have treated bivalves the way your gay postman treats the latest Victoria's Secret catalog: with indifference and even some measure of disdain. Tairagai are a savory portal to a world of bivalves, from whelks to winkles, piddocks to cockles, that have gone tragically untasted by most of us. There are few better ways to make an entrance to that realm than by sampling tairagai as a topping for sushi.

Tairagai are called pen shells or sometimes fan shells in the West. The 1st-century Roman naturalist Pliny was fascinated by tairagai. He claimed they formed a symbiotic relationship with tiny crabs that lived inside the pen shell and shared the fish their host caught. Pliny thought eels grew from horsehairs that fell into puddles, so he is not the most reliable of sources in these matters. In fact, tairagai feed on plankton. The adults are about a foot in length, dull, yellowish brown, and shaped like a half-open folding fan with a sharp tip at the end. The tairagai goes tip first into the mud of ocean floors in the shallows, using a hairy bysuss like a mussel's to hold itself in place. It feeds by opening and closing its two shells and filtering its meals. The adductor muscles that move the shells get a daily workout. Tairagai, consequently, are in great shape. If shell flapping was an Olympic sport and bivalves could enter, tairagai would bring home the gold. Alas, their loss is the sushi tsu's gain. Instead of winning any medals, the tairagai are themselves taken. They're harvested mostly in mom-and-pop operations in the West; in Japan, commercial gatherers scoop up tons of them annually. Tairagai are found in most of the temperate oceans in the world, so it's hard to know where your order originated. While the season runs all winter long, in Japan tairagai is thought of as an autumn tane. In fact, they are available frozen everywhere throughout the year.

As with the scallop, only the adductor muscles of the tairagai go into sushi. The other meat, the viscera and mantle lobes, all have a strong smell. By "strong," we're talking they stink. The itamae will either buy just the adductor muscles or do the job of separating the muscles from the rest of the clam at a safe distance from his customers. He ends up with two, a smaller and larger muscle. The former is sliced horizontally for a tane; the latter is cut vertically, and you can see the distinction if you look closely. Tairagai is rarely used in chirashi sushi; it is a standard, though, for nigiri sushi. It will benefit from a touch in the shoyu dish, but no wasabi on this one. The taste of tairagai is unique; it needs no garnishes.

≋ **By Any Other Name:** As with other adductor muscles, the part of the tairagai eaten for sushi is called *kaibashira*, the "pillar of the shell." So to be more exact, you have to refer to *tairagai no bashira*. "Tairagai" is often translated inaccurately as "razor shell." This goes way back to the British and Italians who, between them, can be blamed for much that is confusing or wrong. In the 17th century, British sailors in Italy tasted razor clams, an entirely different species that looks nothing like a tairagai, more like a folding straight razor. In Italian, these were *capalonga*. Back in England, the sailors started referring to pen shells as "caperlongers," or razor clams. This mix-up is still in evidence today on a lot of sushi menus. Razor clams are delectable, but they aren't used for sushi. The name "tairagai" is best translated from Japanese as "flat shell."

≋ **Watch For:** Tairagai is grilled with *uni*, or sea urchin, as a side dish in the sushi-ya. The combination of flavors will be met with either praise or "Thanks, but I don't need to try that again."

TAKO ⟷ OCTOPUS

Oddball foods in Japan are called *getemono*. Snake innards, bear paws, your Aunt Edna's three-bean casserole—all would be considered getemono. No doubt about it, in a lot of places octopus would definitely fit the definition of getemono. But not everywhere. Picturesque women whack a fistful of raw octopus on stone steps in picturesque Greek villages until it is way past pulp, for instance, and the tourists think it's, well, picturesque. Put a sliver of it on top of rice, and a goodly percentage of the world's non-Japanese population reacts as if you'd served the family cat as tartare. Go figure.

Tako, or octopus, is one of the most common ingredients in both nigiri and chirashi sushi. It has not always been so. In fact, before World War II, octopus was not at all a high-class tane among sushi aficionados. It was relegated in Japanese cooking to other dishes: vinegared, chopped, and added to seafood salad dishes, for instance. About the time Elvis started gyrating, it made an appearance in some Tokyo sushi-ya and quickly caught on, becoming a favorite.

Amazingly intelligent, able to change colors in less than a second, and ranging from thimble size to some that are big enough to dine on *you*, octopus live in nearly every ocean in the world, and there are more than 100 varieties. If you're eating tako in Japan, chances are it came from nearby waters; the tastiest is a species called *madako*. Everywhere else tako is served atop sushi, it is likely to have come from off the coast of North Africa. Wherever it was caught, octopus does not arrive ready to eat. It is tenderized first, then boiled. There's something to be said for that whacking process used to tenderize octopus all around the Mediterranean. The Japanese have taken a different approach to the always necessary method of softening up this tasty mollusk. You won't see any of this in any sushi-ya, true. Still, it is nice to know how it's done. The whole body, tentacles and all, is thoroughly massaged with rough salt and a whole daikon radish that has been grated into a grainy paste. Special attention goes to the tentacles, which have a slimy coating the massaging process cleans off. Once that's done, the tako goes into a pot of boiling water. That's where it changes color (for the last time, the more ironic among us might reflect), going from its natural shade, which is something like the hue of primer on the front fender of a '78 Dodge, to a healthy, lusty pink. Bright red octopus is suspicious: it has probably been dyed to hide less-than-perfect flesh.

Once killed, the meat of tako spoils faster than a kid with rich grandparents at Disney World. The itamae will look for a fresh octopus with a speckled skin, and he'll often give the whole body a shake to see if the tentacles all bounce energetically—two reliable signs of freshness. If the tako has been pre-boiled, he will give one leg a vigorous rub. If that causes the skin to shuck off, he'll pass. If octopus hasn't been boiled, the chef will take care of that quickly. Once done, he uses only the eight tentacles as a tane, which are sliced on a slight bias. If they're going into chirashi sushi, the cut will be straight. If they're going atop nigiri sushi, they are cut in a regular wavy pattern, like a crinkle-cut French fry. (The cut is called *doto* in the slang of the Japanese kitchen, or following waves.) The "waves" help keep the dane from slipping off the rice. For the same reason a belt of toasted nori is sometimes wrapped around tako nigiri.

When tako first made its appearance as a tane, it was often brushed with nitsume. More popular now is the light smear of wasabi that accompanies so many other tane, though you might also have it served with a dash of lemon juice.

≣ **By Any Other Name:** A bit of jargon for octopus that you might hear, especially if the itamae is from Tokyo, is *o-te*. It means a "hand," since the body and tentacles of an octopus kind of resemble the palms and fingers of our hands.

≋ **Watch For:** Slices of tako atop rice should have a slightly unbalanced appearance. That's because a good chef will have sliced off the top part of the cross section of the tentacle, opposite the sucker side. Nothing wrong with that piece, but it is black and unsightly and so it is deftly scooped away with a knife tip.

≋ **Ask the Itamae:** Not so long ago, cooked tako frequently appeared as a sushi topping; ask the itamae if he's prepared it this way. It is thoroughly simmered in water, shoyu, sake, and sugar, then presented just like the boiled version.

≋ **Trivia:** A rendering of an upside-down octopus is a common sight in many parts of Japan, denoting a hot bathing spring or bathhouse. Stylized, the round body of the tako looks like a big tub, and its tentacles going up resemble tendrils of steam rising.

TAMAGO-YAKI ⟿ EGG OMELET

Remember how Grandma used to sift the flour, cut in the shortening by hand, roll out the dough with that patinaed old pin that belonged to *her* grandmother? Add a filling of peaches she preserved herself, after picking them herself, right off the old tree out back? Remember the perfectly fluted crust with the little designs carved in to let the steam out? Remember that first mouthful of her peach pie, the one no one else could make, still warm, that was the perfect finish to a Thanksgiving dinner at her farmhouse?

Well, welcome to the 21st century. Grandma's living in a condo in Boca Raton. This holiday she's serving curried turkey takeout from the local Tastee Thai To Go. Sad but true, tamago-yaki, the sweet egg omelet sushi topping, has undergone a similar evolution. You can spot a real old-timer at a sushi-ya in Japan and even in this country because he will order tamago first. That's because back when Grandma was still young enough to have been climbing around in those peach trees, the standard way to judge the skills of an itamae was to sample his tamago-yaki. Every itamae cooked up his own.

It isn't easy. Unlike a normal omelet, tamago-yaki are cooked in a large square pan. Rather than getting turned once, they are folded again and again, until the thick, eggy block is solid but fluffy and as full of air as a fine soufflé. The mixture itself is a combination of eggs, broth, and mirin. Even for a professional itamae, the process is time-consuming, so much so that most sushi restaurants in Japan and elsewhere have, for many years, bought big blocks of tamago-yaki prepared and frozen from wholesale suppliers. That's why, like a Quarter Pounder, whether you order it in Shibuya-ku or Reno, Nevada, tamago-yaki sushi tastes pretty much the same.

Such uniformity needn't deter the sushi tsu, however. You can still happily make distinctions between thick and thin tamago. The most common fried-egg omelet atop sushi is the *atsu tamago-yaki*, the thicker omelet. *Atsu tamago* is only used for nigiri sushi and Edomae-style chirashi sushi. It is the cake-like omelet with which most people associate the word *tamago*. There is another form of tamago, though, *usu yaki*, or thin omelet. Usu yaki is used instead of fried tofu pouches for some kinds of stuffed sushi, like chakin sushi, hamaguri sushi, and fukusa sushi. In the Kansai region, especially in Osaka, when you order chirashi sushi, you will get slivers of a thin omelet scattered across the top of the bowl. Again, this is usu yaki, or thin, tamago. When it is cut into slivers, by the way, it's called *kinshi* tamago. *Kinshi* is Japanese for "spun gold" or "gold thread."

If you do eat sushi in a place that makes its own tamago-yaki, its texture should be airy and spongy. If it is too thick and tastes a little gooey, more like flan, that's a sign the moisture hasn't been steamed out of it. That is really what the process of cooking is in this case. Frying the egg takes out all the moisture.

Good tamago is actually steamed in the pan. Also check the color: If your tamago has a dark, burned look about it, you may surmise that too much sugar went into the mixture. Examine the layering. Tamago are cooked by folding the egg over and over on itself in the pan, creating layers. A lesser-skilled itamae can't make the layers compact. The results will be too loose and fluffy, which is okay in a chiffon prom dress but less desirable in tamago.

≋ **By Any Other Name:** In the lexicon of the sushi-ya, tamago is *gyoku*. Every sushi *tsu-jin buru*, or poseur, will know this and will be egregious in finding some way to use it, either in ordering or discussing it. These types need to be shut down occasionally. They are irritating to those of us who really are tsu. So when the gyoku schtick comes up, consider asking the clown what he's talking about. Let him explain how that's sushi slang for an omelet and that in normal parlance, it means "jewel." Then ask *why*. He won't know. His type never does. You do, of course. You can explain that it has to do with the *on*, or the original Chinese pronunciation of the character for *tama*. *Tama* refers to spherical objects. So tamago is a combination of *tama* and *ko*, or, as a suffix, go, "a child." An egg is, in a sense, a "round child." "Tama" read with the Chinese pronunciation is *gyoku*, which also refers to round jewels. That's why an egg is a "jewel" and why these bothersome pests will eventually avoid you like a bad rash—and that's not a bad thing.

≋ **Watch For:** *Kurakake* is a "saddle" tamago. The finished omelet is split lengthwise and laid or propped (*kake*) across shari, resembling a *kura*, or saddle. It doesn't taste any better, but it splashes up a presentation of sushi, and it is an indicator that the itamae is willing to go a couple of steps further to make his sushi at least look better.

≋ **Ask the Itamae:** Even though tamago made on the premises is now about as common as Elvis impersonators at the

Vatican, it might still be a good idea to order tamago first, for a couple of reasons. The flavor is among the lightest of any tane and so it is good to start with and will not interfere with tasting the quality of the sushi rice, which, no matter what, had damned well better have been made on the premises.

TOBIUONOKO ⇌ FLYING-FISH EGGS

In the 9th century, for his opposition to the Fujiwara emperor, the scholar Sugawara Michizane was banished to a shrine at Dazaifu, in Kyushu, forcing him to leave behind his native Kyoto and his beloved plum trees, about which he wrote one of Japan's better-known verses when he was only five years old. The plum trees missed him as well, one of them so much that it uprooted itself and flew—these things happen from time to time in Japanese tales—clear over to Kyushu to root itself near the entrance of the shrine. It still blooms today, still called the *tobi-ume*, or flying plum.

In the teaching scrolls of both traditional martial arts and the Noh theatre, a short, quick hopping motion is sometimes referred to as *karasu-tobi*, "crow hopping."

Tobi is used in both instances above to describe airborne movement ranging from an interisland flight of a tree to the short, stuttering hop of a crow. Obviously, the word covers a broad range of action. When it is used as it is in the case of the tobiuo, or flying fish, the verb refers to something somewhere in the middle. While flying fish aren't capable of sustained aerobatics, they can get enough speed up while swimming to propel themselves into the air and buzz along, using their extended pectoral fins, for more than the length of a football field. Tobiuo sail around in waters all around Japan's southern coasts. They often dive-bomb right onto boat decks, which makes it convenient to gather them. Less accommodating schools are harvested with gill nets. Tobiuo are grilled or fried. Early in the summer, when they're spawning, females are also gathered and stripped of their eggs, which go directly to sushi-ya.

Tobiuonoko—in the sushi establishment this long handle is often shortened to *tobiko*—are a rich reddish brown. They are smaller than ikura, or salmon roe, and crunchier. Flying-fish eggs are mildly sweet, though some will complain they are too gritty. They are nearly always served gunkan style or in a heap with chirashi sushi. There isn't any season; once collected they can be frozen and shipped around the world. They are not as glossy as ikura, but they should have a sheen and be plump and not at all wrinkled.

≋ **Watch For:** *Tobi-tama* is a gunkan-style sushi with tobiuonoko as a tane and a raw quail-egg yolk sitting on top. It is another acquired taste, admittedly. Tobi-tama, however, is one of the most beautiful and elegant pieces of sushi, an edible work of art.

≋ **While We're on the Subject:** This is a good place for a brief primer on sushi's other reproductively oriented tane. All of them are available in sushi-ya here nowadays. There is, unfortunately, some confusion about them, and substitutions are made, so the sushi tsu must be conversant and expert.

IKURA are salmon roe (see page 100).

KAZUNOKO are herring roe (see page 126).

MASAGO is the roe of the capelin, a kind of smelt. The *masa* here means, literally, "sand" or "fine gravel," because that's what it looks like. The eggs are smaller than tobiuonoko, very pale orange, and almost sweet. Some itamae refer to crab eggs as *masago*, so if there's any question, be sure to ask if it's kani (crab) masago you are going to be served.

MENTAIKO is the roe of the Alaska pollack, known in Japanese as a *mentai* or a *suketodara*. The mentaiko of the Hakata region in Kyushu is the most famous. The eggs are salted and sprinkled with togarashi, a hot chile pepper, which is why they are also called *karashi-mentaiko*. Mentaiko are deep, rich red; the eggs are just slightly smaller than ikura. Chances are almost certain that if you bite into roe and it is dark red and spicy, you're eating mentaiko.

SHIRAKO are the milt or sperm sacs of a few different fish that are sometimes used as sushi tane, and are presented as a side dish as well. Cod (*tara*) sperm sacs are the most commonly consumed; the poetic epicurean phrase for them is *kumo no ko*, or "children of the clouds." The male reproductive sacs of anglerfish (*anko*) are also eaten in the sushi-ya, along with those of the famous fugu or puffer fish, which has toxins in its liver. So if the sac is not properly prepared, it will kill you. The mere Japanese food connoisseur may therefore opt for a meal of fugu sashimi. The sushi tsu disdains this pedestrian flirt with death and insists if he is going to have a go with fugu, it is going to be with fugu sperm sacs, or one might as well simply stay home.

TARAKO is a generic reference to any kind of cod roe, including, though it should not, the aforementioned mentaiko. Unlike the red roe of the pollack (which is technically a kind of cod), most other cod roe is pale yellowish white and the eggs cling together in chunks. It is a tolerable tane for sushi but not at all in the class of mentaiko. Beware the sushi menu that does not distinguish between these two.

TORIGAI 🐟 COCKLESHELL

Thanks to the level of technology that has revolutionized the way we gather and process and distribute our food, the sushi tsu can, in Houston or Minneapolis or Cleveland, sit down to a meal of sushi composed of seafood that has come, fresh or perfectly frozen, from oceans and seashores his grand-parents had never even heard of. During an ordinary lunch or dinner appear tastes and textures that, even one generation ago, fewer than 1 or 2 percent of the world's population got to eat. The tsu is thankful, but it is in our nature to pine for what we cannot have. That would include fresh, unfrozen *torigai*.

The torigai is a Japanese cockle. Despite the determined efforts of sushi enthusiasts, they are far from endangered as a species. Torigai are abundant in the wild and have been very successfully reared through aquaculture. The torigai is about four inches across, its maroon shell banded on the outside with yellow. It is taken from late summer until late the following spring, to coincide with its two spawning periods in autumn and spring. Torigai are sold at fish markets still alive, although the meat from the shell is sometimes removed immediately after the animal is harvested and is sold separately. It's the torigai's "foot" that is eaten as sushi, about three inches long, more or less, and shaped like a spear point. To the Japanese imagination, the shape was like that of a chicken's beak and so the clam got its name, *tori* (chicken) *gai* (shell). The itamae serves it raw or else boils the foot for just a few seconds and then rinses it in a combination of rice vinegar and a dash of distilled vinegar. The latter preparation is more common in Japan; if you notice a slight sweetness to your order of torigai, that's why. Torigai, incidentally, are loaded with amino acids—that is what causes some who eat them to claim they taste like shrimp—and more protein per gram than any other shellfish.

Aside from its taste, the quality of torigai is measured by the sushi snob in two ways: The thickness of the meat is important. Torigai taken when they are too young or during the spawning season will only yield a thin cross section of meat, and the rice underneath it, when it is used in nigiri sushi, overwhelms the tane. The second standard is the rich black shine of the top of the torigai. If it gets handled too much or if it is left too long in the case, the luster dulls. Glossy torigai is a sign of a competent itamae in any sushi-ya. The taste of torigai is a lot like that of akagai—a very slight, pleasant crunchiness with a delicate flavor that is not at all fishy. Torigai survives freezing more poorly than almost any other shellfish used in the sushi-ya. It is palatable, yet once thawed, there is a rubbery texture that torigai served fresh does not have. Torigai doesn't live on our side of the Pacific; what we have has all been frozen for import and even at that, it is a good tane. But fresh torigai is one of those sushi experiences. . . . Well, it gives us a moment to wonder, despite the advanced state of our food technology, can we really be said to be fully civilized without access to fresh torigai?

≋ **Watch For:** Along with shrimp, torigai is one of the standard tane found in Edo-style chirashi sushi. If it isn't available, one may assume that there has either been a problem with the supply or that the itamae is not as polished as he should be. The former is forgiven by the sushi tsu. The latter is another story entirely.

≋ **Ask the Itamae:** Torigai can be used as a side dish for sushi, presented without rice, along with a small dish filled with shoyu, mirin, and sugar. If you get it that way, dip the torigai in the mixture before you eat it. If you like wasabi, ask the itamae to go a little heavy on the green stuff, which complements torigai-dane.

≋ **Trivia:** Torigai are hermaphroditic and are capable, when there are no other exceptionally attractive specimens of their kind within reach, of fertilizing themselves.

UNI ⮞ SEA URCHIN

Cellophane, along with glues and about 2,000 other things around your house, is made, in part, of kelp. Kelp, as you probably know, are the big houseplant-looking strands of seaweed through which Jacques Cousteau was always swimming, bothering one sort of sea life or another. Kelp is right at the top of the faves list for hungry sea urchins. Sea urchins, in turn, were once kept in line by sea otters. That is, until those frisky furred fellows were nearly wiped out for their skins by the villainous white Europeans who have been busily despoiling and looting the planet since about 15 minutes after they discovered capitalism, if we are to believe most high school history books today. Sea otter numbers plummeted. Sea urchin populations consequently have soared higher than insurance premiums in Belfast. Hordes of them are out there now, nibbling the hell out of kelp beds, wreaking havoc on local ocean ecosystems. And suddenly Mom's paying 29¢ more to buy cellophane with which to wrap the kids' school lunches. The conclusion is obvious: Eating *nama uni*, sea urchin gonads, is an economic and ecological obligation on your part. This doesn't phase you in the least because I lost you when I mentioned gonads.

Let's back up until you get used to the idea. Sea urchins are, along with sand dollars, in the phylum Echinodermata. Maine fishermen call them "whore's eggs." The "urchin" is from the old English word for a hedgehog. Think of a squashed golf ball sprouting some serious attitude in the form of needle-sharp spines. When you run across a sea urchin shell at the beach, it's lost these; it looks like a pincushion without the pins. What is—or was—inside that oblate shell (called a "test") of the female urchin is of concern for the sushi tsu: a star-shaped constellation of five reproductive sacs. They are deep, mustardy yellow–brown ovaries that, unless you and the sea otters get on the ball, will be fertilized by a daddy urchin, resulting in thousands of urchinettes.

Very occasionally, uni will be steamed for sushi. Otherwise, it is served raw. Where it is popular in Europe, the entrails of the urchin are eaten raw too. They are scooped out with a special spoon (it is called a *coupe oursin*—you probably got a set as a wedding gift and returned it for a toaster) and relished with perhaps a couple of slices of bread. The taste has been described as everything from vinegar-flavored pudding to a creamy, buttery, nutty egg yolk. It is strong. So are opinions about it among sushi connoisseurs. Some count it among their favorites. Others order it only if nothing else is available. Few are "I could go either way" on uni. Know that your status as a sushi tsu does not depend on liking it. Even among hard-core connoisseurs in Japan, a fondness for uni is far from universal.

Sushi *tsu-jin-buru*, or would-be sushi snobs, have been overheard gabbing about the relative merits of "Alaskan uni" versus "Californian uni," comparing tastes and textures. This is wrong. Uni is distinguished accurately only by species. The "Atlantic uni" is usually the green sea urchin, which is the same species found in northern Japan, where it is called *Ezo baifun*. (Ezo is an archaic term for the island of Hokkaido; *baifun* is a patty of horse poop, an example of that wacky Japanese sense of humor that saw a similarity of shape between the urchin's shell and equine droppings.) Ezo baifun are why fishermen from Maine to Alaska have been making a fortune the past few years. Instead of throwing the urchins overboard from dredge nets as they've done for centuries, they now ship them instantly to Japan. This uni is plump, just a little sweet, with a noticeable briny flavor and a long aftertaste.

What passes for "California uni" is most often from the short-spined urchin, which is also common in warmer waters all around Japan. There's a burgeoning industry for collecting this variety around Catalina Island in California; it is processed in San Diego. The short-spined uni is sweeter and nuttier than the green species, and a little smaller. Murasaki uni, which is supposed to be the smoothest version, is the purple sea urchin, very common in waters of New England and Honshu. If your sushi-ya is on the East Coast and uses a local supplier, assume it is murasaki uni you're eating.

≋ **Watch For:** Fresh uni is silky and firm enough to hold its shape; the color is bright and consistent. On your plate, it will be served gunkan style, plopped on a nugget of rice and fenced in with a ring of nori. In the case in front of the itamae, uni sits in wooden boxes covered with a sheet of cellophane (see comments above for the irony in this), since it dries out so quickly. But watch out. Not-so-fresh uni is as runny and watery as American "lite" beers. Here's a rhyme every child should know: If the uni is oozing, it's not of your choosing.

≋ **(Don't) Ask the Itamae:** It is tempting to ask the Itamae if the uni in his case is fresh. Uni retains its peak of quality about as long as a government stays stable in equatorial Africa, and if it is the slightest bit off, the taste is god-awful, like a mouthful of tin-flavored soap. (Those who don't cotton to uni will wonder how it could taste any worse. I know.) Since uni is among the most expensive of sushi toppings, there is a natural desire to want to be sure you're going to be able to eat it. But if you can't tell by a look, or, more important, if you don't trust the itamae to be scrupulous in his concern for freshness, you shouldn't be eating there and you certainly shouldn't be eating uni.

≋ **Trivia:** Female uni gonads tend to be sweeter than those of males; speculation on why would lead only to a number of indelicate jokes.

≋ **More Trivia:** Uni is the third leg in the tripartite *tenka no sanmai chinmi*, the "three fabulous and rare foods that are treasures," of Edo-period Japanese cuisine. The other two are *konowata*, or fermented sea slug intestines, and *karasumi*, dried and salted roe of mullet.

UZURI TAMAGO 🐟 QUAIL EGG

A re you losing sleep fretting about the effects of micro-gravity on embryonic avian musculoskeletal development? Me neither. But apparently it has had some scientists in a lather, so much so that one of the first NASA shuttle missions of the new millennium carried aloft an experiment designed to find out what happens to developing chicks if the eggs they are in are subjected to the artificial gravity of the shuttle for a month or so. It wasn't just any eggs they used for the experiment, mind you. It was *uzuri tamago*—Japanese quail eggs.

That perfectly good quail eggs would be wasted on this sort of perverted priority explains a lot about why NASA hasn't gotten around to building thriving colonies on Venus yet or even developing working vehicles like those used on *The Jetsons*. A far more worthwhile experiment would have occurred to any sushi snob the moment "quail eggs" and "space shuttle" were mentioned in the same sentence: that is, in the weightlessness of space, would the taste change if the egg had to be put under the rice to keep it from floating away, instead of on top of it?

Terrestrially, uzuri tamago is served alone in gunkan sushi, or, more commonly, it is plopped sunny-side up surrounded by gunkan filled with masago (smelt eggs) or tobiko (flying-fish eggs). More precisely, it is the yolk that's served; the albumen is removed. Quail egg yolks pack about three times the vitamin B_1 as chicken eggs and about a third less water. It gives them a decidedly more eggy taste than a chicken egg. What makes these combinations of fish and fowl eggs so attractive is the extraordinary interplay of textures. The eggs of the flying fish or smelt have a crisp sweetness about them that goes well with the rich, creamy flavor and feel of the quail egg.

≋ **Trivia:** If medieval Japanese sexual practices interest you, you already know about *asahi o kaeru*. For the rest of you, it is mentioned in some old texts devoted to the venereal pursuits that were popular back during Japan's feudal age. "Returning sunrise" is a good translation. It was a lover's game. One person takes the insides of a quail egg in his or her mouth carefully enough not to break the yolk. Then he or she kisses the other person so gently that the yolk slips into the other's mouth. It goes back and forth until one partner breaks the egg, which is then shared by both. Yes, it's a little weird. No, I do not know of any places in your vicinity where fresh quail eggs may be procured. Ask the itamae at your favorite sushi-ya. He already knows you are odd and won't think much of it.

PART III

The Practice

They are the ketchup and pickles to our hamburgers, the blue cheese dip to our crudités: condiments and sides. In Japanese, condiments are *ashirai*, or *tsuma* and *ken* (used mostly to describe the side condiments for sashimi), or *yakumi*. The last means, literally, "medicine taste," a clue that condiments were used as much to make food healthier as to make it palatable. Sushi would not be at all the same without them.

Shoyu

Until about 25 years ago, you could reliably tell how long a transplant had been living in Japan just by inviting him out for an Italian dinner. If when his plate of lasagna or ravioli arrived at the table, he immediately began casting about as if missing something, you could bet he had been "out East" a while, long enough to habitually bow to a caller at the other end of a phone conversation, cover his mouth while using a toothpick, or fall asleep hanging on to the strap of a metro train. That's because what he was looking around the table for was the bottle of Tabasco. There were once bottles of this hot sauce on virtually every table in Japan's Italian restaurants. Italian food as prepared in Japan was, until fairly recently, so uniformly awful that a healthy spurt of Tabasco shaken over it was more important for palatability than Parmesan cheese.

Given the ubiquity of shoyu—soy sauce—in Japanese cuisine (there seem to be about three dishes in the repertoire of the average home cook in Japan that don't involve either miso or shoyu, or a combination of both), it is reasonable to assign to it a status similar to that of hot sauce on pasta. It is reasonable in theory, but wrong. Shoyu doesn't mask the taste of Japanese food; just the opposite. It is instead the quintessential condiment, a little bit sweet, a little bit salty, a little bit country, a little bit rock and roll. But it is nearly as ubiquitous as those Tabasco bottles once were, and it can be similarly misused. Those who splatter enough shoyu over rice to float the bowl, who drown slices of fresh, succulent sashimi in shoyu, don't understand what shoyu is all about. They miss its subtleties. They're masking flavors, and that is not what soy sauce should be doing. Shoyu complements and enhances the taste of foods, especially Japanese foods, and especially sushi. This means the sushi snob has to know something about it.

So close the blinds. Make a pile of books on top your desk tall enough to fold your arms over and prop up your chin. Mr. Feldman, the World Cultures teacher, had a late evening of it last night, so today's filmstrip day. The epic unspooling, with a flickering whir from the projector, is *Soy Sauce, Ketchup of the Orient*.

An orchestra overture swells as opening scenes show sturdy yeoman farmers harvesting emerald acres of soybeans with combines, the machines' chutes firing the beans into the beds of trucks that trundle along beside them. In the next scene, rosy-cheeked children pause in their play to wave at the friendly truck drivers transporting groaning loads of the soybeans to factories in the big city. Once there, both are roasted in airplane hangar–size ovens. The cooked beans and wheat are then stirred into vats and dusted with an aspergillus mold called *koji*, which is also a handy bit of magic dust to have around when fermenting sake. As that mixture, called *moromi*, cooks up, brine is added. The musical background on the filmstrip goes into a sprightly pizzicato turn as the mash is piped, gurgling, into fermentation silos. Then, after what's been nonstop action, the pace slows a bit during the second act. The moromi just sits in the silos for a year or so. After that, the plot picks up again. The solids of the now well-fermented moromi are strained and the liquid is pasteurized, bottled, and sent off to grateful consumers all over the world, who upend it over everything from rib-eye steaks to vegetable stir-frys to moo goo gai pan to sushi.

Just as the story turns to the intriguing history and lore of soy sauce, the projector jams. The film starts melting, and what remains of Mr. Feldman's third-hour class is spent listening to him reminisce on the summer he spent in Paris. Here's what you missed on the rest of the filmstrip:

Humans require salt much the way popcorn does. People living in early civilizations who ate a lot of meat got some of their necessary quota of salt that way. They augmented it by gathering at mineral licks, where salt concentrations drew hordes of animals as well. Daniel Boone was famous for his encyclopedic knowledge of salt lick locations on the American frontier. Early Japanese got double whammied, however, in their access to salt. Their diet was primarily vegetarian (not only do vegetables contain no salt naturally, but those with potassium also suck salt out of our bodies), and Japan has few natural deposits of the mineral. Seaweeds were cooked down for their salts in Japan. It was a labor-intensive process, the results of which were like a wedding cake—edible but not overwhelmingly tasty—and eventually, cooks in the Yayoi period (300 B.C. to A.D. 300) figured a better way to get their NaCl needs met. They fermented soybeans with grains, essentially a form of miso, koji mold, and salt. The resultant goo was intensely salty. And while it wasn't practical for eating as a way of getting salt in one's diet—it would have been less than spectacular scattered on popcorn, for example—the stuff was perfect for preserving vegetables. So began *kokubishio* (grain salting), the first saline step toward shoyu.

During the 12th century, other parts of Asia contributed to Japan's salt-based condiments and sauces. Vietnamese *nuoc nam* fish sauce, which found its way into Japan, for instance, was almost certainly the inspiration for *shottsuru*, a sauce made of fermented small fish that flavors mostly stews and noodle dishes in Japanese cooking today. In 1228, Mr. Shoyu, a Zen Buddhist monk otherwise known as Kakushin, returned from some postgrad studies at a Chinese temple where he apparently took a minor in cooking. Once home, he introduced *Kinzanji-miso*, an elegant refined miso paste, to Japan. He founded his own temple, Kokoku-ji, in present-day Wakayama Prefecture—I suspect it was more because the springwater there was perfect for his miso enterprise than from any profound evangelical impulses. He quickly had a tidy little industry going in Kinzan-ji-miso. One day, a couple of his workers, probably seeking a cool, shady spot for a nap, crawled under the vats of fermenting miso, where they discovered a briny ooze dripping from between the slats. The ooze is what we now call *tamari*, a sibling of shoyu. First mentioned specifically as such in a dictionary in 1597, shoyu developed through some further piddling with this primordial tamari ooze.

It didn't take long before entrepreneurs in Yuasa, the village nearest Kakushin's temple, got in on the act. By the 1500s, three distinct varieties were being marketed: tamari; *usukuchi*, or shoyu "lite," a slightly less salty version that's a big seller today in the Kansai region; and a darker shoyu called *koikuchi*. It is koikuchi you were dribbling last night on your sweater while dunking your order of maguro nigiri. Dark shoyu accounts for about 90 percent of all soy sauce made in Japan now. The first manufacturer, in business since 1535, was Yamasa Shoyu. By the beginning of the Edo period, the three giants of the shoyu biz were up and running: Yamasa, Higeta, and Kikkoman, all of them in Shimofusa, where the water was ideal for making a quality product. Interestingly, shoyu became one of Japan's first export items. Dutch seamen brought jugs of it to Europe, and it appeared on the table of Louis XIV, who reportedly was nuts about it.

Edo culture gets the credit for generating the particular dark shoyu brands that are sitting in little bottles, beakers, and the small spouted pots called *shoyu sashi* in sushi-ya all over the world. For centuries, the place of shoyu's birth, Wakayama Prefecture around Osaka, Nara, and Kyoto, had been the hot zone for manufacturing lighter shoyu, supplying the Imperial Court in Kyoto with the stuff. So the lighter usukuchi-style shoyu predominated all over Japan. When political power moved to Edo, so did a lot of the shoyu production. Edoites were earthier in their appetites, with less sophisticated and aristocratic tastes in shoyu. They preferred their shoyu dark and salty. So the Edo-area shoyu makers, most of them in what is now nearby Chiba Prefecture, north of Tokyo, accommodated them. That was the end of usukuchi's run; it was soon replaced in popularity by the Tokyo favorite, koikuchi. You are using pretty much the same soy sauce into which those in Edo of old were dipping their sushi, though then as now, hundreds of small, family-run shoyu shops were turning out their own brands everywhere in the country.

Shoyu connoisseurship is an art. Somebody ought to organize shoyu sojourns to Japan, just to tour the countryside and stop at Mom and Pop Suzuki's shoyu shops from Sendai to Shikoku. Japanese do something like that; one of the joys of traveling in that country is tasting the extraordinary variety of locally produced foods, and that includes shoyu. Japanese can get all misty reminiscing over this shoyu or that, which is only available in some remote corner of backwater Japan. There are shoyu makers in rural Japan who turn out only a few dozen gallons annually. It is not different at all from the tiny *caves* of France's wine-growing regions. Those who sample these vintages talk about the perfumes, the roasted undercurrents, the sweet finish. To match these rare shoyu with really good sushi would be among the culinary experiences of a lifetime.

Major shoyu manufacturers, on the other hand, are not into a lot of subtlety. On the contrary, they deal in hundreds of thousands of gallons produced in state-of-the-art factories the size of small towns. While their shoyu lacks some of the personality of the smaller brands, it is consistent, reliable, and overall it's pretty good. And that's lucky for you, since that's what you will be using. Proving the adage that there's no business like shoyu business, the Amoco and Standard Oil of the shoyu world are still a couple of the originals, Yamasa and Kikkoman. They are the brands you are most likely by far to see in sushi-ya. Yamasa is still manufactured in Choshi and imported in the United States. The bottle features a stylized mountain in profile with the character for "above" sitting on the right slope. The 11th generation of the head of the Yamasa conglomerate, Hamaguchi Yozo, is an internationally recognized artist specializing in mezzotints, in addition to his shoyu-making skills.

Kikkoman has set up a huge factory in the United States. That's appropriate, because the majority of even Japanese-manufactured shoyu is made from soybeans grown in Illinois, Missouri, and Iowa. Kikkoman takes its distinctive logo from a polygonal section of a turtle's shell (*kikko*) overlaid with a stylized number 1,000 (*man*), both symbols meant to convey long life. Pour a teaspoon of either of these shoyu into a white dish, just a splash, and you'll see what high-quality shoyu looks like. There is absolutely no sediment. It has an oily silkiness and a consistent color that has, against the white dish, a clearly purplish tinge (hence the sushi slang term for shoyu: *murasaki*, "purple").

As we noted earlier, shoyu complements the taste of sushi. Remember that. Relatively little sushi you will be eating is still alive. It does not, therefore, need to be drowned into submission. Dip your sushi into the shoyu plate. Do not marinate it. You will see how shoyu's various amino acids, along with lysine and threonine, work their alchemal voodoo, drawing the flavors of fish and rice together. Shoyu is to sushi what mayonnaise is to a turkey sandwich. Use it that way instead of the way you would slather gravy on a hot, open-faced turkey sandwich, and vistas of flavor and texture you never knew existed will appear.

There are, to be sure, some inferior grades of shoyu; usually the cheaper stuff has some additives dumped in or has had the fermenting process artificially revved up. Unless you're *really* slumming, you are very unlikely to encounter this kind of cheap shoyu plonk. There might be an occasion, though, when you are presented with Chinese shoyu sauce with sushi. There's nothing wrong with Chinese soy sauce, but it goes with sushi the way a kindergarten class goes with being left unsupervised in a Pottery Barn. Chinese soy sauce—this is a general way to think of it— is used almost exclusively to flavor food while cooking. Japanese shoyu is used for cooking too. It is also, though, used as a dip or condiment, as with sushi. Consequently, even dark Japanese shoyu isn't as strong as Chinese versions. The sushi-ya that does not serve good Japanese shoyu is not worthy of the name and certainly isn't worthy of the patronage of the sushi tsu.

Despite the dearth of smaller, rural brands in the West about which to be snobbish, there is a preponderance of fine shoyu readily available here, so you cannot realistically pine for offbeat brands of shoyu you have never tasted. But what's the point in being a snob if you can't be discriminating? Well, cheer up. There's always a way of discriminating with Japanese cuisine, if you just know how. In the case of shoyu, look for *sashikomi*. It is shoyu that is twice fermented. It is popular in Japan mainly down in Osaka and accounts for only 0.7 percent of production. But sashikomi, also called *kanro*, or nectar, can be found in some high-class sushi-ya in the United States. Or you can buy it in some Japanese-style grocery stores. If you see it, try it, or at least ask the itamae at your sushi-ya if he has it, and you can see and taste most convincingly that not all shoyu are alike and that there's good reason to prefer the best. You may also ask if the itamae makes his own shoyu. Some do, though mostly in Japan. Tamari is boiled and reduced along with sake, mirin, dried flakes of bonito, and other ingredients to create a shoyu unique to the individual sushi-ya. A sushi restaurant that bottles its own shoyu is a serious establishment, needless to say, and should be the immediate destination of any sushi connoisseur who hears of such an establishment.

Before leaving the subject of shoyu, a bit of trivia: Back in the late 1980s, the expression *shoyu gao* was very hip. It referred to a face that was smooth, the epitome of the Japanese idea of beauty, without any of the harsh angles of the Western visage, which was by comparison a *sosu gao*, or Worcestershire sauce face.

Wasabi

The legends are apocryphal, some of them, to be sure. Still, every sushi tsu knows reliable tales of the neophyte who, wondering what that thumb-size blob of green was, popped it whole into his mouth. The temptation to sample is even greater when the wasabi has been pressed into the shape of a small leaf or some other object, giving it the benign appearance of a refreshing after-dinner mint. Hello! That's a way to jump-start those sleepy taste buds, isn't it?

Wasabi is most often explained as "Japanese horseradish." There is some truth to that; details at 11:00. Real wasabi, though, is an evergreen member of the mustard family. A tuber-like rhizome puts up a bunch of stems about 18 inches tall that leaf out, looking sort of like a bonsai version of spinach. The first small leaves and stems of wasabi seedlings are pickled in sake or shoyu as a piquant snack; they have a milder form of the rhizome's jolt. Wasabi takes a couple of years to grow big enough to use. It is more finicky than the houseplants around your place, the ones that wouldn't last a month even if they were under the 24-hour care of the entire staff of *The Victory Garden*. To flourish, wasabi needs plenty of shade on north-facing mountain slopes and sandy volcanic soil bogs with a steady supply of cold, moving water. Wasabi can also be cultivated in soil that is just constantly wet, though the rhizome root system won't be as thick, the flavor not quite as concentrated or subtle.

Real wasabi, accordingly, is rare and expensive. Not as rare as intelligent comedies on network TV, and not as expensive as 50-yard-line tickets to the Super Bowl, but it is rare and expensive enough to preclude all but higher-quality sushi-ya in Japan or anywhere else from using it. Unless or until you have made a pilgrimage to one of these, *People* magazine bags a Pulitzer before you've had a taste of real wasabi. Until recently, that is. The popularity of sushi worldwide has triggered that same inevitable capitalistic impulse in the human soul that inspired ceramic microchips and freeze-dried rehydratable cups of noodles. In places far from the mountains of Japan but similar in soil, elevation, climate, and water supply, wasabi is being grown experimentally with some success. Oregon and New Zealand now have wasabi fields. These commercial farms are selling it on the Internet and by mail for prices roughly comparable to some of your finer grades of cocaine. Expense be damned, the dedicated sushi tsu will avail of the first opportunity to order some.

If you are a regular at a good sushi-ya or two, when your tuber arrives, take it there, and the itamae may prepare it for you. It isn't a tax return–complicated procedure; the root is simply grated and it is ready. Whether it is peeled first or not is a matter of dispute; go with your itamae's predilection. Freshly grated wasabi is used the same way as the instant kind; it just doesn't have to be used in quite the same quantity to get the effect. Here's the cool part: Good itamae insist on using nothing but a sharkskin *korozame* (grater), which they believe gives the wasabi just the right texture. The life of a good sharkskin grater isn't much longer than that telemarketer's call to you last night during dinner, so cheaper versions made of pricked copper or ceramic are also available. If you're springing for fresh wasabi, you ought to at least ask your itamae if he is using sharkskin to prepare it, and you can nod sagely if he is, and sigh with resignation if he has to admit he isn't. (Of course, you want to know what *kind* of sharkskin, don't you? It's angel shark. And watch to see if he grates properly, going from the stem end of the rhizome down, not the other way around or crosswise.)

Given the price and scarcity of real wasabi, though, even the dedicated and serious sushi tsu must settle for the ersatz versions for most of his sushi meals. There is a choice: powdered wasabi (*kona wasabi* in Japanese) to which water is added, or the stuff that comes out of what looks exactly like a toothpaste tube. (If that similarity inspires in any way a really, really good practical joke, we had nothing to do with it.) Both are made of horseradish (called *wasabi daikon* or *seiyo-wasabi*), cornstarch, and other ingredients. The difference in taste between these and real wasabi? It's like the difference between Jif and Peter Pan. Fake wasabi isn't bad at all. It just lacks the elemental zing of the real thing.

Faced with the fact that availability and price make it inevitable for the tsu to have wasabi out of a can or a tube on a lot of sushi, you have two options: You can grouse and whine and generally make an annoying ass of yourself, or you can be gracious. Ignore your nature's first impulse and opt for Plan B. Here's the deal: when you decided (a) to become a sushi snob and (b) to reside elsewhere than in sushi's homeland, you accepted that (c) some accommodations had to be made. Grumbling that, for instance, the domestic sake you are drinking in a Japanese steakhouse in Wichita hasn't been made with springwater from Mt. Daisetsu, like the stuff bottled by Otokoyama in Hokkaido, is like going to backcountry Japan and complaining that the veal piccata just isn't up to the standards of that little place in Florence. This is not the attitude of the snob. It is an unreasonable expectation and an affectation of the jerk. There are elements of sushi the tsu should expect to be the very best, lots of them. You must also be gracious and accept, as long as the sushi-ya does not put on pretentious airs or misrepresent itself, that lesser standards of quality are not unreasonable in some situations. Wasabi is one such situation.

Assuming you do get a shot at it, here are some things to know about real wasabi:

What makes it hot? It's elementary. I sure don't need to tell you what happens when a glucoside is hydrated by the enzyme myrosinase. Quick like a bunny, you've got yourself a heapin' helpin' of allyl isothiocyanate, right? That's the juice that gives wasabi its punch. What you may not know is that isothiocyanate, unlike the active ingredients in chile peppers, is water soluble. That's why, after too much wasabi, a sip of tea or water and a moment or two will almost immediately restore all your taste and olfactory systems to normal levels. It's strictly bush league compared to the fire of a habanero or Scotch bonnet pepper. Too big a nibble of those, which are not water soluble, will have you coughing flames through a mouthful of seared flesh 20 minutes and several margaritas later.

Early medical texts in Japan mention wasabi's medicinal properties. Premodern Japanese widely believed the root to be an antidote to food poisoning. That may be why it ended up paired with raw fish originally. There are laboratories full of experiments with wasabi right now. It may actually prevent cavities. (You can try that defense if you go for the toothpaste-wasabi tube switch mentioned above. Good luck.) Its demonstrated anti-inflammatory powers ameliorate the damage of a heart attack for a longer period than aspirin. Maybe in the future, victims might head for the nearest sushi-ya for a life-saving platter of sushi.

And finally, just because you don't have access to real *Wasabi japonica* doesn't mean you can't use a discussion of the green heat to advance your standing. Take the experience of Myrna, for instance, whom we join as she is describing, to officious sushi tsu wannabe Lenora, her latest evening of sushi at Setsu's.

"Setsu's!" exclaims Lenora with smarmy, pretend disbelief. "Oh, I suppose it's okay for some. But that fake wasabi. I guess after Pascal and I flew to Osaka to eat at Katatsumuri and had the real thing, well, I just can't get too excited about sushi here in the States."

"Katatsumuri?" says Myrna with the unflappable equanimity of the seasoned sushi tsu. "They told you the wasabi was real there?" She shrugs, ever so slightly. "All depends on how one defines 'real,' I suppose."

Lenora can't resist it; Myrna knew she couldn't. "What do you mean?"

Myrna explains gently, as to a simple-minded child. "Their 'real' wasabi is *sawa* wasabi. It means 'swamp' wasabi; it's the kind that's cultivated. Sure, it's okay, and certainly better than the fake stuff at Setsu's. But *yuri* wasabi, the stuff that grows wild up in the mountains . . ."—She closes her eyes at the pleasure the thought affords her. "To me, that's real wasabi. If I can't have that, I'd just as soon settle for the powdered kind."

Accommodations must be made, as I said, for even the most dedicated sushi snob. But as Myrna's exchange demonstrates, there are times when it is all worth it.

Shoga

Shoga is the Sancho Panza of sushi-dom, an unfailing, always amiable companion. No matter what crazy, off-the-wall kind of nigiri sushi you order, the comforting mound of ginger slices is always right there next to it. Would that your friends were as dependable, eh? The piquant palate scrub of shoga is not only a necessity, without which sushi would not seem like sushi, it also has a long history in the kitchens of Japan.

The chances that Japanese food will be confused with, say, Cajun cuisine are remote. Spices and strong flavorings have never figured prominently in Japanese recipes. The exceptions have usually been imported, either from China or by Western-ers. Ginger was introduced to Japan from China, and while no one knows when, it must have been a long time ago, because shoga is mentioned in two 8th-century texts, the *Nihon Shoki* and the *Kojiki*. It was probably first used for its medicinal benefits and because it acted as an agent to kill bacteria in foods. Shoga is a rhizome. In other words, it's an underground stem of the plant, with flowers above and roots below. It is the stem part, fresh stems taken in the spring when the skin is still tender and thin, that is used to make the slices on your plate. The process is not difficult. The ginger is sliced, then boiled, then pickled with rice vinegar, salt, and sugar. (A good

Japanese cook will also know the secret of pickling shoga slices. It is a bag of small stones put on top of them in the pickling crock, so they don't float.) This is shoga *ama-zuke*, or sweet pickled. In the sushi-ya, pickled ginger is often referred to as *gari*. There is more than one theory on why. *Agaru* is the verb for "to rise" or "ascend." So perhaps the nibbles of ginger between orders of sushi are a step up from one course to the next. A possibly more hip term for pickled ginger (in the sense that it is slightly archaic and, for the sushi tsu, the older the better in many cases) is *sudori shoga*. *Sudori* is "to pass through quickly," and the ginger slices are called that since they are just a quick respite from the last order of sushi, in anticipation of the next.

The pink pickled shoots you may see next to grilled fish in a Japanese restaurant, by the way, are also ginger. They are young shoots, pickled much the same way as gari, and known, for their color, as *hajikomi* (blushing) shoga. Ginger pickled with a sweet-and-salty brine, then cut into threads and used for some cooked dishes, is *beni-shoga*. It's too salty for use with sushi.

Shoga in the sushi-ya is a palate cleanser, it needs to be reiterated. A couple of slices are all that is necessary for the task. The sushi tsu should not need to be told that eating the entire hill of shoga is a waste. You have seen people, maybe even in Japan, who add shoga to their nigiri sushi and eat the combination, but you should avoid that kind of silliness. And you do not even *know* anyone who dunks shoga into a plate of shoyu before eating it, right?

Other Condiments

The other common condiments and side dishes of sushi aren't as notorious as wasabi or as familiar as shoga. Even so, they are important for the tsu and contribute to a lot of the more subtle tastes of sushi.

AKA-OROSHI ▼ Another name for momiji oroshi (see page 209).

ASATSUKI ▼ A true chive, asatsuki is finely chopped to go atop sushi tane like bonito or mackerel. In the United States, green onions are often substituted for asatsuki.

CHIRIZU ▼ A piquant dipping sauce for shiromi-dane, chirizu doesn't get the attention it deserves in most sushi-ya outside Japan. The sushi tsu should ask for it, and a good itamae will know how to make it. Chirizu is a combination of sake, lemon juice, grated daikon, shoyu, and red pepper flakes.

DAIKON ▼ "Big root" is the best known of Japanese vegetables, a white radish that grows to the size of a small pumpkin or as long as your shin. Grated daikon occasionally appears as an ingredient in chirashi sushi; it's a fixture as a side dish for sashimi. In either case, fresh daikon is run through a serrated cutter so what comes out are long, fine filaments that explain its name, *shiraga*, or white hair daikon. You might instead get a hill of *oroshi daikon*, or ground daikon, with your sushi, or more likely, with an order of sashimi. Daikon is widely believed to be good for digestion. Older Japanese sushi tsu and itamae alike might recognize the old—and now quaintly literary—word for daikon: *suzushiro*, or "white bell."

KIKU-AMA-ZUKE ▼ These are pickled chrysanthemum leaves. They are usually purple, sitting in a mound beside your sushi. Kiku-ama-zuke are a favorite of older Japanese; they aren't common in sushi-ya here but they are an excellent condiment for nigiri sushi.

KINOME ▼ The young leaves of the sansho, or Japanese pepper tree, have an aromatic, minty flavor. They look like miniature fern fronds and are used as a garnish for several kinds of nigiri sushi.

KIZAMI-NORI ▼ Slivered nori is a common addition to chirashi sushi.

MOMIJI OROSHI ▼ The translation is "maples grated." A fresh daikon is stabbed repeatedly with a chopstick and into the wounds are stuffed red chile peppers, then the entire daikon is grated. The resulting rough paste is as pink as early autumn's maples. Momiji oroshi is used as a condiment for several sushi tane.

PONZU ▼ The recipe for ponzu is almost as mysterious as that for Dr Pepper. It's a citrus concoction made with the juices of bitter orange and *kabosu* and *sudachi*, both varieties of lemons. Ponzu is a sauce for dipping and is added to lots of stews. It figures in the sushi-ya as a dip for some kinds of nigiri sushi.

SHISO ▼ This aromatic plant, whose leaves are eaten, is kind of a cross between sweet basil and mint. See page 44 for a full description.

TONBURI ▼ These are seeds from a species of cypress in Japan, the *houkigi*. They are a favorite condiment for temaki sushi in Japan and are also used as one of the seasonal ingredients mixed into the rice used to stuff inari sushi. They are available in the United States now, and more and more good sushi-ya are using them. The flavor is like a mild form of juniper berry.

WAKEGI ▼ *Wakegi*, an onion somewhat like a chive, matures in the autumn and, finely chopped, is used to garnish nigiri sushi. The chopped green stems of green onion that you see on sushi in this country would much more likely be wakegi in Japan. The flavor is more delicate and the stems are thinner.

YAMANOIMO ▼ Cultivated varieties of this "mountain yam," also called *yamaimo*, are used along with those taken from the wild, and are grated to go atop some sushi as a garnish. The grated yam is *yamakake* or *yamaimo-kake*, and you're most likely to see it on chunks of raw tuna. The flavor is mildly bitter; it's the slippery texture that is its most attractive characteristic. Yamanoimo is traditionally considered an aphrodisiac, an image reinforced not so subtly when it is used on top of various roe in sushi.

WASHING IT DOWN:
WHAT TO DRINK WITH SUSHI
AND WHAT NOT TO

Remember in *You Only Live Twice* when Bond reminds one of his superiors that he took a major in Oriental languages at Oxford and therefore won't have any trouble passing himself off as a native Japanese, especially not with that ever-so-believable temporary plastic surgery eyelid job? Okay, so then in *Tomorrow Never Dies*, how come Bond can't even read a computer keyboard with Chinese characters? More to the point, this is the same Bond who impresses the head of some Japanese secret agency in *You Only Live Twice* by knowing that sake is served at 102.9 degrees. "Very good, Mr. Bond, you must know your sake," Tanaka-san tells him. Maybe, but he doesn't know squat about drinking it. The best, premium-grade sake is actually better when savored cold, and even medium-grade sake doesn't benefit much from warming.

I dump on 007 here as a way of noting that Western "experts," as well as some commonly held ideas about anything Asian, are not infrequently unreliable. It is the same sort of pseudoexpertise that has paired, in the minds of many Westerners, sake with sushi. Maybe they think it is a sort of culinary total immersion experience. I'm eating the quintessential Japanese food; might as well have the essential Japanese spirits. That might work with ouzo and a gyro platter or (I'll take your word for it) haggis and a fine blended Scotch. But sushi and sake go together like cherry Kool-Aid and Twinkies. It is overload, without any contrast. Sushi, being mostly rice, and sake, being made from rice, are too much of the same. If you want to be a sake snob, you've gotten the wrong book. You should know, however, that in Japanese restaurants and at meals, sake is rarely served where rice is present in any quantity. Sometimes it is served with a platter of sashimi when it is part of a larger multicourse meal. But there is a whole class of snacks that go with sake called *sake no tsukudani* or *sake no sakana*. Salted, slightly fermented fish guts and bite-size vegetables boiled in a thick sauce of shoyu and sugar are typical *tsukudani*. Sushi is not a tsukudani. That's another reason sake doesn't go with sushi. The idea behind an *izake-ya*, or sake pub, is to leisurely while away a few hours, nibbling and sipping and hiding from spouses, work, or other obligations. The sushi-ya, however, has traditionally been a fast-food outlet, with volume a big consideration. When you are serving raw fish, you've got a limited window of freshness, obviously. You don't really want to encourage customers to linger by offering the temptations of drink.

I hasten to add that just because sake is not a good accompaniment to sushi doesn't mean you can't indulge your desire for alcohol along with a visit to the sushi-ya. Sushi and beer are an okay combination. So pour a cool one of your choice if you like, although many sushi tsu disdain any kind of alcohol, insisting it can dull the taste buds. The sushi snob should know that, historically and for some other reasons, tea is probably the best liquid with which to wash down sushi.

Tea

As we will see in the section "Tableware and Utensils" (page 216), *yunomi*, or teacups, for the sushi-ya are economy size. That's because back in the days when the itamae worked alone at their streetside stalls, they didn't want to spend a lot of time topping off beverages. Water was difficult to come by for early street peddlers of sushi. The solution: fire up a huge kettle at the start of business, throw in some tea leaves, and let it steep. When a customer arrives, splash enough boiling hot tea into a cup to float a small pleasure craft and be done with it. It isn't much different today. You can depend on tea at any sushi-ya. But you, the sushi tsu, need to know a little more about it.

If you ask the itamae in most American sushi places what kind of tea you are having, he's likely to tell you it is *kona-cha*. *Cha*—or more politely *o-cha*—is tea; *kona* refers to any kind of flour or meal. *Kona-cha* is a generic word for cheap tea. It's the dust or "flour," powdery bits and pieces, twigs, and stems of tea left over from processing. Sushi-ya buy it by the train car–load because it is inexpensive and because it infuses in hot water almost instantly. But "kona-cha" describes the texture of the tea more than the type or kind. There are different kinds of o-cha poured in a lot of restaurants, starting with the bottom-of-the-barrel stuff and working up to the expensive brews.

Bancha is at the bottom of the heap, a rough grade of green tea. It is what ordinary Japanese drink every day, made from stalks, stems, and fragments of dark green roasted tea leaves, and it is almost always the main component in kona-cha. Bitter as a custody battle when it cools, bancha is immediately recognizable in your cup; it has a pale yellowish hue.

Roasted leaves of bancha-grade tea without the assorted detritus will give you a cup of *hoji-cha*. The color is a light tawny brown; it has a subtle but distinctive smoky taste. A lot of Japanese like hoji-cha at night because it is among the teas that are lowest in caffeine. You might run across it in some sushi-ya or other kinds of Japanese restaurants since it is quite drinkable even when it's cool.

Mix bancha with tiny kernels of popped, hulled, and toasted rice kernels and you will get *genmaicha*. It has a fragrant, nutty aroma. Genmaicha is often associated with winter to the traditional Japanese palate, and while it isn't often poured at sushi places, if you see what look like little popcorn kernels and rice hulls floating around in your cup, it is genmaicha you're drinking.

You might also encounter *kukicha*, or twig tea, in some sushi-ya. It's made from the stems of tea leaves and has an almost sweet, grassy flavor. Another, more poetic, term for kukicha is *karigane-cha*, Japanese for "wild goose." Migrating geese were believed by the Japanese of old to be able to rest on tiny twigs floating in the ocean, similar in size to the twigs and stems from which this tea is brewed. Kukicha can only be infused once; second steepings are weak and for that reason a lot of sushi places avoid it, but it goes well with sushi, and if you find a place that serves it, by all means compliment the sushi-ya.

Sencha is inevitably the sushi connoisseur's choice of drink. Most of the time, sencha is prepared in grapefruit-size clay pots called *kyusu*, with a handle at 3 o'clock and the spout at noon. The tea leaves that go into the pot look like small, wrinkled pine needles, dark, dark green. The taste is unmistakable once you've had it. Ever been in a barn's hayloft right after the bales have been stacked? Ever remembered to bring the blanket along to spread out on those bales, simultaneously assuring your companion that Farmer Brown hardly ever comes in here this time of day? You're correct; none of my business. But those big lungfuls of air you were taking in afterward are what sencha tastes like. Imagine drinking a cupful of a meadow of sweet, grassy, pleasantly astringent alfalfa. Sencha is absolutely the best tea to drink with sushi. Tea-growing nations all over Asia harvest sencha; most of the results end up in Japan, where it is the base for *macha*, the emerald powder that is used for making tea in the tea ceremony. It is available here, but it isn't cheap. If you find a place that will spring for the expense of serving sencha and you can afford the prices, chances are good you've got a sushi home.

Tea, even the less expensive kind, goes so well with sushi because it is astringent; it sweeps the palate clean. A lot of fish used for sushi are oily, like mackerel. Even the more delicate fish, like flounder, have long chains of proteins that hang around on your palate, lolling about on your tongue the way your brother-in-law does on your lawn furniture every Labor Day. Flushing them away cleans the decks for the next round. No drinkable liquid does that better than tea.

In the sushi-ya, by the way, o-cha isn't called "o-cha." It is called *agari*. There are two possible reasons why. The less interesting one is that tea is usually drunk at the end of a meal, which has long been known in colloquial Japanese as *agari-doki*. The more entertaining version is that tea, in the businesses of feudal Japan devoted to life's baser pleasures, was known by the slang term *agari-bana*, or floating flowers. Gambling dens, brothels, cheap taverns—workers in all of these used the word. Their expression *agari-bana o hiku*, which means, literally, "to grind tea," referred to having to kill time in between customers.

Sushi and Other Drinks

Beer, yes. Water, fine. Dr Pepper, whiskey, iced tea, martinis, vodka, chicory coffee, hot chocolate, rum, frappés, gin fizzes, eggnog, egg creams, birch beer, or buttermilk, no.

Sushi and Wine

There are those who have done in-depth, clinical studies to match sushi to Western wines and who have hosted gatherings that pair various kinds of sushi with these wines, and there are even restaurants that devote much time and attention to such matchings. There are also those people who think romance novels qualify as fine literature, those who refer to dinner jackets as "tuxedos," and others who wear pinky rings.

The sushi connoisseur recognizes that such people exist.

TABLEWARE AND UTENSILS

The *Ruijuzoyo-sho*, a 12th-century scroll that chronicles this and that of courtly life in the Heian era (794–1185), depicts a massive, sit-down soiree among the upper crust of old Japan. The illustrations make it look like something of a church social for the gentry and include several close-up paintings and drawings of the plates and bowls used for the feast. Another text compiled around the end of the 13th century, *Chujinruiki* (A Kitchen Miscellany), provides extensive details about the same Heian-period tableware. So we know that dishes and other utensils have played a role in Japanese cuisine for at least 1,000 years or so. Actually, they go back a lot further, into the 4th century at least.

What you need to know first is some basic concepts about the way in which food is arranged in the traditional Japanese style. By now you may have picked up on the idea that not a lot in feudal Japan was left to chance or spontaneity. Let me give you an example: Despite their well-known proclivities for technology, feudal Japanese did not have e-mail or cell phones. The Japanese used smoky fires for signaling information over long distances, especially as a communication device for troops in battle. So what, you say? Native Americans and others used smoke signals too. That's not the point. The point is that it was the Japanese who codified these techniques into a formal curriculum, with scrolls written to teach the techniques, including "secrets" of the art that were passed on only to trusted initiates. That's the way it was with everything. Japanese of the feudal era had schools (*ryu*) with specific curricula for incense appreciation, horseback riding, and using every weapon you've ever seen in a samurai movie and many more that look like they were confiscated from a prison riot. So it is no surprise, or shouldn't be, that by the 17th century, there were at least half a dozen formal and distinctive schools of etiquette, including one, the Ogasawara ryu, that had the official approval of the Imperial Court. The Ogasawara school, in turn, fostered another school, the Shijo ryu, which is devoted specifically to the preparation and presentation of food. These two schools have influenced Japanese cuisine. Even an ordinary box lunch bought at a train station in Japan will usually have some pattern, some attention to aesthetic detail based on the principles of the Ogasawara or Shijo traditions. The most extreme expression of formal food presentation occurs in *kaiseki*, the meals served during very formal tea ceremonies. Sushi is a long way down the spectrum from kaiseki. It has an elegant look about it when masterfully prepared, but sushi, as we saw in the section on its history, has a distinctly plebian background. So a lot of the rules of food presentation are more relaxed and informal for sushi dining. An intense, exhaustive knowledge of *moriawase* or *moritsuke*, the rules and principles of food presentation, is thankfully outside the realm of study for the sushi tsu. Even so, there is a definite pattern to the way utensils and other objects are used and how the sushi is placed before you.

Plates and the Stuff Put on Them

To the Shaker Heights dowager, nothing may bespeak the elegance of refined beauty quite like her matching set of china, every piece identical in pattern, right down to the olive platter that you, you little ingrate, chipped when you knocked it off the Thanksgiving table, trying to hit your sister with a bread knife. By the standards of Japanese aesthetics, though, that kind of consistency in tableware says "beautiful" the way a text on Euclidean geometry says, "Just let me finish this chapter, honey, then I'll join you in bed." Boring, boring, *bor*-ring.

Thanks to the Greeks and Romans, symmetry of form has an appeal to the Western senses. Japan developed an aesthetic based more on the model of nature, which tends to be just the opposite: asymmetric and irregular. That is why Western music has a regular, four-beat measure that's comfortable and enjoyable to our ears and why, for the most part, Japanese music sounds like Picasso's *Guernica* looks. Sure, in comparison to the concertos of Bach, Japanese music sounds atonal and discordant, to say the least. Only when you compare it to the sounds of a summer thunderstorm or the permutations of a brook as it flows, splashing here, gurgling there, quiet for moments while collecting in pools, can you appreciate a different standard. A lot of Japanese art tends to follow this sort of inspiration, drawing on the inconstancy of nature. That is the perspective from which you have to look at the dinnerware and presentation used for sushi.

Dishes and any other kind of tableware for a Japanese meal almost never match one another in pattern, size, or shape, or even in the way they are arranged on the table. There are also a lot of them. Accustomed as we are to a single plate with two or three servings of foods on it, the spread of a typical Japanese meal looks crowded, almost cluttered. What's even stranger is that you notice one plate has only half a dozen boiled green soybeans piled on it; the bowl beside it, scarcely more than a smidgen of sautéed carrots. It isn't so much the quantities; it is the way they're arranged that matters. Foods, even just a couple of diminutive mouthfuls, are stacked or bunched or piled so they look most attractive. The dinnerware is there to enhance them. The effect is achieved or heightened by contrasts. Things are deliberately mismatched. It is more interesting that they have different shapes and textures. Think of clouds passing over on a July afternoon. If all of them looked like a triceratops eating Abraham Lincoln's nose, they wouldn't be as much fun to watch.

That is not to say that the selection of dishes set before you at a sushi-ya or any other Japanese restaurant is a random collection of yard-sale odds and ends. The dishes in a meal like sushi don't match one another. They do match carefully, though, the foods served on them. It might be more accurate to say they complement the food. They do this, generally, in one or more of three ways, which have to do with shape, season, and texture.

SHAPE ▼ Japanese serving dishes, plates, and bowls have never been confined to the round shapes found in Western-style dinnerware. The sheer number of them used, even for an informal meal like sushi, offers a chance to mix and match that adds different dimensions to Japanese cuisine. Consider that the circles of maki sushi arranged on a round plate would be making the same statement twice. The eye goes round and round and doesn't stop anywhere. Round maki sushi on a rectangular plate is a contrast of shapes, and so becomes at least eye grabbing if not actually interesting. If an order of maki sushi is placed on a circular plate or serving dish, the pieces will be aligned in a diamond pattern or some other linear form, again, as a contrast. Hexagons, squares, ovals, folding fans, or the leaves of plums or maples: The variety of shapes in Japanese dishes is nearly endless, especially when you consider some of the natural materials like split sections of bamboo or sea shells that find their way to the table. What's important is the way they interact, in terms of their shapes, with the arrangement of the food.

SEASON ▼ In the hottest days of summer, your side dish of pickled ginger might come in a cool, pale blue (in Japanese the color is called *mizukiri*) plum blossom–shaped container. The hue, the smooth glaze, even the shape of the container are all meant to be refreshing. In the winter, your sushi might arrive on a heavy slab of hand-thrown ceramic, dark brown with scarlet undertones to the glaze to make you feel warmer. In Japan, as noted, sushi is frequently served using a lot of natural materials: wrapped in young cherry leaves in early summer, for instance, and placed on persimmon leaves just turning orange in the autumn. This attention to matching foods to their dishes with a sensitivity for the season is a part of *shun*, the taste for freshness that is almost always a factor in Japanese cuisine.

TEXTURE ▼ An entire multicourse formal meal in a Western setting can be eaten without touching a plate or bowl with one's fingers. Japanese tableware, though, almost asks to be touched and handled. Etiquette actually demands that diners touch bowls and some smaller dishes, manners that come from Japan's long and treacherous civil war. If I've one hand on my chopsticks and the other wrapped around my rice bowl, I don't have a spare one with which to stick a knife into you, making for a more relaxed and civilized meal all around. That etiquette aside, much of the appeal of Japanese pottery and porcelain is in their feel, grainy and rough or wonderfully smooth, shaped to fit in the palm of the hand or rested on the fingertips.

It isn't just the feel; texture also has a visual appeal. How do you arrange two slices of gossamer, nearly translucent hirame atop two snowy pillows of rice? Arrange them on a dish of white porcelain and the effect is monotonous. Contrast them by putting them on an irregularly shaped slab of rough, black, unglazed pottery and it makes the hirame look even more delicate and delicious.

In more modest sushi restaurants here and in Japan, limits on storage space and budgets will mean there won't be this kind of variety in tableware. In better establishments, though, you can count on it, and you should start watching to see how the itamae and the rest of the kitchen staff match foods to dinnerware.

Plates and the Stuff Left off Them

In the language of Japanese aesthetics, there are more than a dozen words to describe things that are not there. *Yohaku* is the white space left empty on an ink painting. *Yoin* is the "reverberation" or sound that lingers on mostly in your mind after the ringing of a big bell. Plates or bowls, no matter what their size, are almost never completely full when they come to the table. There is always an empty space. What is empty gets filled in with your imagination. We'll go into more about this when we discuss presentation, which is right now.

Presentation

You didn't think this was just going to get left to chance, did you? Were you paying attention back there when we were talking about the Japanese mania for formalizing everything? Let's review: There is a proper way in traditional Japanese etiquette to cut up a dessert persimmon and, as graphically illustrated technical scrolls for professional sword testers who used condemned criminals as the targets of their craft show, to cut up human beings as well. The way a cord is knotted around a wrapped present signifies something about the occasion for the gift. So given that kind of pickiness, you can damn well assume there will be rules for presenting food on a dish. There are the rules, noted earlier, that are known as moritsuke or moriawase. And the rules themselves have rules: Food is arranged in formal (*shin*), semiformal (*gyo*), and informal (*so*) styles. (Although, to make it more fun, within the formal style are formal-formal, formal-semiformal, and formal-informal, and the same for gyo and so. So there are actually nine different permutations.) The same shin-gyo-so approach is found in the tea ceremony, calligraphy, flower arranging, and other arts where spatial factors figure.

There are some basic methods of moritsuke used to present sushi, and some others that dictate the way side dishes are arranged. Again, cuisine doesn't get much more informal, in Japanese terms, than sushi, so the rules are fairly relaxed. Note, though, that the underlying principles of the rules are going to be observed and it is the perspicacious sushi tsu (and there should be no other kind) who recognizes and appreciates them.

The *hiramori* style of food presentation is what you are most likely to see on your plate in a sushi-ya. Your order of nigiri kisu has just been handed to you, let's say. Resist the urge to shovel it in as swiftly as civilized table manners will allow. Take a moment to consider the way it has been laid out on the plate. The most common order of nigiri sushi is a pair. Notice, though, that that the pair of kisu is deliberately situated. The pieces are neither horizontal nor perpendicular, but rather slanted on the plate, and overlapped just enough so the piece closest to the front of the plate is closest to your right hand. Part of the reason is practical. It is easier to pick up the pieces of nigiri than it would be if they were lined up evenly, side by side. It also has more eye appeal. This slanting arrangement of a pair of pieces of food is the simplest form of hiramori, or "flat-style" moritsuke.

Sashimi is typically arranged in a flat style, the slices of fish drifting across the length of the plate. If you have a couple of orders of nigiri sushi, they might well be arranged similarly. If so, you can begin to see some of the more subtle elements of the flat style, which, while simple, is far from simplistic.

This sort of flat style, with a single row of food lined up horizontally, is called *ichimonji*, after the brushstroke for the numeral 1, which it resembles. Printed with type, 1 is written with just a single, horizontal stroke with a little bump on the right end. When a calligrapher writes the character, though, he draws the brush up from left to right as he goes across the paper. The line of your nigiri sushi slants the same way. It adds a dimension to the presentation that would be missing if the sushi were lined up exactly straight across the plate. In fact, if you draw a line vertically or horizontally on your plate, your sushi will not be along either axis, or squarely in the middle where the lines cross. It will always be grouped along an angle or in a quadrant, off center, to avoid what would otherwise be monotonous and predictable.

A potential problem with the ichimonji line of sushi is that it threatens—we're going into Art Appreciation 101 here, I know, but follow me—to rise right off the back of the dish, compositionally speaking. So that's where a mound of pickled ginger slices is stacked, usually below the ascending side of the sushi line, as a compositional counterweight. There will always be something on the plate to anchor the line of ichimonji.

If the counterweight consists of ginger slices, they will be arranged *sugimori* style. A *sugi* is a cedar tree. The mound of ginger (or any food served sugimori style) has the same shape as that tree; bunched up something like a plump pinecone. When a garnish or side dish is put on a flat plate, like the ginger beside your nigiri order, it is an informal version of sugimori. More formal versions would be set in a bowl or deep-sided container. Sometimes they're used in sushi-ya, placed beside the plate of sushi. If the itamae does serve ginger in a separate bowl, he will take time to place it just so. The mound of ginger will be just tall enough to peek over the rim of its container, like the summit of a mountain appearing above the mist, or sunk below the sides of a deep bowl, to resemble a cedar growing far down in a valley. Most of the other side dishes that might accompany sushi, such as edamame or tangles of shredded daikon, are arranged in an informal sugimori style or in *mazemori*. A *mazeru* is a mixture. Mazemori arrangements will look spontaneous if they are done properly, as if they were just plopped onto the plate or into the bowl. But if you look, you'll see they are placed so they add a balance or dimension to the overall composition.

Round, coin-shaped maki sushi are either laid flat or tilted against one another like a pile of toppled dominoes. If they were placed in the single line of the ichimonji, however, even slanted, the row would be dull to contemplate. So the itamae bunches them in diamonds or parallelograms. If they are tiled against one another, or *kakemori* (*kake* means "propped"), the inner ingredients can be seen and appreciated; the sides of the maki sushi sticking up add another dimension to the arrangement. Every now and then, an itamae will stack maki sushi in a staircase-step arrangement, in the *tawaramori* style. A *tawara* is an old-fashioned rice bale. It looks like a small barrel; a stack of maki sushi resembles a pile of tawara.

There are those occasions—parties, after-hours office get-togethers, anywhere there is a hungry crowd expecting food—when the sushi tsu finds himself behind fabulous amounts of sushi arranged in shallow-sided tubs as big around as a motorcycle tire. The moritsuke style of arranging sushi in these tubs will be one of three used for big, multiple servings of nigiri or maki sushi or both combined. In that fleeting moment between the time it is served and the time your companions hit it like a pack of hyenas tearing into a drought-weakened water buffalo, you may notice the nigiri and maki sushi lined up with one row slanted left, the next slanted right, back and forth in a zigzag formation. That's a *nagashi* (flowing) arrangement for a multiple order of sushi. A *hosha-mori* is a pinwheel pattern of sushi, spiraling out around the tub in concentric circles. These two arrangements can be combined, with a few rows of sushi across the center of the tub and then spirals wheeling out to the edges.

There are at least two other ways of arranging big orders, but they've gone out of culinary fashion in sushi circles and if you happen across one, it is like a step back in time, a little more than half a century back, to be exact, to the war years in Tokyo, when rice and fish were in short supply. During that era, itamae sometimes arranged party-size sushi orders by stacking them in two layers to make it look like there was more there, in a *kasane-mori*, or heaped-up style. Or, for the same reason, they piled it differently (this was mostly with maki sushi) to create a pyramid effect called *jiro-mori* (castle style).

Having now some basic grasp of the aesthetics of tableware and presentation, let's turn to the items themselves. Memorizing the names for all the utensils and tableware is of debatable value for the sushi tsu. Consider: "My, what an elegant *muko-zuke* the chef has chosen in which to present the takuan; obviously a fine example of Seta ware." Way, *way* over the line, and it violates the maxim of George Apley's that must be embroidered on the heart of every snob of every persuasion: "If you've got it, don't flaunt it." Just have some idea of what things are on the table in front of you.

Dishes

The most common plate on which your sushi's going to be delivered in most sushi restaurants is a simple rectangle of some kind of porcelain (*jiki*) or ceramic. It may be cheap and factory-made or expensive. In Japanese, it is a *shiho-zara*, a "four-sided plate." The plate or shallow bowl on the side for pickles or other condiments is a *ko-zara* or *ko-bachi* ("little dish" or "little bowl"). The dish you fill with soy sauce is a *tsuke-zara* or "dipping dish." In the lexicon of the sushi-ya, the tsuke-zara is called a *mura-choko*.

One piece of dinnerware that is not quite a dish and not quite a tray but something in between is the *geta*. You've certainly had sushi presented on one of these. It is a wooden rectangle, usually unpainted, with perhaps a light varnish, and a couple of struts or "teeth" supporting it underneath. It is named after the traditional Japanese footwear that it resembles. Another in-between piece of tableware for sushi is the lacquered stand fitted with holes for holding temaki, nori cones of sushi. It is a *sushi-dai* or just a *dai*, a generic word for any object designed to hold something. Sometimes a "dish" will be carved out of a vegetable. A hollowed section of a daikon radish might be filled with pickled ginger slices, or a sliver of cucumber folded over like a miniature rice-winnowing sieve might hold a daub of wasabi. These are called dai too.

At some very high-class sushi-ya, chopstick rests, *hashi-oki* or *hashi-kake*, might be provided. Ceramic or made from other materials, they come in all kinds of shapes, looking like little gourds or kites or what have you. Some Japanese collect them, but you'll find precious few opportunities for stealing them from the typical sushi-ya for the same reason Burger King doesn't provide napkin rings. They are a formality of dining that is out of place in a sushi-ya environment.

Soup Bowls

Though misoshiru, or bean-paste soup, is not served in every Japanese sushi-ya, it has become almost a standard fare at sushi restaurants elsewhere. It is served in a *wan*, a Japanese-style bowl. The Japanese soup bowl is no less beautiful or functional than the wider, more shallow European model. It merely takes the concept as a container for soup in a different direction. Soup has never been a separate course in the Japanese meal. Instead, it is drunk during the meal, acting as something of a beverage as well as a food. That's why in Japanese, soup is *nomimasu* (drunk) and never *tabemasu* (eaten). And it is why a request for water at a Japanese restaurant is met with a glass the size of that paper cup you rinse with at the dentist's office. The soup needs to be fairly steaming throughout the meal, and the lid (*futa*) facilitates this, as do the steep sides and deep center of the bowl. A wan is shaped more like a bouillon or consommé bowl, and for the same reason: to keep the contents hot. Lacquer assists here; it doesn't conduct heat well. That is why you can hold a bowl of misoshiru while a soup of similar temperature in a ceramic soup bowl would scorch your fingers. That's good, since soups in the sushi-ya and other Japanese restaurants are meant to be sipped without the intercession of a spoon. In many Japanese-style restaurants and sushi-ya, if you are not a regular and don't look Japanese, the server might bring a spoon to the table. Ignore it. The bowl, even if you wanted to try, doesn't accommodate spooning motions. It is too deep and too small. It is, though, just the right size to fit balanced on the pads of your thumb and fingers, where it belongs. As you drink it, notice how the depth of the bowl creates an additional dimension for the ingredients inside. Whether it is cheap plastic or fine lacquer, the interior of a wan is nearly always dark red or black. Black was the only model available in soup bowls until the 10th century or so, when red was introduced and promptly appropriated by the ruling classes. The color works to accentuate the "clouds" of miso grains suspended in the broth, revealing on and off, as the liquid swirls around, cubes of tofu, leaves of wakame, or other ingredients. Remember this: The attraction of watching these lazy, billowing miso clouds in one's soup bowl has taken many a sushi tsu through otherwise interminable meals with in-laws, bosses, and a host of less-than-engrossing dining companions. Its entertainment value under such circumstances should never be underestimated.

Trays

You won't see these too often in a sushi-ya. You are apt enough to run across them, though, in Japanese restaurants, and you need to know the terminology. The Japanese invented the TV tray at least as early as A.D. 100 and then waited patiently for centuries for the TV to come along. The individual trays that were placed right on the floor among the hoi polloi for dining are called *oshiki*. Upper classes dined on *zen*, trays with short legs and more specifically called *oshiki*, *hassun*, or *bon*. A bon with raised edges that looks as if each of the corners has been sliced off is a *sumikiri*, "cut corners," bon. *Hassun* is for formal kaiseki-style food.

The tray that holds *bento*, or prepackaged boxes in which sushi is sold at train stations or other places, including grocery stores here in the United States, is called an *ori*. It comes from the verb *oru*, meaning to "fold" (*origami* means "folded paper"), since these boxes were originally made of thin wood folded into squares.

At sushi-ya that also serve tempura or other Japanese cuisine, you can order a sort of blue plate special, which might include sushi and tempura or some other food, served in a tray like the one used in your high school cafeteria, with little compartments. These were once popular meals served between acts of long Kabuki plays, hence the name *makunouchi*, or between the curtains. The name for this tray is *shokado bento*. It is about the width of one's comfortable grip when carrying it in both hands, with the elbows held at the sides.

The big tubs used for large group orders of sushi are called *oke* and are made of lacquer. Sometimes an itamae or Japanese-speaking server in a sushi-ya will refer to them as "sushi-dai." Sushi for large groups may also be served in trays that look like a model ship. That's kind of what they are. Wide and high-prowed, they are *takara-bune*, a "treasure ship," named after those that regularly traveled to China and returned full of goodies still rare in ancient Japan. By association, the ships became linked in popular culture with all sorts of prosperity and good fortune, much like our horseshoe, and much more appropriate for serving sushi.

Teapots and Cups

A ceramic teapot is a *dobin*. A *kyusu* is a smaller version with a lug handle that juts out from the body of the pot. Iron teapots are *tetsubin*. Teacups are *yunomi*. As we discovered in the section on what to drink in the sushi-ya, tea is probably the best liquid accompaniment for sushi. The two have been matched since proprietors of outdoor stalls were peddling sushi back when the last of the shogun were around.

There are three basic shapes of yunomi used in the sushi-ya. The most common is the *tsutsu-gata*, a tall cylinder. A shorter version of this is the *han-tsutsu-gata*. *Gokezoko-gata* are cylindrical too, though fatter and squatter than the first type. *Gokezoko* refers to the wooden bowls where stones for the game of *go* are stored; the cup sort of looks like one. No matter the shape, yunomi are properly filled to about a finger width or two below the rim. If the server is pouring more than that, it is a sign of sloppiness, because it ignores a function of the yunomi. Earlier we noted how a lacquered soup bowl insulates your fingers against the heat of the soup inside. The yunomi, made of porcelain or clay, requires a different approach to keep you from burning yourself. A space is left between the hot tea and the lip of the cup, enough space for you to put your forefinger to it. Your little finger goes on the "foot" (*kodai*) of the cup. You can then wrap your other fingers and palm closely around the hot cup to warm them on a cold night, or keep them at a distance if the cup is too hot. If the person pouring your tea takes it up to the brim, you can't hold the cup correctly.

Chopsticks

The length of joined wood in the paper sleeve beside your plate is a pair of chopsticks. No doubt you realize this. However, there is still some work ahead.

Chopsticks are *ohashi* in Japanese. The *o* here is an honorific; *hashi* is of indeterminate origin. Some philologists venture that the word comes from an archaic term for a bird's beak, but no one really knows. And as Japanese language texts and teachers never seem to tire of explaining, *oHAshi* is the word for chopsticks, while *haSHI* is a bridge. Lots of Japanese words depend on these pitch accents. Even so, as culturally deaf as Japan can be, it is not likely that asking for *ohaSHI* in a Tokyo sushi-ya will result in the staff setting off to locate for you the nearest trusses or spans. If you are ever in the presence of one of these irritating fussbudgets who delight in correcting nonnative speakers whenever this word comes up, here is how to handle it. Say "Yes, my Kyo-ben keeps giving me away, doesn't it?" Then explain with just a soupçon of condescension that in Kyo-ben, the dialect of Kyoto, the pitch accent for these two words is reversed. And if the person in question hasn't by then slunk away in abject humiliation, deliver a final kick: note that were you in the presence of another sushi tsu like yourself, you would not even have used the word in the first place, and were doing so only out of consideration.

In the argot of sushi-dom, ohashi are called *temoto*, or hand things. Unlike the tapered and usually lacquered hashi used at home, some Japanese restaurants and all sushi-ya use *waribashi*. These are machine milled and unvarnished, with a groove that allows them to be split for use. *Bashi* is just the suffix form of *hashi*; *wari* is from the verb *wareru*, "to split."

Theoretically, you could eat sushi for the rest of your life and never pick up a pair of chopsticks. You could also change a Mack truck transmission without staining your hands. Neither is likely, is it? Eating chirashi sushi or misoshiru or other foods served along with sushi requires some dexterity with chopsticks. You cannot avoid it. If you want to be an active member of the sushi fraternity, you're going to have to learn to use ohashi as if you have been doing it all your life. That is the bad news, particularly if you haven't—and maybe even if you have, since older Japanese constantly complain that the younger generation cannot use ohashi properly. The worse news is that this book can't teach you how. Nor can any other. Nor can those weirdly illustrated and worded directions printed on the paper sleeve in which your chopsticks are wrapped. The worst news is this: Far too many a would-be sushi snob assumes he is adept with chopsticks. And unless you have been wielding them since you were still drinking from a sippy cup, your use of ohashi can mark you as an amateur from clear across the room. What you've got to do, unless you have a lot of familiarity with them, is practice—a lot. And as much as you practice, watch others to see how it is done. Like wintertime driving, positions of sexual congress, and investing profitably in the stock market, it is easier to tell you what *not* to do than to describe how to do it correctly:

1 While using chopsticks, don't use your elbows as much as you would when wielding a knife and fork. Notice how native ohashi wielders tend to use their wrists more, leaving forearms or elbows on the table. Novices also tend to freeze their finger grip on the stick, keeping their wrists stiff. That's one reason they look so awkward. Another is that the less-than-expert users choke up on their ohashi, putting their

grip near the center of the chopsticks' length or at the front third. Don't. Hold them as far back near the end as you can. Notice too, that in many instances, especially when the food is in a bowl, as with soup, the bowl is picked up and held a few inches below the mouth. When you have a bowl of rice with your sashimi, do not leave the bowl on the table as you would when eating from a bowl during a Western meal. Pick it up. You'll be pleasantly surprised how much easier it is to use chopsticks with the rice bowl in your other hand. Speaking of the other hand, do not put a bowl right at your chin and shovel in the food. In the case of chirashi sushi or other sushi in bowls, they are not lifted when you eat from them, but you can lean a little as you're eating. So anything dropped goes back into the sushi and not on the table or in your lap. In the West, etiquette demands we keep one hand in our lap when eating with the other. In Japan, in the case of bowls like those used for serving chirashi sushi, it is just the opposite. The nonchopstick hand should be at least touching the bowl. Who knows why? Probably, as with most forms of etiquette in Japan if you look deeply enough, it has to do with keeping both hands in sight when you're eating in company, lest the one hidden be readying a weapon.

2 Ohashi bear no morphological relationship to ice cream cones, cake batter beaters, or your lover's ear, and thus are not for licking. During Japan's feudal period, upper-class women wore thick lipstick. One way to tell whether a woman was well mannered was to watch her eat a bite of rice. If she was good, she could take the bite without smearing her lipstick or getting any on the ohashi in the process. You aren't going to be held to similar standards, but try to put just the last half-inch of your chopsticks into your mouth when you eat.

3 Japanese rarely use their ohashi in between bites to perform percussion solos on the tabletop. Not that we want to "be

Japanese," but neither do we want to use the dead time between sushi courses as an opportunity to imitate the drummer from Kiss. Apparently, about 30 years or so ago, word got out that rapping with your ohashi on your plate or teacup was the way to get the attention of a server in a Japanese restaurant. While it may work, it is about as polite as just throwing your ohashi.

4 Don't wave your chopsticks around over your food trying to make up your mind about what to eat. Don't wave them or gesticulate at others with them unless you are very angry during the course of a conversation and want the other party to believe you might well make a stab at him. Never spear food with your ohashi. Do not use them to pull a bowl or plate toward you, and don't keep them in your hand if the itamae or server hands you a dish or some other serving.

5 When they aren't in use, ohashi are laid horizontally across the plate, pointing to the left. Many sushi-ya have succumbed to the Western concept of where service belongs, and put the ohashi in their paper sleeve vertically alongside the plate. It isn't the worst gaucherie imaginable, true. Give some extra points, though, to those places that lay the ohashi horizontally, as they would in Japan.

6 There are a couple of other taboos about ohashi that you probably already know. Passing food directly from one pair of chopsticks to another is reminiscent of a similar act done with the cremated bone fragments at a Buddhist funeral. Sticking your chopsticks into a bowl of rice and leaving them there as if you've just planted a flag on some territory you're claiming is another symbolic funeral gesture. Don't do either.

7 Okay, and here's the big "don't," the habit you're most likely to acquire by hanging out with the wrong crowd, that

is, those sorts of wannabe aficionados the sushi tsu never, ever wants to emulate. It is an affectation of those types to slide the ohashi out of their paper sleeve (it is called a *hashi-bukuro*, by the way), break them, then vigorously rub them together as if they were making fire. Why? Ask one of them. He'll be thrilled to let you in on the arcane lore that it is to rub off the splinters.

Think about it for a minute. Rubbing ohashi together to get rid of a mouthful of splinters you might otherwise be chomping on is sending a kind of message to the sushi-ya's owner and staff, isn't it? Why don't you bring along a dust rag and give the tabletop a good polishing while you're at it? The teacups might have a spot or two that require your attention. Sushi-ya can thrive or dive based on a lot of criteria; providing eating utensils that need minor carpentry before use would be an unlikely way to get patrons lining up out the door, now, wouldn't it?

Here's the story: The wood for crafting ohashi is soft. Ohashi come out of the sleeve and get broken for use in a splinterless condition. Rubbing ohashi together like a cricket going into mating-call hyperdrive will actually *raise* splinters, or at least roughen the surface. Interestingly, this is exactly what some customers at Japanese restaurants want to do, specifically at places that specialize in noodle dishes, especially those noodles served in bowls of broth. The rougher surface provided by rubbing them together gives the ohashi a little fuzz that ensures a better grip on the slippery noodles. Somehow, some way, someone saw this and decided the ohashi rub was de rigueur any time they were used. Consequently, we now have thousands of people in sushi-ya all over the planet, whittling or scraping or rubbing their ohashi together. Eat with ohashi or don't. (We'll get to that next.) But please, refrain from any impromptu refinishing with them.

This brings us to a more fundamental ohashi-related subject. Should you use them at all for sushi? Their use for the sushi tsu is essential to be sure, simply because in your travels along the path to expertise, as I've already noted, you will encounter other comestibles, misoshiru for instance, where ohashi dexterity is demanded. And obviously, scattered sushi in bowls is going to be a lot easier and look distinctly more civilized when consumed with chopsticks. In the case of nigiri sushi, though, you are usually better off getting hands-on. The section on rituals (page 263) has more on this subject.

Let's get back to the subject—if you'll forgive the pun—at hand. What you are holding in yours are probably made of *sugi*, a Japanese cedar. It is a softwood, as mentioned above. The bulk of sugi for ohashi, 400 million pairs of them annually, in fact, comes from Wakayama Prefecture. Before you determine to head out for the woods of Wakayama to take up residence in the sugi forests to protest this outrage against the environment, calm down. Consider: These sugi forests are tree farms planted specifically for harvest. Ohashi are also milled of Canadian aspen, which is also commercially grown for that purpose. So no old-growth forest died for your ohashi. They died for all that beautiful woodwork in the sushi-ya, perhaps, but not for the chopsticks.

Cheap, disposable chopsticks are in keeping with the outdoor-stall informality of sushi. That is not to say, however, that there isn't a connoisseurship attached to them. To the average sushi enthusiast, the pair of waribashi sitting in their envelope at the sushi counter are eating utensils and nothing more. The tsu knows to take a closer look and discerns at least eight different kinds of waribashi. Look for the crosscut shape and the manner in which the joined waribashi have been cut to see exactly what kind they are.

CHOROKU are plain and square and are the cheapest kind of waribashi. You will rarely run across them in a sushi-ya. They are found primarily with box lunches or other such items at Japanese 7-Elevens or similar places.

KOBAN are milled so they're shaped in crosscut, in a broad oval, like the *koban*, a common coin of the feudal era. Koban-style waribashi are a favorite of noodle shops.

GENROKU-STYLE waribashi are probably the most commonly used ohashi in sushi-ya, both here and in Japan. Look at them from the ends when they are still joined and you will see that they are rectangular, but each right angle has been shaved off. They're also indented where they are joined, so in effect, they are seven-sided. They break apart easily and the angles make picking up food, especially rice, easy. Genroku-style chopsticks are precut anywhere from about one-half to one-third of their overall length. The Genroku period in Japan (1688–1704) was an era that saw some severe economic depression in Japan, one in which parsimony was an important virtue. Genroku waribashi are named after that period because they use the least amount of wood of any kind of chopstick.

TENSOGE are square if examined from the tip, but at the butt, they are cut at a steep slant. Tensoge-style waribashi are comparatively expensive to make. They are nearly always a sign of a better-class restaurant. "Tensoge" simply means "split from above." The precut split in tensoge waribashi is usually only about one-third the overall length of the chopsticks. So they require a little more care when breaking them apart, lest they split unevenly. Some Japanese sushi tsu think it is an affectation to have them in sushi-ya. If the restaurant specializes in sushi but has other Japanese cuisine on the menu, okay. If a sushi-ya is using tensoge, though, it can seem pretentious and a sign you might be paying for atmosphere rather than for the best-quality sushi.

The above are the waribashi most often seen in restaurants with Japanese food. Just in case you are wondering, the following are the other forms of this kind of chopstick.

RIKYU-STYLE waribashi resemble the Genroku chopsticks above, except that the center indentations are offset, so one of the two joined pieces looks to be sitting above the other. They are named after Sen no Rikyu, the famous tea master, who carved them for serving kaiseki, or formal tea ceremony, cuisine. Rikyu waribashi are generally used now in kaiseki for eating sweets.

KAISEKI waribashi are like Rikyu-style chopsticks, but thicker in the middle than on each end. They are used for courses in kaiseki-style cuisine other than sweets, and are often carved specifically for the event out of green bamboo.

TAKE, bamboo waribashi, are very inexpensive chopsticks, usually tossed in with an order of take-out sushi or other cheap food. Students and other unfortunates living on the cheap sometimes wash and reuse them, but they grow a slimy film of mold quickly if they aren't dried properly.

MARU-GATA are round wooden chopsticks, which come separated. They are most often used for special meals at New Year's.

Even if waribashi do not require cutting vast acres of virgin timber, the argument can be made that it is a hell of a waste of wood to produce all those millions of waribashi that get used once and then are thrown away. The sight of them, by the thousands, tossed in trash cans or littering the gutter after a big festival is disturbing, even if your idea of defending Mother Earth is little more than asking for paper rather than plastic at the grocery store. International pressure has been brought to bear on Japan, not in any big way yet, but noticeably, to think about using recyclable materials for waribashi. It isn't a bad idea. In the meantime, if you are feeling particularly guilty about your own waste of waribashi, make plans to go to Yugawara, a little resort town south of Tokyo at the base of the Izu Peninsula, next summer. Every August 4 there is Hashi-no-hi or "Chopstick Day," and at a local temple, used ohashi of all kinds are solemnly burned in a ceremony to demonstrate how much they have meant to grateful eaters all year long.

So now we have pretty well covered the disposition of your sushi, condiments, and drink, along with the plates, dishes, platters, and cups used in presenting it. There shouldn't be a lot of surprises for the sushi tsu familiar with these. That is not to say, however, that these descriptions are unbendable rules or that they are an infallible yardstick by which to take the measure of the sushi-ya or the itamae. Itamae may experiment, they may play some epicurean riffs on these basic patterns or utensils. They may ignore them altogether. What we're talking about are some basic concepts that guide the presentation of sushi. Life is uncertain. It is spontaneous. You are up to any challenge and are unfailingly gracious. So if you run across presentations of sushi that defy what you have learned here, you needn't assume the itamae is an idiot or a boor. If he's violating the fundamentals, though, he ought to have a good reason to do so. And with the above information, the knowledgeable sushi tsu has the skill to make the call on that.

ACCOUTREMENTS AND FURNISHINGS IN THE SUSHI-YA

From eateries as breathtakingly expensive as any haute cuisine French restaurant to prepackaged plastic boxes of maki sushi at the local Stop & Shop, sushi has gone both up- and downtown and to every neighborhood in between. Ballparks offer it along with hot dogs and nachos and warm, overpriced beer. Not long ago, I ate very credible Osaka-style pressed sushi in a Japanese restaurant on the northern edge of the Missouri Ozarks, within sight of a highway that was, back when it was a dirt path, traveled by the James-Younger gang. (I like to think Jesse would have liked the salmon-skin rolls.) The point is, there isn't any "typical" sushi restaurant. So it is impossible to predict exactly how one will be set up or furnished. There are features you'll see in most Japanese restaurants, though, that specialize in sushi. Knowing what they are and why they're there is an important part of being a sushi tsu.

Noren *(Doorway Curtain)*

There will probably be at least one in the place, hanging in the doorway as you come in, up over the restaurant's kitchen door, or above the entrance to the restrooms: a split curtain hanging down that's brushed aside or ducked under when passing through. (In Japan, a *noren* hanging outside is very often a sign the place is open; no noren and it's closed.) Noren have been in use as a kind of entrance to Japanese businesses since at least the 9th century. They have cousins in the door family in the swinging bat-wing doors of Old West saloons and in those hanging strings of beaded curtains in the apartments of college students. That is, noren are more like dividers than doors proper. They close off space or create separate spaces in a symbolic way. There's a lot of this in Japan, from the hanging twisted straw ropes that section off the sacred areas of a Shinto shrine to the *byobu*, or decorative screens that can be folded or unfolded in a room to create smaller or larger spaces. (Incidentally, this whole idea of having a bit of space, even if it is only in a symbolic sense, will have a lot more meaning once you've ridden the Toei Shinjuku train out of Shinjuku Station at, say, about 6:30 on any given weeknight, sharing a car with what seems like 70 percent of the entire population of Japan.)

Noren have been around so long they figure in lots of colloquial expressions in Japanese. When a shop owner allows one of his employees to open another place, it is called *noren wake*, or dividing the noren. *Noren ni kizu ga tsuku*, meaning "the noren has been damaged," is another way of saying that the good name of a shop has been besmirched. Struggling at some hopeless task is *noren ni ude oshi*, or beating against a noren.

The writing on a noren is a fully functional part of these curtains, since almost as soon as they were used in business doorways, those businesses used them as advertising. So what's almost always written on a noren in a sushi-ya will be the name of the restaurant or the characters for "sushi."

Sampuru *(Menu Samples)*

In a display case in the window or near the entrance to a lot of sushi-ya will be rows of samples—*sampuru*—of the establishment's offerings. These are standard at many kinds of Japanese restaurants. Originally, sampuru were the real thing, laid out to show what was available inside. The drawbacks to this approach are obvious. "Gee, that bowl of chirashi sushi with the flies crawling on it sure looks tasty." So shop owners came up with wax imitations. They were okay, though they tended to look a little wilted and less than appetizing during the hot summer months when a plate of wax cucumber rolls melted into the pair of shrimp nigiri next to it. In the early 1950s, plastic vinyl began to be used as the material of choice for sampuru, and the art was revolutionized.

Sampuru is almost an art form. Nearly all of it is made in one neighborhood of Tokyo. Shops specializing in it have jealously guarded their secrets for making fish look glossy and still wet from the sea and nori appear to be crackly-crunchy fresh. Some sampuru is just a straightforward depiction of the menu. Others demonstrate a creative side of the makers, with a pair of chopsticks pinching a bite of nigiri sushi, for instance, which looks as if it's about to be lifted by an invisible hand.

Guidebooks for travelers in Japan often tout the critical role sampuru can play for the prospective diner who doesn't speak Japanese. Just point to what you want, the books advise. If the selection of sampuru is inside the place, that's not a bad idea. It is probably not a great notion, however, to grab a server by the hand and try to drag him or her outside so you can point out your choice.

Daruma (*Resolution Reminder*)

Bodhidharma was a guy who didn't do much halfway. The average ascetic monk of the 6th century, for instance, was content to sit and wait for the ferry when he wanted to get to the other side of a river. Bodhidharma was in such a hurry to get the word of Zen Buddhism spread from its native India into China that he crossed rivers, balancing on a single stem of a rice plant. While other Buddhist monks put in some pretty impressive hours sitting and meditating on the road to enlightenment, Bodhidharma sat and faced the wall of a cave for nine years without moving. He sat for so long, we are led to believe, that his legs more or less dissolved. When he fell asleep once during meditation, he awoke so put out with such slacking off that he cut off his eyelids to make sure that wouldn't happen again. (The lids didn't go to waste, so the story goes. When he tossed them outside the cave, they took root and sprouted into tea bushes. That explains why tea was originally cultivated by the Buddhist monastic orders, who drank it to ward off visits from Mr. Sandman during their meditations.)

What we are left with in the tradition of Bodhidharma is a legless guy whose stare was so intense that Japanese kids having *niramikura*, or staring contests, chant *"Daruma-san, niramekko shimasho!"* which means, roughly, "I'm turning my Mr. Daruma high beams on you!" (His full title is Bodai Daruma, the Japanese pronunciation of the Sanskrit *Bodhidharma*.) You'll see Mr. Daruma in some sushi-ya, a roly-poly figure in a scarlet robe, heavy of eyebrow, bearded, and bug-eyed. Temples all over Japan sell effigies of Daruma. They are papier-mâché figures with big, round, empty circles in place of where the patriarch's eyes should be. At *Daruma-tera*, temples specifically devoted to the patriarch, where stacks of these are on display for sale, the effect is weird, not unlike a convention of extremely hirsute Little Orphan Annie impersonators. Purchasers take their Daruma home—they are especially popular around New Year's—and paint in the pupil of one eye. At the same time, the owner of the Daruma makes a resolution: When the goal is achieved, the other eye gets painted to celebrate the accomplishment. It is a neat way to remember your resolution, really, that one eye noodging you day after day, never blinking, until you either go quite insane and bash the figure to bits with a softball bat or get on with it and do what you, in one of your more foolishly optimistic moments, vowed you were going to do.

A one-eyed Daruma in the local sushi-ya means that the itamae or someone else there has made a resolution. A Daruma with a double-barreled 20/20 means mission accomplished.

Tanuki *(The Raccoon)*

This is an amiable-looking little fellow, a sort of chipper, upbeat Rocky Raccoon with a serious beer gut, a broad-brimmed straw hat cocked far back on his head, and a gourd and some *ude-nenju*, or Buddhist prayer beads, clutched in his paws. It is a *tanuki*. In Japanese sushi-ya and other restaurants where this jolly quadruped sits in a foyer or on a shelf to greet customers, the animal is sometimes the real thing, a taxidermy mount of *Nyctereutes procyonoides*, a distant canid cousin of the raccoon, minus the tail rings, that is native to Japan. Most places, though, have on display tanuki statues cast in painted ceramic of some sort. The sedge-grass hat, the Buddhist rosary, the gourd ewer for water or sake sustenance are all trappings of the mendicant pilgrim, off on a shrine-hopping tour of the countryside and stopping off at this fine establishment for a snack and a cool one.

Aside from serving as a setup for some good jokes ("We don't get many tanuki in here." "No, and at these prices, I can see why."), the actual appearance of a tanuki in a sushi-ya or anywhere else would have been met with some consternation in old Japan. Along with foxes, tanuki figure in all kinds of Japanese folk tales and stories of the supernatural. They were, these tales have it, capable of enchanting humans to work their will on hapless victims, or actually taking human form and generating all manner of mischief. A fun fact for the sushi snob: Legend has it that rhythmic bass reverberations sometimes thumping mysteriously from far up in the mountains in wild Japan are the echoes of tanuki playing a paradiddle on their round bellies. That's the modern, expurgated, cleaned-up-for-the-tourists version. For the original, take a closer look at what's between the tanuki's legs. Yep, they're what they look like. A pair of massive, what in vulgar Japanese are called *kin-tama*, "golden orbs." *That's* what the tanuki were really supposed to be playing.

Manekineko *(The Original Hello Kitty)*

A Japanese saw cuts on the pull stroke instead of on the push, like those in the West. You pull a Japanese-style woodworking plane, where you'd push the Western kind. A Japanese counting on his fingers will begin by folding his thumb into his palm, then his forefinger, middle finger, and so on, instead of starting with his little finger like most of us do. So you ought to figure that what seems to be a gesture of goodbye is actually a howdy-and-come-on-over. That explains why the doe-eyed feline squatting on the shelf in many sushi-ya appears to be waving *sayonara* to you even though you just walked in. It is a *manekineko*, a "beckoning cat."

The manekineko is kept around sushi-ya and other businesses to wave in business, money, and success. A male and female pair of manekineko the size of fireplugs guard the inner sanctuary of the Imado Shrine in Tokyo's Asakusa neighborhood, where couples seeking a good marriage come to pray. Both are calicos, the original and still most popular color for beckoning cats; however, manekineko now come in several colors. Here's a quick rundown of what they indicate: The all-black version has a certain rakish savoir faire and is seen more often in the big cities; his job is to keep evil on the run. Pink manekineko are supposed to usher in love, red manekineko promote good health, and the gold cats are beckoning for money to come into the establishment.

If the manekineko is wearing a collar, it is probably adorned with a pendant with the character for "good fortune" or "long life." The observant sushi snob will notice that in some sushi-ya, manekineko are waving with the right paw, and in others, with the left. The conclusion that the difference might indicate the political sensibilities of the sushi-ya is a reasonable one and would make, I admit, a great bit of trivia. Alas, the real reason is less intriguing. Different manufacturers make different molds for the good-luck kitties, so some are right-handed and some are southpaws. In the paw that is not bidding you a happy entrée is clutched an oval gold coin from the feudal era, called a *koban*, a not-so-subtle invitation to stay a while and enjoy yourself and spend big while you're at it.

Kumade *(Good-Luck Rake)*

The image of Japan as a land of nuance, subtlety, and understatement loses some of its luster once you've attended a "Penis Festival." Celebrated in one way or another in most regions of Japan, these rowdy street fairs feature Buick-size phalluses paraded through town, amidst general festivities all aimed, in origin at least, at promoting the fecundity of the precincts. Nothing quite that salacious is to be found at our typical sushi-ya, perhaps to your disappointment. Nevertheless, the symbolism of some of what you will find decorating the place is not terribly obscure or difficult to fathom. Take the "good-luck rakes" that adorn the walls of some sushi restaurants. Raking in the cash is an idiom that transcends culture; that's what the *kumade* not so obliquely suggests.

Lavishly decorated rakes are sold by the millions at Otori Shinto shrines, found in several places in Japan, including a famous and popular one in Asakusa, a section of Tokyo. Samurai going into battle once prayed to the resident deity of these shrines; later the deity became a general-purpose player for anyone looking for a larger-than-usual slice of luck. Special celebrations are held at these shrines on the Day of the Rooster according to Japan's old calendar, where these rakes are offered to celebrants.

Good-luck kumade are so heavily adorned that you may barely see the bamboo tines at all. What are plastered all over them are *engimono*, symbols of prosperity and luck: a tortoise with gold coins for the plates of its shell, bright scarlet tai (sea bream), cranes, and depictions of any or all of the Seven Gods of Good Fortune, who will appear as the crew of a treasure ship.

Folk Art Masks

These are a popular decorative item in sushi-ya and other Japanese restaurants. A more expensive sushi-ya might have some masks used by the Noh theater. You can pick those out easily, as they're minimally decorated with soft colors. More likely, you'll see a gaudily painted pair of masks representing Okame and Hyottoko.

Okame is a chubby girl with the fat, rosy cheeks the Japanese call *pocha-pocha*, the kind of face we'd expect to see on the "before" picture of a weight-loss ad but that said clearly and appealingly to feudal Japanese, "My daddy can afford enough rice to keep me looking this healthy and happy." Hyottoko looks slightly deranged, his pursed lips twisted to the side, with a long cloth usually wrapped around his head. He is supposed to be blowing a spark into a flame. This pair appear in all sorts of folk dances, and they are frequently seen cavorting at festivals. The masks at your neighborhood sushi-ya don't have any deep meaning; they just add to the atmosphere of the place.

Oshibori *(Moistened Towels)*

Back in the early innings of Western civilization, when the plagues were batting a consistent .350 against most of Europe, Japan suffered nary a sniffle. Through the whole of its culture, in fact, Japan has never experienced a major plague. True, famine in Japan was common up until modern times. Earthquakes and typhoons hit with the regularity of UFO sightings in rural Alabama, and the nation has been periodically ravaged by giant, surly, radioactive beasts of one kind or another. But again, there have been no serious plagues. One theory suggests this is because of the near-obsessive preoccupation the Japanese have always had with bathing and hygiene in general, evidenced by public baths, self-sanitizing toilet seats, and the face masks cold sufferers don to avoid spreading germs. Whatever other attributes may be ascribed to the whole of Japanese civilization, at least its collective ears have been well scrubbed. And your little contribution to keeping that aspect of Japanese culture alive comes in the form of a moistened towel called an *oshibori*.

In summer, these tightly wrapped cylinders of cloth are chilled; in winter, be careful. They can come to the table almost throbbing with microwaved heat. Either way, their purpose is for wiping your hands and face. It is refreshing, it is sanitary, and it is one of those minor rituals surrounding a sushi meal that, given enough repetition, is performed with the understated panache that marks the true sushi tsu.

Oshibori began as a courtesy extended to guests visiting in one's home during Japan's feudal era. You could expect to be met with a folded, damp towel at the entryway of a house when you came calling, especially in the summer months. One reason for the custom is that the humidity levels in most of Japan during the warmer parts of the year could wilt a Panamanian sweatshop worker. A cool, moist towel provided a reinvigorating welcome. Later, the hot oshibori became the winter equivalent and eventually, during the middle of the 20th century, restaurants adopted the custom. At most Japanese restaurants, the oshibori will be removed from the table once it is obvious that you've used it. At a lot of sushi-ya, however, the towel will be left so you can use it to wipe your fingers throughout your meal.

A fact for the sushi snob to file away: In *oshibori* the *o* is an honorific; *shibori* means "to wring out." That's what an oshibori is, a cloth with excess moisture squeezed out. Ethnologists have observed that when Japanese wring out a wet cloth, they do it with the palms up, thumbs in opposite directions. Westerners tend to make the same motion the opposite way, with the thumbs facing each other. The rack or tray on which the oshibori comes, by the way, is an *oshibori-ire*.

Sasa-beri *(Those Green Pieces of Plastic)*

During slack periods in the old days, itamae honed their knife skills by carving delicate shapes into leaves of aspidistra, or baran. These could be fabulously complex, like tatted lace, or relatively simple patterns. While there aren't many itamae left today who practice this, it is still around, in the form of the thin plastic sheets cut like a picket fence and used to decorate sushi presentations. *Sasa-beri* means a "lacy fringe."

Tatami *(Floor Mats)*

Feminine beauty in Japan has been traditionally measured by such anatomical locales as the nape of the neck, the arch of the eyebrows, the shape of the chin. Legs, though, have never figured prominently into the equation. The legs of Japanese women are often dismissed by both sexes as *daikon ashi*—legs (*ashi*) like a plump, thick radish (*daikon*). Daikon ashi aren't as common as they once were; those who monitor such phenomena point to the comparatively scant time young women now sit on the floor, legs tucked beneath them. Now they sit mostly in chairs. Women in their great-grandmothers' generation, in contrast, could have gone their entire lives and sat in chairs no more than a few dozen times at most.

The Japanese have, until fairly recently, sat on the floor, worked there, and slept there. Not on the floor itself, but on tatami. These are densely woven mats fitted together to cover an entire floor, made so ingeniously that they can serve as a box spring for a mattress, dinner seating, or a place to change the baby's diapers. Mats of one kind or another have been used by the upper classes since the 8th century. Tatami as a common form of flooring are basically a 15th-century improvement over the original loose rice straw that was scattered atop the dirt floors of most Japanese homes. Tatami—the word comes from the verb *tatamu*, meaning "to fold"—caught on quickly. In a sense, they are more than just a flooring material. The size and architectural layout of Japanese homes, even now, are described and designed according to the number of tatami the rooms hold. So you will hear of "six-mat rooms" or "eight-mat rooms," or that standard of cozy huts built for the tea ceremony or the even cozier apartments of space-starved Tokyo, the four-mat room.

Since sushi-ya began as street-side vending stalls, few sushi restaurants here or in Japan will have a lot of tatami seating. Usually just a corner of the place will have a raised platform lined with tatami. Diners sit on the tatami at a table with their legs dangling into a well, built below. At any rate, the sushi snob is bound to encounter tatami. Here's what you need to know about them: The greener they are, the fresher they are. Tatami are expensive; a sushi-ya will try to make them last. That is why you are likely to see tatami the color of wheat, and slightly frayed. New tatami are a pale green and have a wonderful, fresh-cut-grass aroma that's unforgettable. (There is a sardonic adage in Japanese, "Wives and tatami are both best when they're new."

The more elaborate the cloth binding that borders the long sides of the mat, the more expensive the tatami. Cheap tatami tend to have plain borders of a single color. More expensive tatami have lush, fantastic brocade borders. Plain or expensive looking, avoid stepping on these edges, which can be crushed easily. You know not to step on any part of a tatami while you're still wearing shoes; even in stocking feet, try not to walk like John Wayne ambling across the corral. Shuffle-slide, moving from your knees. It is a gait less likely to pulverize the tatami core or its delicate surface. (Rice straw and other material are packed inside tatami, incidentally, but the woven strands on the surface, the *tatami omote*, come from the stems of a kind of swamp rush.)

You won't sit directly on tatami. *Zabuton*, or seat cushions, are provided, or occasionally *warouda*, round seat pads made of tightly woven rush or straw. Sometimes a kind of stadium seat with a back support might also be available. If not, an evening enjoying sushi while sitting on tatami can be a mixed experience of pleasure and discomfort. Console yourself by remembering that few Japanese nowadays are comfortable with it, either. Don't sit in the posture of *seiza*, with your lower legs tucked straight under your thighs. This is appropriate for a formal outing like a tea ceremony, or in a martial arts training hall. Don't sit in the lotus position (it's called *fuza* in Japanese). A sushi dinner is informal; your best bet is to sit *agura*, or cross-legged, relaxed, as if you were around a campfire and the guitar was about to come out.

Incidentally, even though the Japanese government uses statistics based on tatami to measure house sizes, the exact dimensions of a tatami are not standard. In general, tatami made and used in the Kyoto region are a little larger than those in Tokyo, for instance. That's why you might hear Japanese describe a room as a "six-mat *kyoma*," or "Kyoto-style dimensions," when they want to distinguish the difference.

Kakefuda *(List of Available Fish)*

On a wall, often above the counter of our typical sushi-ya, is a wooden rack. It is a menu listing the fish that are available, along with, perhaps, whatever specials might be offered in the place. The frame of the rack is made so that narrow boards with both specials and fish currently available written on them in a vertical script can be slid on and off the *kakefuda*. Sometimes, if a fish or other sushi ingredient isn't available, the shop will just turn over the appropriate board. Sushi kakefuda may also be arranged by price. So there will be a sign for 200 yen and underneath it all the sushi in the place at that price; next to it a list of all available for 300 yen, and so on. In general, this approach is taken by a lower-quality sushi-ya.

If you've gone to the trouble of memorizing the characters for some of your favorite sushi, you might scan the kakefuda, growing more and more dejected as you go down the lines of writing. The kakefuda could be providing the standings for the Malaysian Ice Hockey League, for all the sense it makes; you don't recognize a single character. Don't despair. Even if you were fluent in written Japanese you might have some trouble reading much of it. That's because the lettering on most kakefuda is written in *sushi-moji*, the alphabet of sushi. (It just never can be easy, can it?)

Think about it: When's the last time you saw obscene graffiti on a public toilet wall scrawled in Gothic script, or a taco-stand menu written in the flowing cursive of a high school graduation announcement? We have not only a rich tradition of writing and printing styles, but also a cultural sense of what kind of writing is appropriate for different situations. Japan, which borrowed much of its writing from the Chinese, has the kanji characters, as well as a much more abstract kind of shorthand called *kana*, which spells out the syllables of Japanese phonetically.

It would seem these two methods of writing would be enough. Over the centuries, though, dozens and dozens of variations have crept in. One of the most distinctive was perfected in the mid-18th century by a famous calligrapher, Mikawa Jiemon, who adopted the artistic name of Negishi. He designed a style of calligraphy for the *banzuke*, the broadsheets that were posted just before major sumo tournaments, listing all the participants, with the reigning champions in "Elvis Found Alive In Fiji"–size print, the lower ranks in the microscopic lettering found now in appliance warranties. This style of kanji calligraphy, called *Negishi ryu* (the Negishi style or tradition), was quickly adopted with very slight variations by the Kabuki world, which used it in its advertisements and programs. Some woodblock artists adapted it as well; you can see it on *ukiyo-e* prints by Hiroshige and dozens of others.

The Negishi style of script has an elegant look about it, characters rendered in a ribbony series of graceful swoops and curves, and it may suggest a certain aristocratic sophistication. But sumo and Kabuki, far from being diversions of the upper classes, were much the feudal Japanese equivalents of professional wrestling and mime, and the woodblocks were as classy as paintings of bullfighters on black velvet. They appealed to the masses. Sushi-ya were becoming popular eating establishments during the same period; the street stalls were peddling fresh fish and vinegared rice to the crowds out shopping or carousing. The Negishi style of writing was a natural favorite for sushi-ya advertising and menus. It's been that way ever since.

As a sushi tsu, you should, of course, learn to decipher the characters for the fish you like best, and with some practice, you'll be able to read a lot of these basic kanji when they've been rendered into Negishi script. (You should know, though, that thousands of kanji were modified after World War II, streamlined and made simpler. Negishi calligraphy universally ignores these changes, opting for old, sometimes ancient characters that virtually no one born before the advent of MTV can read.) But look to the right of the vertical lines of calligraphy on most kakefuda and you'll see a supplementary kana form. These are the phonetic pronunciations of the characters. There are 47 of these, and you should learn them first.

Sometimes, if the itamae or the shop owner is an accomplished calligrapher, he might write his own characters for the kakefuda, or start playing around with the characters themselves, making puns or using kanji so antiquated only a few scholars would recognize them. Don't fret. Just recognizing that the kanji are not the standard form is an accomplishment.

THE ITAMAE

We've used this word about 1,000 times already, studiously avoiding the most common and misleading translation of "sushi chef." No account of the kabbalism of sushi would be complete without an explanation of the guy who is making it. He is usually wearing white, though he might be dressed in a colored jacket. In Japan, most itamae work in *geta*, or wooden clogs that have exceptionally high teeth. They allow the itamae to see over his counter and keep an eye on everything that's going on in the place. The towel wrapped around his head is a *tenugui*, worn both to keep any drops of his perspiration from dripping onto the fish or his work space, but also to give him, the true son of Tokyo, a sporty, jaunty look near and dear to the heart of the Edokko.

To understand how an itamae gets where he is, keep this in mind: in the more than two millennia of Japan's evolution as a culture and a nation, egalitarianism and democracy arrived in that country, comparatively speaking, about a week ago last Thursday.

Japan is on the cutting edge in a lot of ways, from light-speed trains to laser nose-hair trimmers. So it is easy to be fooled. But you don't have to look too deeply to see that aspects of feudalism remain all over Japan. Institutions with a feudal mentality abound. You can find them in martial arts training halls and in schools for the tea ceremony or flower arranging. Traditional restaurants of all types maintain a lot of this feudal culture. It is a pyramid. The owner or head chef is at the top of the heap, and he doesn't tend to share power or prestige. Even if it is a chain restaurant, the man in charge of a particular place is going to have the final say, bear the ultimate responsibility for the place. Under him are layers of assistants, subassistants, general workers, and apprentices. In a sushi-ya, the itamae may also be the owner, in which case he's on top of the whole enchilada. If not, he is still, without exception, the *kaicho*, the "boss" of the kitchen area. That's where his name comes from, in fact. The itamae is the person "in front of the cutting board." The average sushi chef begins his career right out of high school. (I say "his" because the vocation of itamae has historically been a province of the male gender.) That is when he still has a *nyuanshin*, a flexible mind that can be trained and influenced by his elders. (Parents of teenagers reading this: get a grip, it isn't *that* funny.) Begin the training of an itamae much later than that and his personality becomes so set that he brings elements of it to his work. Supposedly, according to sushi lore, a person entering the sushi trade at that point will never develop completely as a master itamae, and sushi tsu in Japan claim they can watch an itamae work for a while and tell you if he began his training as a teenager or later.

Apprentices who suffer supersize helpings of harsh discipline and severe tests of their spirit are standards of success stories in Japan. It is part of a process called "eating cold rice," although the average starting apprentice at a Japanese sushi-ya is lucky if he even gets to see rice of any temperature. For a couple of years he is washing dishes, knives, and other utensils, mopping floors, and making or picking up deliveries. He's a *deshi-kozo*. *Deshi* means "student"; *kozo* is an old word to describe a Buddhist priest in training. The word has the connotation of a young whippersnapper. If the deshi-kozo can make it through a couple of years of this "Oliver Twist Goes to Boot Camp" life without chucking it all, dyeing his hair green, and joining an apocalyptic cult or a rock band, he graduates to *shikomi*, beginning an actual education in sushi.

The deshi-kozo period is tough—in some cases it actually becomes abusive—but it has some advantages. It weeds out the less-than-sincere candidates, and tasks like scrubbing the cutting boards provide plenty of opportunity for the smart apprentice to see the master itamae in action, to *minarau* (learn by watching) or do *mitori-geiko* (training through observation). It is an axiom of all traditional Japanese arts that you truly learn not through direct instruction but by *nusumu no gei*, or stealing the art, from an accomplished teacher. It isn't a coincidence that the Japanese word for an apprentice is the noun form of *minarau: minarai.* Being on the bottom rung of the sushi ladder offers lots of chances for that kind of educational theft for a minarai. It also acquaints the future itamae with every aspect of running a sushi kitchen, from the ground up. Having washed his mentor's knives day after day, month after month, the apprentice has a feel for that tool even before he's given his first lesson in using it. That comes when he is promoted to the job of rough-cutting the fish. Guts, gills, skins, and fins: The apprentice at shikomi level gets up close and personal with those parts of the fish that don't make it to the table. In the parlance of the sushi kitchen, this is *shita-koshirae*, or making from the bottom.

At this second level of his training, the minarai is introduced to preparing rice. As you know, rice is essential to the whole business. Once he is allowed to rinse and wash the raw rice and season it after it's cooked, the apprentice knows he has at least been accepted as a part of the restaurant. In some cases, that may be as far as he ever gets. He becomes the sushi-ya equivalent of what are called in Japanese businesses by-the-window employees. Businesses the world over have these employees. You know, the doltish nephew of the boss, or his daughter's "unusual" fiancé, the ones who aren't exactly scaling professional peaks at Ferrari speeds but who can't comfortably be sacked either. They are given desks with a nice view, away from the center of activity, and they spend their lives at mundane, make-work chores. In the sushi-ya, these types don't get a window seat; they are relegated forever to the back parts of the kitchen, making rice and cleaning fish, a career—unless they get fed up and take off to try some other occupation—of apprentice-level chores and duties.

If he has got the talent, the apprentice takes the next step, which is a big one: He's promoted to *shimoita*. It means "below the board." Walk into a sushi-ya laid out in a traditional way, and the guy standing behind the counter closest to the front door is the shimoita. He's sort of a journeyman. The shimoita will assist the itamae; most of the time he still won't be allowed to make sushi on his own for anywhere from three to six months. What he does make is considered practice, good enough for the help to eat though nothing the sushi-ya would present to the customers. When his skills have progressed to that point, when he is actually serving customers and fashioning sushi (still under the discerning eye of the head itamae), the shimoita has about three years ahead of him before he can be considered fully trained. In some sushi-ya, there is an intermediary step beyond shimoita. The chef working to his right is a *nakaita*, a chef at the "middle board." Technically, he is a fully fledged itamae at this point. If the chef above him dies or retires or decides to go out on his own and open a place, he then becomes a *kami* (upper) *itamae*. The upper itamae is the one behind the counter farthest from the door when you walk in, and the one you want to watch if you want to see sushi made by a master.

Sushi itamae see themselves as part of a tradition that goes back to the Edo period, when the capital city was the center of all that was hip and chic in Japan. The 19th-century guy from Edo would have had a lot in common with the typical New Yorker today, each taking for granted that he was at the hub of all that mattered and not the least bit hesitant to let you know about it. Flippant, smart-mouthed, snide, and jocular, the style of the Edo hipster was personified in the itamae. At a lot of old, established sushi-ya in certain parts of Tokyo, itamae still engage in good-natured harangues with customers, laced with the rough male Japanese equivalents of "Wazzup wich you?" and "Fuggedaboudit!" The style doesn't translate well to, say, Houston or Milwaukee, true, but joking and schmoozing are a big part of the itamae's job, no matter where in the world he's doing it. He is constantly interacting with his customers, knows the regulars by name and preferences. About the closest we have to it is the bartender at your neighborhood watering hole.

Now, have all or even most sushi chefs in the United States gone through this kind of grueling, time-consuming apprenticeship? Hardly. Even in Japan, the full regimen of traditional training, though it is still standard at high-end sushi-ya, is becoming less common. In the past couple of decades, the demand for sushi has resulted in "sushi academies," instructional schools that teach sushi making. There are several of these in Japan and elsewhere now. There isn't any shame in having learned the craft in one of them, but it isn't something worth bragging about either. A sushi-ya or itamae who makes a big deal out of being a graduate of a commercial sushi school should be viewed with some suspicion. Sushi making has always been a traditional craft, taught through the apprenticeship system. Proudly advertising that an itamae has opted for a trade school education in the art is, at best, déclassé. It can also be a sign the place doesn't really know what sushi is all about.

Outside Japan, your sushi maker could have trained, depending on the restaurant, completely in the old style we've just described. Or he may have been an ambitious dishwasher trained and promoted to his post behind the counter by someone who never got any extensive training himself. Or (most likely) his sushi education has been somewhere in between. Sushi schools have opened in the United States, and in big cities some supermarkets have in-store classes where they teach the rudiments of sushi preparation. Recent immigrants from the Philippines, Thailand, and other places in Asia are often working behind the counter of many sushi-ya in the United States and elsewhere outside Japan. This leads us to the tricky subject of whether one must be Japanese to be a great or even good or competent itamae.

Do you know the expression *nihonjin-ron*? You do if you've spent more than about a week in Japan. Nihonjin-ron is a concept as deeply regarded in much of Japan as cherry blossoms and overstuffed commuter trains. It is the notion that "we Japanese" are special, unique, utterly unlike any civilization elsewhere on the planet. Nihonjin-ron accounts for, in part, the Japanese reasoning with a perfectly straight face that foreign-made skis should not be sold in Japan because the snow there is "different" from snow in other ski resort climes, and only Japanese-manufactured skis will accommodate it. Nihonjin-ron is used to explain why imported rice was banned for decades. It wasn't protectionism, you see, but rather that Japanese intestinal tracts were unlike those of other humans; for health reasons, only Japanese rice should pass through them.

At its worst, expressions of nihonjin-ron like this are simply xenophobia and bigotry. Be prepared. As a result of having read large parts of this book, you might know more about sushi than most of the adult population of Japan. (You're welcome.) This will fascinate and impress many of those you encounter in the sushi-ya of your future, but you will, eventually, run across those Japanese who will resent your expertise. And while your objections to this resentment might not be on an economic scale similar to that of the ski manufacturer or rice exporter, they will understandably be real. You will be *kakka suru*, which is to say "really angry." When that happens, when you encounter racism in the sushi-ya and are tempted to bring up the subject of that photo of General MacArthur towering over short-stuff Hirohito, consider the case of Hawaiian Chad Rowan, better known in sumo circles as Akebono.

Stressing the scales at 200 pounds before he was shaving, Chad gave up any plans he may have had for a future in ballet. Scouted by a relative in the sumo biz, he left Hawaii for Japan at age 17 to join the ranks of professional sumo. If you thought the description of an itamae's training sounded harsh, you ought to forget completely about becoming a sumotori. Trainees are regularly beaten, are forced to train through injuries that would have most of us in a hospital, and spend their every waking moment outside the training stable cooking, cleaning, and catering to the needs of their seniors. Dickens could have chronicled the itamae's life. It would take a Solzhenitsyn to do justice to the training of a sumotori. For Rowan, who was given the sumo name Akebono, it was even tougher, unused to the language and food and customs as he was. He also had to contend with a coach who didn't believe he'd make it in sumo because of his long legs, a serious handicap in the sumo ring. Akebono persevered and shot up to the level of *ozeki*, or "champion," in near-record time, the second non-Japanese to reach that level.

Given his success, talk of a promotion for Akebono to *yokozuna* began in Japan. A yokozuna is a grand champion, but it really doesn't translate. The title's been bestowed very few times in the 2,000-year history of sumo. Even after the Sumo Council made its affirmative decision, there was a lot of grumbling from several directions in Japan about the promotion. Some death threats were made against Akebono. It wasn't at all clear he would be accepted as a "real" yokozuna. What changed things, to some considerable degree, was Akebono's official ascension to the title. It occurred in a Shinto shrine in Tokyo. At the center of the ceremony is the sumo wrestler advancing to the main part of the shrine and announcing formally to the deities there that he has been named a yokozuna. It was cold and snowing in Tokyo that day. This part of the ceremony requires the yokozuna, nearly naked, to squat and address the spirits in a long monotone that includes a lot of classical Japanese. Akebono was advised to authorize a slightly altered form of the ceremony that would have kept him warmer. He refused. He went through the ceremony as other yokozuna did it, with snow falling on him. That did it for at least the majority of

Japan. Akebono is arguably among the most popular yokozuna of recent times. He is a beloved figure everywhere in Japan, even though he has retired from competition. And this is because he was willing to do it *the Japanese way.*

The masses of Japanese, just as they gradually came to consider Akebono as a legitimate yokozuna, are willing to consider eating sushi made by Western hands. But just as in Akebono's case, those hands must have done things the Japanese way.

The problem for the non-Japanese itamae is that the Japanese way can be tough to describe, and even tougher to understand. Here are some qualities to watch for, some ways you can judge the training and caliber of an itamae, no matter what his race or background:

1 *How he handles the product.* Obviously, his product, his sushi, has to be good. Sushi that is the least bit off in freshness, taste, quality, or rice that's too mushy or hard in the center or in any way less than perfect aren't acceptable. These might have been the result of poor help, but the blame always goes to the itamae. He sits at the top of that pyramid we mentioned earlier, and he is the one who takes the heat when anything anywhere in the structure underneath him goes wrong. If you have complaints about the ring in your server's eyebrow or the hair in your tuna roll, in the sushi-ya they get addressed to the itamae. If he attempts to shift the blame, to pass off anything rather than taking responsibility for it, you've got an itamae who doesn't know his business.

2 *How he handles his tools.* As early as the Muromachi period (1333–1568) cooks were known as *hochoshi,* or kitchen knife masters. A good itamae is obsessive about his tools, especially his knives. He keeps them sharpened on a daily basis and has a special place, usually a cloth bag, to store them when he's not working. Anyone even touching an

itamae's knives, just to move them out of the way, is risking amputation or worse. The knives a skilled itamae uses will usually be worn at the handle, and carry a dark patina on the wood. They look used and lovingly cared for. Everything else behind the counter will be spotless. It's a point of pride for a well-trained itamae; it is a certain sign of a good sushi-ya. After all, you're eating raw fish. Cleanliness and attention to details in caring for the equipment is not just an aesthetic choice.

3   *How he handles his customers.* As I said, the itamae's ancestral inspiration is the devil-may-care sushi chef of the 19th-century Edo Period. There is even a word in Japanese to describe the attitude: *inase*. It means "hip" or "chic" or "with it." But it doesn't have any connotation of arrogance about it. He is supposed to be accommodating and ingratiating. A lot of good-natured teasing, especially if the customer is fluent in Japanese or the itamae is fluent in English, is expected. An itamae willing to teach you about sushi is even better. But if the guy behind the counter adopts a sushi-er-than-thou attitude, if he condescends, no matter how good his sushi, he doesn't deserve the patronage of a serious sushi tsu. Likewise, an itamae who gets flustered, or gets absorbed in his tasks and ignores the clientele, or is so busy chatting with the regulars that other customers are passing out from hunger, is not at the top of his craft.

And finally, in explaining the qualities of the expert itamae, there is the matter of *dosa*. Dosa is a sense of presence. It is the way an itamae conducts himself as he moves and works, and while Japanese can be rightfully scolded for a lot of their silly nihonjin-ron, there's no denying this ineffable quality in people of various Japanese professions who really know what they are doing. Part of it springs from a culture that does have some particular ways of doing things, and has been doing things a certain way for a long time. Non-Japanese martial artists, Kabuki or other dance performers, even potters or calligraphers have to deal with this. Their technique might be great, but there may still be something missing. The itamae who is technically proficient will still be lacking in the eyes of a lot of Japanese if his comportment and bearing don't reflect dosa. You, the barbarian sushi snob upstart, may be tempted to dismiss this dosa as another example of nihonjin-ron. Spend enough time watching a good itamae in action, though, especially in those busy times around lunch and dinner when he is handling multiple orders, and you will see. He's composed and efficient; he doesn't waste a lot of movement. At the same time, he seems to have a command of everything going on behind the counter, and he is keeping up conversations with patrons in front of it. Sometimes it is worthwhile to get a table away from the counter when you go to a sushi-ya, but close enough to see this going on. Dosa is something you can learn to see; it just takes practice to know what to look for. As it is with all forms of connoisseurship, judging the itamae has to take into account the surrounding circumstances. Sitting down in Paris to a meal of *le Grand Mac* and *pommes frites*, the would-be snob looks a bit silly complaining about the accompanying wine being a *vin ordinaire* rather than a Côte de Nuits. You get the idea. Expecting a master itamae at a quick-stop sushi bar in a suburban strip mall—and criticizing the one there because he isn't—is just poor form for the true sushi tsu. On the other hand, if the place advertises itself as a traditional sushi-ya, certain standards that must be met. Gauge your expectations accordingly.

Dismissing an itamae because he isn't Japanese can be racist or reasonable, or both. Obviously, there isn't anything in the gene pool that makes Japanese good itamae. That nearly all the best are Japanese is explicable in the same way that most great running backs are American. They have both had a lot of exposure to these activities and a lot of culture growing up that makes mastery easier. A boy from Biloxi, Mississippi—or a girl, for that matter—can become just as good an itamae as someone from Kanda or Nagano. All it takes is hard work, talent, and a willingness to excel in one's chosen art. That's peachy news for you, since the same can be said about becoming a sushi tsu, right?

SUSHI RITUAL

Sock, shoe, sock, shoe, or sock, sock, shoe, shoe? Jelly spread on top of the peanut butter, or on its own slice of bread? Tail of the toilet paper roll over or under? Whatever it is, in so many facets of life, we crave or at least enjoy ritual. Since in all probability these rituals figure significantly in our not reverting to complete barbarism, the majority of us are generally in favor of them. Japan, as a culture, has tended to agree with us. When you've got several million people living in a place the size of California, you are going to have to develop some rituals that make life bearable. That is one reason classical schools of etiquette taught up to a dozen different ways of bowing in old Japan. It made everyone feel better, smoothed over potential touchiness, and, as with rituals and manners everywhere, it made it easier to put people in their place. If you didn't know the proper way to open a sliding door or pour a flask of sake, chances were your breeding and background were less than those who did know the approved etiquette for such tasks.

There are some rituals in eating sushi as well, of course. And what's the fun of knowing something if you can't lord it over those who do not? The problem with insisting on all the proper mannerisms and rituals of sushi is at least twofold: One, not knowing the correct rituals, the aspiring sushi tsu can be caught and exposed to public humiliation. What's worse is he is tempted to invent or to follow the inventions of others, subscribing to sushi rituals that never existed.

So it's best that you know something of the etiquette and ritual of the sushi-ya. This is not as easy as it may seem, since opinions may appear to differ significantly about certain aspects of the whole process of going to a sushi-ya, ordering, and eating. Browse through some of the many introductory books available on sushi and you will see they tend to vary wildly in their dos and don'ts. Those who want to learn the "correct" way of doing things are caught between strictures and admonitions so exact they are intimidating, and exhortations to eat sushi however the hell they like provided no really important federal regulations are trampled. The sushi tsu knows, of course, that the correct approach is somewhere in between. While an adherence to form is utterly necessary for learning, one must demonstrate the panache and confidence to wing it from time to time. Knowing the right thing to do is as important as enjoying yourself.

You may have turned to this section first, thinking logically that if you can eat it correctly, it won't matter quite so much what you eat. There is a certain truth to this. On the other hand, if you gain enough competence in other realms of sushi—recognizing different forms of sushi, speaking knowledgeably about tane in season—you are apt to feel more relaxed and confident about conducting yourself properly in the sushi-ya. Compare the penitentiary lifer with the newcomer on the cell block: The former, based on his experience, is a lot more comfortable leaning over in the shower. Okay, poor comparison, but you get the point.

Let's take it step by step and go over some of the things you will want to keep in mind.

What to Say

The itamae, his staff, any waiters or waitresses, all let go with a hearty "Irrashaimassssse!" when you walk in the door. It is a folksy, hail-to-thee kind of greeting, perfectly suited to the sushi-ya's convivial informality. Sometimes it is just *"Irashai!"* In Kyoto, you will probably hear the local dialectical variation, *"Okoshi-asu!"* or *"Oide-asu!"* The urge to make some kind of response is natural. There ought to be, it seems only natural, some ritualized comeback. But there isn't. The best you can do is simply to nod. Don't bow. As a guest, you're not in a position to initiate a bow or to do so in response to the welcome; though it might seem appropriate, it isn't. Then take your seat and maybe offer a "Good evening" in English or Japanese.

Where to Sit

When they were mobile street-side stalls, a choice of seating at a sushi-ya was moot. Everybody stood. The sushi bar itself has evolved as a combination of a restaurant with seats and that outdoor stall, moved inside. If you're there strictly for sushi, belly up to the bar and have at it. If, on the other hand, you are out for an evening of sushi along with conversation with your spouse, racquetball partner, client, or parole officer, then get a table. If you want to wax philosophical with your cohort, get a table. Want to order some dishes other than sushi during the course of the evening? Get a table. Taking a seat at the bar implies that sushi is your main objective. That's not to say that proper sushi bar behavior is diving face-first into your cucumber roll if you are sitting at the bar, raising your head only to order more. It's just that you need to have some consideration for space in the restaurant. Arriving with a party of six and taking up seats at a sushi bar that only seats seven, and then ordering a couple pieces of nigiri and drinking and talking for three hours isn't going to win you any friends at that sushi-ya. Use some sense and adjust to what is going on around you.

If you have opted to sit at the bar, this advice applies as well to any verbal intercourse with the itamae. If the itamae is lingering, you're one of half a dozen customers in the place, and he is chattering away at you about the chances of the local team making the playoffs, feel free to reciprocate. If the line to be seated is out the door and the itamae looks like Lucy working frantically on the automated cake line, it is not the time to try to draw him into a protracted conversation about U.S.-Japan relations, the foreign exchange student from Kobe you dated back in high school, or the superiority of the Kawasaki motor-cycle over the Harley-Davidson.

As you have learned, itamae tend, as part of their profession's traditions and lore, toward the witty and garrulous. They take pride, in general, in their ability to engage in snappy repartee. There isn't any part of the job description, though, that demands it. Some itamae are naturally more reserved. They just don't care to engage in a lot of banter with customers. They may not even want to answer simple questions about sushi, which is okay. Consider that there may be language limitations too. From his station behind the counter, Ito-san might be jabbering incessantly with other native or fluent Japanese speakers, but don't assume he is equally eager to chitchat with you in English. Play it by ear.

If you do sit at the bar, it is obviously the best place to watch the itamae in action. However, remember that sushi-ya depend, even more than most restaurants, on a rapid turnover. Don't be in a hurry, but don't linger either. If you want to make a long and leisurely evening of your sushi meal, again, take a table.

Preliminaries

If there is an oshibori placed beside you, usually in a tray, use this damp hot or cold towel to wipe your hands and face. It is refreshing, sanitary, and, in a traditional sushi-ya, it's the only "napkin" you're going to get. It doesn't belong in your lap, however, unless you want a really interesting stain. Leave it folded beside you on the counter or table. You will be asked what you'd like to drink. And then you'll probably be given a plate or tray with some kind of snack, called *otsumami* or *tsukudani*, on which to nibble. It can be anything from boiled soybean pods (*edamame*) to tiny dried fishes (*niboshi*). Think of them as appetizers.

Ordering

Take your time. Tamago and kohada are some of the traditional tane with which to start a meal of sushi, as we learned in the sections on them. It used to be that every sushi-ya prepared its own omelets, which explains the tamago as a first order. You could get an idea of how skilled the itamae was. Similarly, most establishments had their own particular recipes for marinating kohada, giving you a reasonable clue about the prowess of the man in charge. Modern methods of production have pretty much tossed those old indicators out the window, so unless it is a gesture to tradition, there isn't much reason to begin your meal with either of those. Most sushi tsu, if eating nigiri sushi, order a succession of tane that goes from the leaner cuts to the fattier ones, much the same way a wine connoisseur arranges a tasting. Lean cuts like hirame or kasugo keep the palate sharp. As the tane become fattier, the rich globules start sticking to your tongue and it is harder to pick out some of the subtleties of taste. If you are eating chirashi sushi, the shrimp is eaten first. If you've got a combination of nigiri and maki sushi, eat the maki sushi with the nori wrapping first, before it becomes tough and gummy.

Consider beginning your meal, as many sushi tsu in Japan do, not with sushi, but with an order or two of sashimi. It is an excellent way to take the edge off your hunger and judge the quality of the fish so that you can order sushi at your leisure and with some insight into what's good and fresh. Another good reason to start with some sashimi, particularly if you aren't familiar with the sushi-ya, is so you can watch to see how orders are taken there. Different sushi places have different methods. In most in the United States, you are handed a printed list with the sushi menu on it. (Immediately give some extra points to the establishment if some part of this menu has been hand-written, indicating that they have some specials, depending on availability of the fish or other ingredients.) You mark your choices and hand it back to the itamae or the server, or you simply give the server your order verbally. The entire order is filled and comes all at once, on a platter or a *sushi-oke* tub. In other restaurants, the itamae wants to get your orders one at a time and he'll make them as you ask for them. Again, some common sense is necessary here and there's nothing wrong in asking a server how it goes in this establishment. There is also nothing wrong, if you want a more leisurely meal in a place that takes the orders all at once, in asking the server to accommodate you and take them one at a time. Do not believe that ordering either way is the only "real" procedure.

If it is a top-class and authentic sushi-ya, you and your fellow diners at the counter announce your individual orders to the itamae, no matter what he's doing. And he repeats it—loudly—to acknowledge he's heard.

"Chu-toro!"

"Chu-toro!"

"Ika-nigitte!"

"Ika-nigitte!"

You'll be tempted to order "Cheeze-booga!" just to hear the echoing shout *"Cheeze-booga!"* like on that old *Saturday Night Live* skit with John Belushi.

There is another, lower-decibel method of ordering sushi, common in Japanese sushi-ya of middle level or cheaper quality, one that's never really caught on in a lot of U.S. sushi places and is often an excellent buy. A selection of sushi can be ordered by the set. Sets consist of several different kinds of nigiri, ranging from the cheaper to the most expensive. It is sort of like a prix fixe meal. If the sushi-ya offers these, they'll be listed on the menu or on the wall and they are usually identified by A, B, and C, or as *ume* or *bai* (plum), *chiku* or *take* (bamboo), and *matsu* or *sho* (pine), in ascending order of expense. The plum will always be the cheapest, the pine the most deluxe. There may also be various kinds of deluxe offerings, with names like *kiku, hana, yuki, tsuki* (chrysanthemum, flower, snow, and moon). This is sushi *moriawase*. You may find it listed that way on some sushi-ya menus. It is a nice alternative to ordering by the piece, particularly if you would like to spend your time eating and talking with companions rather than focusing on a menu. Remember, though, that ordering this way almost always implies that it is the chef's choice.

Finally, you can consider ordering *omakase*, an enjoyable if chancy way to eat sushi. The root of the word means "to trust" or "to place confidence in," or, in some contexts, "to submit." When you say to an itamae, *"Omakase itashi-masu,"* you are leaving your meal entirely up to his discretion. It isn't much different from jumping on a ride at the carnival you've never ridden or seen before. You don't know where you are going or how you're going to get there, but it is probably going to be a good time. The competent itamae is challenged by an omakase order. It brings out his competitive streak, his artistic inclinations, and, of course, if he is Japanese and you are not, his almost genetically instilled inclination to shock or amaze you. For years, savvy Westerners in Japan have repaired to the big department stores there, to the floor devoted exclusively to foods. Clerks will press samples of everything on the gaijin, sometimes out of a sincere desire to expose the non-Japanese shopper to their wares, and often to see if they can present something the foreigner won't or can't eat. (Either way, it works out great for the Westerner, who can make a moving buffet out of the adventure.) Omakase meals can produce extraordinary creations that never appear on a menu, as well as perfectly coordinated courses of sushi that constantly expand on the palate from start to finish. They are the consummate opportunity for the itamae to demonstrate his chops, and rarely will one pass up such an opening.

There is no doubt that eating sushi omakase style is one of the most rewarding experiences the sushi snob will have in his journey to connoisseurship. It is, though, like telling a good dirty joke to the pope. It can be enjoyable and successful, but you have to be quite careful exactly how you go about doing it. Here's one way *not* to. "Omakase, please, but I don't like cucumber rolls or uni, and I think I'm allergic to any shellfish taken from the Pacific." If you are going the omakase route, let the itamae do the driving. If you have limitations, order from the menu instead. An itamae might appreciate your letting him know if you have some favorites. He, though, best ascertains these by seeing you at his sushi-ya often enough so he gets to know you.

It is fine to let the itamae know, if you aren't a regular customer, approximately what your level of sushi expertise is when ordering omakase. Just don't be a boor about it. *Good*: "I was eating sushi for at least ten years before I learned about omakase. That must've been six years ago, and now whenever I'm in a new sushi-ya, I love to order that way. I haven't had a bad experience yet, and I have gotten to eat a lot of really unusual stuff I didn't know about." *Bad*: "Having been initiated into the world of sushi as a child by our loyal housegirl Yumiko, I'm something of a sushi expert, old boy. So only your best for me this evening, and chop-chop about it."

Interaction with an itamae is always a subtle exchange, and never more so than when you allow him to create an entire meal for you. If he is good, he can size you up by the way you drink your tea, handle your chopsticks, and so on. If you are disappointed in what he gives you, either go to a different sushi-ya or come back again, remind him of what he served last time, and tell him you'd like to be more adventurous this time. Given the expense of sushi, especially when it is omakase, this approach can seem extravagant, of course. And it is.

Speaking of money, to the uninitiated, omakase dining has the air of "money is no object" about it. That is not entirely accurate. It is gauche to ask to be put in the hands of the itamae and then tell him what you can and can't handle. It is perfectly acceptable, however, to know how much dinner is going to set you back. In some sushi-ya, omakase prices are listed on the menu or on the signboards. If they aren't, you have to ask. You may ask the itamae or a server. You can say something like "My well-heeled friend here would like to spend $1,000 tonight; can you feed the two of us for that?" This is particularly effective if you are speaking Japanese at the time and your wealthy friend doesn't understand a word of it. He'll finish the evening with a wonderful story to tell about how frightfully expensive *real* Japanese sushi is, and you will leave very, *very* well fed. If, on the other hand, you're picking up the check, don't hesitate to be more modest. "Can you feed me well for $50?" isn't inappropriate, unless this is a fabulously expensive sushi-ya with some big-name "chef" running it. A couple of by-the-ways here: Do not confuse omakase with *osusume*, which means "What do you recommend?" Second, don't believe the myth that only sushi must be ordered from the itamae and that you are insulting him by asking for another cup of tea or a beer. Itamae have always taken these requests. What they'll do is turn to a server or assistant and have them serve you. But you're not breaking some sushi-ya protocol to request items other than sushi.

If you make a single order of nigiri sushi, expect it to come in pairs. It's a tradition in the sushi-ya and has been since the Edo period, when nigiri sushi developed. There are a couple of explanations for this, one a little far-fetched, the other more likely. One of the many beautiful things about being a sushi tsu is that you will know both and can one-up anyone who offers the other when the subject arises.

The far-fetched story has to do with an unfortunate double entendre. *Hito kire*, or one slice, can be written with other characters pronounced the same way in Japanese for "to kill a man." *Mi-kire*, or three slices, can also mean "to kill myself." So to avoid any homicidal or suicidal overtones, sushi-ya went with serving two pieces, or *ni-kire*. That is the story anyway. If you buy it, however, you're probably the sort of person who actually believes the cable guy really will show up next Wednesday between noon and six. In the first place, the construction of the Japanese language is such that, with some imagination, literally thousands of words and phrases can have odd, salacious, or potentially embarrassing or inauspicious double meanings. (We're talking about a language where *komon*, depending on the emphasis of syllables, can mean either an anus or a consultant.) In the second, sushi has never been ordered like pizza, that is, by the slice. No one says *ni-kire*, or two slices, when ordering. (In most cases in spoken Japanese, "two slices" is more grammatically expressed as *futakire* anyway.) So those words wouldn't have been part of the parlance of the sushi-ya in any case. The correct numeration for sushi is *nigitte* or *sangitte*, "two pieces" or "three pieces." There's nothing wrong with simply naming your preference—uni, for instance, and adding an *o kudasai* after it, to make an order. (*Kudasai* is a polite way of saying "please.") If you want an order of sea urchin, just say *"Uni o kudasai."* If there is no mention on the menu of the number of pieces making up an order, simply hold up the requisite number of fingers.

The second, more believable explanation for the pair of nigiri sushi you're served has more to do with the Japanese sense of aesthetics. Nigiri sushi comes in twos because one would be chintzy all by itself and not very attractive, no matter how it was placed on the plate. Three orders of the same tane, while they could be arranged nicely, would be almost too much of a good thing for Japanese appetites. So two it is, even though it is one of the rare times an even number will figure in a presentation. You must remember as well that it isn't usually just two objects on a plate of nigiri sushi, not when you count the mound of pickled ginger or other side dish that invariably accompanies the order. The addition of a garnish can also offset the presentation and make it more balanced and attractive.

All that said, many sushi restaurants in the United States and elsewhere outside Japan have gotten tired of trying to explain why one order of nigiri really means two pieces are going to be served, and they have adopted the convention of serving just one piece. Also bear in mind that even in those sushi-ya that do observe the tradition of serving two pieces as a single order, this does not apply to temaki sushi or maki sushi.

It is a sad development, since two pieces of most tane is just the right amount. Still, life goes on. The lack of a standard also means you may have to ask how many pieces come to a single order.

Assuming you're at the bar, the itamae will respond to your order in one of two ways: He may set out a plate or a footed wooden geta board with your sushi on it. You take it down, eat, and then return it for the next round. Alternatively, he might give you a different dish each time you order. There isn't any deep meaning either way; it is simply a preference of the restaurant or the itamae. If the sushi-ya prefers putting out the wooden geta with sushi atop it, do not reach up and take the sushi with your chopsticks. You've either got to move the geta down on the counter beside you or simply take it from the geta with your hands. However you've gotten it, your sushi is finally in front of you and it is almost time to eat.

Eating

There's a bottle full of shoyu on the counter in front of you. Alongside your order of maguro or saba or kappa-maki is a vernally green blob of wasabi. You have seen it a hundred times before, of course. Shoyu goes in the *kosara*, the small dish that's been placed to the side of your sushi plate. It's followed by the dollop of wasabi. Stir with the chopsticks until the surface of the dish is an iridescent greenish-purple pool suitable for baptizing your nigiri sushi all night long. This is a can't-miss step in the course of sushi ritual.

Wrong.

Yes, it's true, you see it everywhere. But here's what the sushi tsu knows: most sushi fans outside Japan are chronic wasabi abusers. They're gorging on the stuff like a horde of diet-maddened Weight Watchers on a hot fudge bender at Baskin-Robbins. They have convinced themselves that sushi just wouldn't be sushi without a lusty dip of what is called *wasabi-joyu*, wasabi and soy sauce soup. It's hard to blame them and easy to understand how the habit has metastasized into a shrieking, biting, not reliably housebroken monkey on their backs. This addiction to wasabi is probably the natural result of the Sears Christmas catalog cornucopia of tastes we have at our disposal in today's abundance of multiethnic, seasoning-spangled eating arenas. Wednesday's dinner is a jambalaya. Thursday's is Jamaican curry. Friday it's a rich duck confit. When Saturday rolls around and you're off to the sushi-ya, your taste buds are more jaded and overstimulated than a bunch of adolescent boys spending the entire summer at the beach. So naturally, they need major stimulation to make the gastronomic point that one is indeed eating again. Traditional Japanese cuisine, whatever its other attributes, does not bring a lot of spiciness to the soiree. The vocabulary for *textures* of food is far more extensive in Japanese than the ones devoted to spicy *tastes*. This serves to make at least two points: (a) that seeking to make foods taste zestier by adding stuff like wasabi in baby fist–size doses is contrary to the aims of the cuisine, and (b), that there are foods to be better appreciated by far without the stimulation of additional hits of wasabi. Those foods include most of what you normally eat during a visit to the sushi-ya.

Here is one explanation for how the wasabi and soy sauce soup ritual got started. The elixir of wasabi-joyu is an essential component in eating sashimi. What is the crucial difference between a plate of sashimi and an order of sushi? Yes, you've been paying attention: the rice. Rice for sashimi is ordinary gohan. It is the sushi-meshi that makes the sushi, and that addition of sugar and vinegar adds components to the rice that can easily be overpowered by a lot of wasabi or any other strong flavors. Somehow—and this has happened in Japan as well, so the clueless clowns of the West can't be blamed—the perfectly reasonable practice of dipping slices of sashimi into wasabi-joyu has been transferred to sushi, where it does not belong. Be that as it may, wasabi-joyu has become deeply ingrained in the "traditions" of sushi, so much so that anyone questioning it will be faced with an outrage similar to what would happen were you to tell the patrons of Wrigley Field that mustard on hot dogs isn't acceptable. Not only might you be threatened with grievous bodily harm if you should publicly suggest the wasabi-joyu baths are not the best way to eat sushi; you will, if you do not follow the tradition, probably soon be shown the "right" way by "expert" and well-meaning diners close by. To have any chance against such assaults, the sushi tsu had better be packing some serious culinary firepower. To assist in the lock-and-load process, this is a good time for the story of a couple of lovers.

Let's call them Sherry and Tommy. Both are footloose and fancy free in Paris that first summer after college graduation, and they meet one sunny afternoon in the Louvre when they find themselves staring at the same painting. Within about four seconds after Sherry begins speaking to him, Tommy thinks he might be falling in love. He suggests repairing to a nearby café he discovered only just this morning, for a little refreshment. What do Tommy and Sherry order? A bottle of wine, a wedge of cheese, and a loaf of bread, right? That's because what is going on between Tommy and Sherry isn't about getting in their daily nutritional needs. The sharing of the wine and cheese and the bread is an excuse for them to spend some more time together. It serves as a kind of bonding agent, bringing two hithertofore disparate and uninvolved components together in a harmonious fashion.

Wasabi is the cheese and bread of sushi. The restrained smear of wasabi added by the itamae when he makes the sushi joins the slightly sweet and vinegary shari with the luxuriant fats and protein of the tane, adding just a hint of a spicy spark that brings the two separate components into a happy, healthy whole. Shoyu adds the same dimension as the wine at Sherry and Tommy's first little tête-à-tête. It is lubrication. Neither the wine nor the bread and cheese are the center of things here. It is all about Sherry and Tommy. All right, now imagine that same date in the same café. Only instead of the bread, cheese, and wine, Tommy and Sherry sit down to an entire roast goose, candied yams, and more. It's a whole different scenario, no? The food would be at the center of the experience and Sherry and Tommy would be concentrating on that rather than on each other. They'd be too stuffed to want to do anything but waddle back to their respective hotels and fall into a calorically induced coma for the rest of the day. You want Sherry and Tommy never to get together, fine. Whip up your slurry of wasabi and shoyu and ruin it all for them. Just don't count yourself much of a romantic—or a sushi tsu.

I hope the tale of Sherry and Tommy will convince you to at least try sushi with just the wasabi put on it by the itamae, and dip it just a little bit in unadulterated shoyu. It might not be easy. But just knowing that you've got a problem is the first step, and we're all here for you.

Before leaving the subject of big-time eating don'ts, we also need to address another gaffe that is too common in sushi circles. You may have seen someone use chopsticks to lift tane off nigiri sushi, then dip it into the plate of shoyu, replace it on the rice, then eat the whole mess. If you have seen this, chances are very good that it was a woman doing it, a Japanese woman, to be exact. This is a habit some women (and men too; it's just more common among the former) have at the sushi-ya. Look, being a sushi snob is a whole different matter from being a social snob. So we are not going to go too far down this road. Here's the essence of it: Removing tane from nigiri sushi to dunk it in shoyu and then replacing it on the rice to eat is regarded in Japanese culture as a kind of lower-class habit. That's not to say you won't see people doing it or that you should make any inferences about them if you do. It is only to say that if you do it, inferences can and may be made about you. You can't please everybody in life. Just know that this habit has social implications among many Japanese that are less than admirable.

Eating nigiri sushi correctly is mostly a matter of doing it so the whole package gets to your mouth in one piece, doing it so it tastes as good as it can when it gets there, and doing it in such a way that no one in your proximity loses their appetite during the process. It isn't much more complicated than that. We are talking about nigiri sushi here, the standard form, with shari and a slice of tane of some kind on top. Place your thumb and middle finger (and ring finger if you need it) on either side of the rice. Your forefinger goes on top of the tane to help hold it in place. Make one quick stop before the final destination, to quickly roll the nigiri into the dish of shoyu. The key here is to briefly flip the entire piece upside down just long enough so the tane side is touched with the shoyu. It's a corkscrewing motion, left or right, your choice. What does matter is that the tane, rather than the rice, goes into the shoyu. This would seem self-evident. Introducing a composite material to any liquid not limited to but including shoyu, is going to radically reduce the cohesive properties created by the glutinous factors of the rice's natural starches—combined with sugar and vinegar and reinforced by the pressure of the maker's hands—causing the individual grains to separate from the whole. Is this really that complicated? Stick shari in a dish of shoyu and it is going to come apart. Do it enough times, and your shoyu dish looks like the ink-dark sea after the *Titanic* went down, with pale, pitiful little survivors bobbing sadly about on the surface. It isn't pretty. If you take nothing else from this chapter, know that the unmistakable trail of the sushi parvenu is marked with the flotsam of rice grains in the shoyu. It isn't just an aesthetic consideration that should guide your hand. Sushi-meshi has its own unique flavor. The itamae or one of his staff worked hard to get the combination of rice, sugar, and rice vinegar just right. Don't blot it out by soaking the whole piece in shoyu. It is the fish or other tane that can benefit from the saltiness of the soy sauce. There are, even now, legions of would-be sushi enthusiasts out there who don't think their nigiri sushi has been adequately doctored unless the bottom is as brown as the shoulders of a beach babe from Ipanema. The sushi tsu is never among this crowd.

Some other minor points of eating etiquette to observe:

▾ Don't smoke.

▾ If you're eating off a communal plate of sushi and using chopsticks, turn them around and use the rear ends to take food from the plate. This is an obvious gesture of hygiene that's observed for any Japanese food that is being shared.

▾ Try to avoid leftovers. Japanese etiquette has always had some fussiness about leftovers of any kind at the table. During the feudal period, diners at formal meals brought small packets of paper tucked into their kimono sleeves for folding into squares and filling with fish bones or other inedible and unsightly leftovers. Then too, given the history of food shortages and famine in Japan, leftovers can be an expression, even if unintended, of careless gluttony. (Many a Japanese mother used to tell her children that every un-eaten grain of rice left in the bowl represented a tear from a farmer whose efforts were unappreciated.) The portions of most kinds of sushi and the progressive method of ordering it are such that with little effort, you should confirm your membership in the Clean Plate Club in the sushi-ya without much problem.

▾ It is fine, though it is certainly not expected, to buy a beer or sake for the itamae. He will probably drink the latter from a tea mug if he's Japanese or has been trained in Japan. It is an old custom, dating back to the time when tea mugs were the only drinking cups available at a sushi stall.

And before leaving the subject of how to eat sushi, here's a word about falling into the habit of ordering the same kinds of sushi again and again. "In the tea room, the fear of repetition is a constant presence," Kakuzo Okakura wrote in the classic text on the tea ceremony, *The Book of Tea*, back at the turn of the 20th century. Had he been writing today, he'd have added that a similar fear occurs when checking the movie schedule for

HBO, which seems to feature the same six movies all month. As it was in the tea hut then and on HBO today, repetition makes for a dull evening. The same goes for your sushi diet. Certainly you will have favorites. But don't be afraid to take the chance to try some new fish or tane. Establish yourself as a regular at a good sushi-ya and the itamae will reward you with some interesting tidbits that you might otherwise never get an opportunity to savor.

Paying the Bill

On just about every other city block there will be a sushi authority who can explain to you that the itamae is never to be asked for a bill and that it is a serious breach of sushi etiquette to do so. Once again, they are confused. If you'll review the section on the history of sushi, you will see that outdoor sushi stalls were strictly one-man operations. The itamae made the sushi and collected the bills, among other duties. So there isn't any ancient tradition that itamae are some kind of sensitive artisans who are above the bourgeois concerns for lucre. (That's also why, as we explained earlier, it is fine to ask the itamae for drinks or whatever else you might need during your meal.) In fact, in a really traditional sushi-ya in Japan, the itamae keeps a running tab of every customer in his head. You have to ask him for an accounting, as he's the only one who knows what you ate. It is true that in Japanese and Japanese-style restaurants in general, workers who handle money don't handle food, and vice versa. If you ask the itamae for the bill, he will alert a server or a cashier to write it up for you. A more subtle way of letting the itamae know you are ready to pay and leave is to either ask for tea (even if you've already got a cup) or to mutter *Gochisosama-deshita*, a ritual phrase spoken at the end of any Japanese meal. Back in the 1950s and '60s, the customer would say *Ichinin-mae,* or an order for one person, to the itamae as a way of alerting him to the fact that this would be the last course ordered. It is a phrase still heard everywhere in Japanese sushi-ya, though not as often. In Japanese sushi-ya, the bill is almost always paid at the cashier's. In the United States, it is more common to have the server bring the check to the table.

Should you be in a thoroughly authentic sushi-ya, there might not be any written bill at all. The itamae, as we have noted earlier, keeps the tab for each customer in his head. It is part of the ritual of sushi, and it is an expected skill of the itamae in places that are still run the old way. You might be wondering if he may forget something, trying to keep straight what everyone at the bar has been eating since you began. Just don't wonder out loud. Never question the bill of an itamae who's been keeping the tab mentally. If you think he is egregiously off and has given you a bill far higher than it should be, pay it. And don't go back. And tell your friends not to go back. But don't argue the point. In truth, you may be charged a little more on some nights, a little less on others. It works out if you're a regular customer. Regular customers are what a sushi-ya that observes this kind of tradition is all about. You're the one who walked in; they didn't drag you off the street. A sushi-ya, traditional or not, that deliberately cheated customers would not stay in business long. The likelihood you are being scammed at one is not great. Chances are much, much higher that if you have actually found a sushi restaurant where the itamae has the bills in his head, you've stumbled onto a paradise that would be the envy of many a sushi tsu, even in Japan.

Here's a final word about patronizing sushi-ya. If you are in a large metropolitan city, there might be several dozen sushi-ya within easy striking distance. The temptation to want to sample them all is natural. Give in to it. It wasn't that long ago that sushi could be found only in a few restaurants on the East and West Coasts. Elephants outnumbered sushi-ya in the Midwest and South by a wide margin. So celebrate a little. Try out these places. Use your sushi explorations to hone your skills. Once you have canvassed what is available, however, you need to begin developing a good relationship with a local sushi-ya—and an itamae. Again and again, I have stressed the point that becoming a regular at an authentic sushi-ya has enormous benefits. Your sushi-ya fidelity need never be absolute, just enough to make you a respectable sight ambling in to your favorite haunt. It is the best place to put into practice all the etiquette outlined here, and to learn new subtleties that will reinforce your status as a sushi tsu.

Sushi-Ben, the Language of Sushi

Not to be precious here, but it goes without saying, or should, that the ultimate *lingua franca* of the sushi-ya is the most difficult of all to master and appreciate: silence. Someday you might reach the point where you slide onto your regular seat at the sushi-ya and the itamae gives you a perfunctory nod. You might talk about the Yakult Swallows or the rising crime rates in Japan, which are all due, everyone in the country knows, to foreigners who have no respect or understanding of the Japanese way. You might discuss the weather or the stock market or life in general. But you won't exchange a word about sushi. Why? The itamae knows your tastes. He knows too the depth of your wallet. He serves you what he knows you like, or if he's got some tasty tidbit on hand, he puts that out for your enjoyment. You and your regular itamae are, as they say, *ki ga awanakatta*. Your spirits are in harmony and so communication on matters such as this aren't necessary. The sushi tsu who enjoys such a relationship is at the top of the game and is to be emulated and admired. If we are not at that rarified level, though, we have to ask about the day's ingredients, consult on what to order, inquire about what's what.

For the most part, ordinary English or Japanese will do. If you aren't fluent in either, you can probably get by just by nodding, pointing, and grunting, truth be told. After you have spent a little time in a sushi-ya, however, you may begin to hear some words and expressions that, even if you are fluent in Japanese, sound odd or are totally mystifying. It could be that you don't understand because everyone in the place is actually from Venice and they're speaking Italian. If that's the case, you will probably be able to figure it out on your own. If you've eliminated that as a possibility, consider the chances that you are hearing some *sushi-ben*—"sushi slang."

Sushi-ben are words heard, for the most part, only in the confines of a sushi-ya. They may have roots in the lexicon of the world of the workaday Tokyo crowd of a century or so ago. Some might have vaguely underworld origins, or they may be a part of the fish dealer's slang or the specialized vocabulary of the Japanese restaurant trade. Whatever their source, know when it comes to the customer's use of sushi slang, there are two conflicting opinions: One party of sushi tsu in Japan delights in indulging in this linguistic arcana. Like pidgin in Hawaii, conversance in the "insider" slang of sushi is a way of demonstrating one's identification with a certain group. Using slang is a way of showing that you belong, that you are hip to the scene around you, that you have a familiarity with it all that the outsider does not.

Another group of Japanese sushi snobs takes the opposite position. Just trying to show that you belong, they insist, is a sure sign you really do not. If you are a college-educated professional in Japan who also happens to be a sushi snob, it does not make sense for you to speak perfect Japanese all day long and then suddenly resort to sushi-ben when you walk into a place selling sushi. It sounds affected, they say. In general, the Western sushi tsu ought to give careful consideration to this latter position. Imagine the fresh-off-the-jet tourist in Waikiki who approaches a local young lady and, wishing to find a good place to eat, says, "Excuse me, Ms. Wahine, could you recommend a restaurant with ono-licious grinds?" He's got some pidgin words right, but the execution definitely has something missing. The nonnative Japanese sushi tsu has enough challenge in correctly pronouncing the standard Japanese necessary for conveying his connoisseurship. Playing around with sushi-ben can be a stroll through a linguistic minefield. Making a mistake while trying to speak ordinary Japanese is explicable if you aren't a native. Making an error while trying to appear like you are an expert in sushi-ben makes you look like a fool. Japanese has some nuances that can make even a nearly perfectly fluent speaker sound odd. No matter what your skill level in the language is, it's best to play around with sushi-ben carefully and judiciously. You should never, ever look as if you are trying too hard to fit it. It is a ploy that always looks desperate and contrived.

Whether you choose to use it or not, naturally, you will want to know what sushi-ben is. So I've included a list. Many of these have already been explained previously. Not even a majority of these terms are exclusive to the sushi-ya, by any means. Those slang expressions that are normally used only around sushi are denoted with an asterisk.

AGARI* ▼ See page 212 for an explanation of tea.

AWASE-ZU ▼ The mixture of rice vinegar, sugar, and salt that seasons rice for making sushi-meshi.

DEMPYO ▼ A formal word for the bill. It can be fun to use this in a Japanese restaurant of any kind. It has a slightly archaic ring about it. Asking for the dempyo in Japanese sounds something like asking for the bill in English by saying, "There, kind fellow, an accounting of our debt, if you please."

DOSA ▼ The bearing and posture of an itamae as he works.

GARI* ▼ Sushi slang for shoga, or pickled ginger.

GYOKU* ▼ Literally, "jewel," a term for tamago or omelet.

HIYA ▼ Water. This word, usually said *o-hiya,* is pleasantly old-fashioned. A more modern word for water is *mizu.*

ICHININ-MAE ▼ "An order of sushi for one person." A few decades ago, this was what the customer said to the itamae to indicate he was ordering his last course. It's still used, but not quite as commonly as before.

IKIJIME ▼ Fish kept alive until just before they are filleted for sushi; the opposite of *nojime.*

INASE ▼ The Japanese equivalent of "hip," "inase" is a term much beloved by the itamae, or at least much esteemed. He considers himself to be inase.

ITADAKIMASU ▼ A ritual expression at the beginning of a meal. It means "I'm receiving your offering," but it is said, or at least mumbled, by everyone at the table. It isn't appropriate in a restaurant, though you may hear it when a family or friends are all together and eating out.

KAMI* ▼ The word literally means a "deity" or a "spirit from above." It's used to describe the gods or spirits in Shinto, among other things. In the sushi-ya, it is a slang title for the chief itamae, used in a jocular way.

KANJO OR O-KANJO ▼ The normal word for a bill.

KANPAI ▼ "Cheers" or "To your health"; this is the standard Japanese toast, and even if you're in a sushi-ya where drinking isn't the focus of attention, you'll often hear this expression.

KIKAI-MAKI* ▼ *Kikai* is an "instrument" or "an apparatus." Since maki sushi is made not just by hand but with a bamboo rolling mat, it is called, in the sushi-ya, kikai-maki.

KUCHIAKE ▼ Literally means "open mouth." It is what you call the first customer in the sushi-ya for that day or evening.

KYO WA NANI GA OISHII DESU KA? ▼ "What's good today?"

MURA-CHOKO* ▼ Classic sushi slang for the small dish filled with shoyu and used to dip nigiri sushi. The *mura* is from *murasaki* (see below); *choko* is a word for a sake cup.

MURASAKI ▼ A famous sushi-ben way of referring to soy sauce. The word in normal Japanese means "purple," and you can see how the dark, rich, iridescent tones of shoyu have a purple hue. "Murasaki" as a sushi-ben term is a matter of some contention. In some places, using it at all is considered an affectation.

NAMIDA* ▼ "Tears"; sushi-ben for "wasabi," for reasons obvious to anyone who's gotten a little too much of the stuff in his mouth.

NAMINOHANA ▼ "Flower of the waves," or salt.

NIGEMONO* ▼ Cheaper tane.

NOJIME ▼ Fish that have been cleaned and filleted and prepared for use in the sushi-ya ahead of time, as opposed to *ikijime*, which are alive until just before they're used.

O-AISO* ▼ Sushi-ben for the bill. It comes from the word *aiso*, or "goodwill," with an honorific "o" tacked on. It means you're wishing the owner goodwill at the same time you ask for the bill. See also *tsuke*.

OMAKASE ITASHI-MASU ▼ An order to the itamae that you're leaving the choice of sushi up to him.

SABI* ▼ An occasionally heard variation on "wasabi." It's almost always used as part of *sabi-nuki* (see below).

SABI-NUKI* ▼ "Without wasabi." If you don't want wasabi on your order, tell the server *"Sabi-nuki o kudasai."*

SU-MEZU ▼ Another term for *awase-zu*.

TE-ZU ▼ "Hand vinegar." This is the term used for the rice vinegar mixture the itamae rubs on his hands to keep sushi-meshi from sticking to them.

TSUKE ▼ Another word for the bill. The derivation of "tsuke" is from *tsukeru*, or "to write down." Way back when sushi-ya moved from outdoor stalls to indoor permanent restaurants, clients would ask the itamae to put the bill on their tab. "I'm writing it down," the itamae would reply. And so *tsuke* became a way of referring to the bill itself. It is used mostly by older people and in neighborhood taverns and other types of local restaurants.

Afterword

merica has embraced food fads more enthusiastically than probably any other civilization in history. From Watergate salad to Buffalo wings, from Tex-Mex to Thai, a succession of foods and cuisines has been paraded out and presented to the American table. And while some have faded in popularity—lime Jell-O with cottage cheese passed quietly, without much mourning—others endure. The hamburger, for instance, it is safe to venture now, has found its place in the American diet, for the time being at least.

Sushi, without a doubt, got its start in America as a food fad. It is too soon to tell how far sushi will go beyond this culinary realm into the mainstream of our eating habits. For us, it does not matter. The course set by the sushi tsu will not deviate. Your compass is fixed. Knowing the best, appreciating it, and seeking it out is your destination, and if there are dabblers along the way, smile and wish them well and leave them dribbling grains of rice in the soy sauce of your wake.

Your passion is not an easy one to satisfy. You must contend not only with a foreign language but with a specialized idiom as well, with oceans of fish the exact identification of which would make even the seasoned ichthyologist hesitate. And there is the certainty that the best sushi will always be scarce, rare, and expensive. You go forth determined to seek it nevertheless, infused with the spirit of the gourmand, with the exacting standards of the connoisseur, and above all, with the confident, understated élan of the snob. This book should serve as something like a series of charts to assist in your exploration. Make no mistake, however. If you really want to be a sushi tsu, you must be always prepared to learn and expand your sushi horizons when the opportunity presents itself. Sharpen your palate like the keen edge of a samurai sword. Refine your taste so that no combination of rice, vegetable, or fish will ever be greeted as a stranger.

On the other hand, you could just order some take-out Chinese this evening. . . .

Index

abalone, 64–67
abura-age, 19
agari, 215, 283
age sushi, 20
ahi, 139
aji (horse mackerel), 4, 53–56
aji-tataki, 55
ajoiso, 44
aka-amadai, 173
akabana, 116
akagai (red clam), 56–58
akakuzuna, 173
akami, 32, 142
aka-oroshi, 208
akashidai, 176
Akebono, 257
aki-iwashi, 105
albacore, 140
almaco jack, 116
almond kozakana, 106
ama-ebi, 73
ama-kuchi, 5
amadai, 173
amberjack, 33
    hamachi, 75, 76
    hiramasa, 86–88
    kanpachi, 114
anago (conger eel), 58–62
anakyu-maki, 14
anglerfish sperm sacs, 187
anko, 187
aogisu, 129
aori-ika (cuttlefish), 98
aoyagi (trough shell clam), 62–64
arai style, 172
ark shell, 57
Asakusa nori, 49
asanomi, 20
asatsuki, 209
ashirai, 196
atsu tamago, 183
avocado roll, 15
awabi (abalone), 64–67
awase-zu, 4–5, 283
ayu (sweetfish), 67–70

bachi-maguro, 138
bakagai, 62

bamboo shoots, 44
bancha, 213
bara sushi, 24
baraboshi, 63
baran, 28
bashira, 94
basho-kajiki, 109
battera sushi, 27–29
beefsteak plant, 44
beer, with sushi, 215
beni-mazu, 156
beni-shoga, 208
benitade, 20, 158
    in chirashi sushi, 23
benizake, 156
bento, 227
beta-beta, 3
bigeye tuna, 139
binnaga, 141
Biwa, Lake, xvii
black abalone, 65
black aji, 53
black sea bream, 175
blackfin sea bass, 171
blackfin tuna, 140
blue king crab, 113
blue sillago, 129
blue swimmer crab, 113
bluefin tuna, 138–139
bo sushi, 30
bocho, 14
Bodhidharma, 240
bon, 227
bonito, 76, 120–126
The Book of Tea, 278
botan-ebi, 73
bream, 32, 33, 173–177
    in battera sushi, 28
    kasugo, 116–120
bunsen-maki, 17
burdock, 38–39
buri, 75
buta-guchi, 166
byobu, 239

cabio, 88
California roll, 16
California uni, 191

capelin roe, 187
carrots, 43
  in chirashi sushi, 23
cha, 213
chakin sushi, 19
chariko kasugo, 118
chi-in ken, 11
chiai, 77, 141, 143
Chiba nori, 49
chidai, 118, 175
chinu, 175
chirashi sushi
  types of, 21–24
  variations on, 24–26
chirimenjako, 44
chirizu, 209
cho, 77
chopsticks, 229–230
  caveats about, 232–233
  in serving from communal dish, 278
  types of, 234–236
  using, 230–233
choroku, 235
chu-maki, 13
chu-maki shrimp, 71
chu-toro, 142
chuba-iwashi, 105
Chujinruiki, 216
chum salmon, 102, 154
clams
  akagai, 56–58
  aoyagi, 62–64
  hamaguri, 78–81
  hokkigai, 91–93
  mirugai, 146–149
  torigai, 187–189
Clavell, James, xvii
cobia, 88
cockles, 57, 187–189
  in chirashi sushi, 22
cod
  roe of, 187
  sperm sacs of, 187
coin roll, 17
condiments, 208–210
  shoga, 207–208
  shoyu, 196–203
  wasabi, 203–207
conger eel, 58–62
coronado, 76
crab, 110–113
  roe of, 187
crabeater, 88

crake, 69
cuttlefish, 98

dai, 225
daikon, 209
  pickled, 44–45
  shoots, 40
dango, 104
daruma, 240–241
date-maki sushi, 20
dempyo, 283
denbu, 38, 43
dishes, for serving, 225–226
dobin, 228
dosa, 260–261, 283
dragonet, 131

ebi (shrimp), 37, 70, 74
  in battera sushi, 28
  in chirashi sushi, 22
  types of, 71–73
ebi no marugata sushi, 28
echizen-gani, 113
edamame (soybean pods), 266
Edomae sushi, xix
eel, 36
  in chirashi sushi, 23
  conger, 58–62
  types of, 59
egg omelet, 182–185, 266–267
  in chirashi sushi, 22
engawa, 89
engimono, 244
Ezo baifun, 191
etiquette
  eating, 273–279
  greeting, 264–265
  ordering, 267–273
  paying, 279–281
  schools of, 217
  seating, 265–266
Ezo hatahata, 82
Ezo-awabi, 65, 66
Ezo-sazae, 162

fan shell, 178
fish paste (surimi), 168–170
flat sea bream, 176
flathead, 131
flounder, 33, 88–91
flying-fish roe, 102, 185–186
folk art, in restaurants, 244–245
four seas roll, 17
fugu sperm sacs, 187

fuji-no-hana sushi, 19
fujiwara sushi, 19
fukko, 173
fukube, 40
fukunagai, 75
fukusa sushi, 19
funa sushi (funa-zushi), xvii
funa-gata, 10
funamori sushi, 18
furishio, 134
futo-maki, 13

gari, 208, 283
genmaicha, 213
genroku-style chopsticks, 235
geoduck, 147
geso, 99
geta, 225, 252
gin-anago, 61
gizzard shad, 35, 133, 134
    in battera sushi, 28
gobo, 38–39
gokezoko-gata, 228
goma, 39
goma-saba, 150, 151, 152
gomoku sushi, 23
goshu-maguro, 138
greeting, in sushi ritual, 264–265
grouper, 84–86
gu (fillings), 22
    types of, 38–45
gugansha, 38
guji, 174
gunkan sushi, 18
gyoku, 184

ha sushi, 31
hajikomi shoga, 208
hako sushi, 27
hako-gata, 9
halfbeak, 158–160
hamachi (yellowtail), 32, 74–78
hamachi-cho, 78
hamaguri (clam), 78–81
    shioyaki, 80
hamaguri sushi, 19–20
han-nare sushi, xvii
han-tsutsu-gata, 228
hana sushi, 18
Hanaguchi Yozo, 201
hana-katsuobushi, 126
hanasaki-gani, 113
Hanaya, Yohei, xviii
hana-zukuri, 172

hangiri, 4
hara-itcho, 141
Harada Genai, 58–59
harasu, 157
Hasegawa, Machiko, 162
hashi-oki (hashi-kake), 225
hashira, 57
hassun, 227
hasu, 39
hata (grouper), 84–86
hatahata (sandfish), 81–83
    sushi-zuke, 83
hatsume, 119
hatsuo-gatsu, 121
Hawaiian roll, 15–16
hedai, 176
herring, 126, 134
herring roe, 126–128
hickory shad, 133
hikari-mono, 35
hikiwari natto, 42
himo, 57
himokyu-maki, 14
hira-saba, 150
hira-suzuki, 171
hiramasa (amberjack), 86–88
hirame (flounder), 88–91
hiramori style, 222
hirenaga kanpachi, 116
hiya, 283
hoji-cha, 213
hokanomono, 37
hoki-hata, 86
hokkigai (surf clam), 91–93
    kobashira, 93
hokkoaka-ebi, 73
hon-akagai, 56
hon-katsuo, 124
hon-maguro, 137
hon-saba, 150
horenso, 39
horotto, 96
horse clam, 146–149
horse mackerel, 53–56
hosha-mori, 224
hoshi shiitake, 44
hoso-maki, 13
hotate-gai (scallops), 64, 93–96
Hyogo nori, 49
Hyottoko, 245

icefish, 167
ichimonji, 222–223
ichinin-mae, 283

Ieyasu, xx, 47
ii-zushi, 83
ika (squid), 97–100
    no sugata sushi, 99
ikijime, 34, 283
ikura (salmon roe), 100–103
inada, 75
inari sushi, 20
inase, 260, 284
indo-maguro, 138
ishidai, xi, 176
ishikari-nabe, 154
ishinagi-zoku, 171
isonori, 48
itadakimasu, 284
itamae, xxii, 252
    attitude of, 260–261
    expertise of, 259–260
    interactions with, 270
    and omakase, 269–270
    tradition of, 255–256
    training of, 253–256
ito-kezuri-katsuobushi, 126
iwashi (sardines), 104–106

jackfish, 76
Japanese cucumber, in chirashi
    sushi, 22
Japanese shad, 135
Japanese whiting, 129
jigami-gata, 9
jiro-mori, 224

kabosu, 210
kabu, 40
kahata, 83
kaibashira, 64, 94, 179
kaiseki, 217
kaiseki chopsticks, 236
kaiware, 40
kajiki (swordfish), 107–110
kaji-maguro, 109
kakefuda, 249–251
kakemori, 223
kakomi sushi, 18
Kakushin, 199
kama, 76
kamaboko, 169–170
kamaboko kani, 111
kami, 284
kaminari-uo, 83
kanburi, 77
kani (crab), 110–113
kani masago, 186

kani-miso, 113
kani-shabu, 113
kanjo, 284
kanpachi (yellowtail), 114–116, 165
kanpai, 284
kanpyo, 40
kanpyo-maki, 14
kanro, 202
Kansai-style chirashi sushi, 21
Kanto-style chirashi sushi, 21–22
kappa-maki, 14
karakuchi-iwashi, 106
karashi, 126
karashi-mentaiko, 187
karasumi, 192
karigane-cha, 213
kasane-mori, 224
kasugo (young sea bream), 116–120
kata (shapes), 9
katakuchi-iwashi, 168
katsu-aji, 55
katsuo (bonito), 120–126
katsuo-tataki, 55
katsuo-zuke, 125
katsuobushi, 126
kawari sushi, 17
kazari sushi, 17
kazunoko (herring roe), 126–128,
    186
kazunoko-konbu, 128
kazunoko-wakame, 128
keiji, 156
ken, 196
kenzake, 156
ki-aji, 53
kichinu, 175
kihada, 139
kikai-maki, 284
kiku-ama-zuke, 209
king amberjack, 76
king crab, 112, 113
kingfish, 76
kinome, 20, 209
    in chirashi sushi, 23
kinshi, 23
kinshi tamago, 183
kintoki, 43
kinusaya (snow peas), 43
kiri sushi, 27
kisu (sillago), 54, 129–131
kitsune sushi, 20
kiwade maguro, 139
kizami-nori, 209
knives, types of, 14

ko-aji, 54
ko-bachi, 225
ko-maki shrimp, 71
ko-zara, 225
koba-iwashi, 105
kobako-gani, 111, 113
koban, 235
koban-gata, 9
koboshi, 63
kochi (flathead), 131
kochi-kochi, 3
kodai, 117, 118
kodai suzumi sushi, 29
kogayaki, 26, 40
kogyu, 69
kohada (shad), 35, 132–136, 267
   in battera sushi, 28
koika, 97
koikuchi, 199
Kojiki, 207
kokuchi ishinagi, 171
kokuchi-aji, 5
komai rice, 2
kombu-jime, 159
komichi-wakame, 128
kona wasabi, 205
kona-cha, 213
konbu, 40–41
konbu-hata, 85
konbu-maki, 18
konnyaku sushi, 18
konoshiro, 132, 133, 135
konowata, 192
koppa, 173
kori-kori, 92
koromo, 91
kotsubu natto, 42
koyadofu, 41
kozokura, 75
kuchiake, 284
kudari sakana, 121
kukicha, 213–214
kumade, 244
kumo no ko, 187
kurai-ebi, 71
kurakake, 184
kuro-maguro, 138
kuro-aji, 53
kuro-awabi, 65
kurodai, 175
kuro-goma, 39
kurokajiki, 109
kuruma-ebi, 70
kushi-gata, 10

kuzu uchi, 166, 172
"kyo wa nani ga oishii desu ka?," 284
kyuri, 22, 41
kyusu, 214, 228

lemonfish, 88
lotus root, 39
lox, in sushi, 156–157

ma-aji, 53–54
macha, 214
mackerel, 35, 149–153
   in battera sushi, 28
   horse. *See* aji
madai, 174, 175
madaka-awabi, 65
madako, 180
madregal, 76
magochi, 131
maguro (tuna), 32, 136–137
   cuts of, 143–146
   freshness issues, 34–35
   technique for cutting, 141
   types of, 138–141
maguro suji-yaki, 145
ma-hata, 85
maika, 97
ma-iwashi, 105
makajiki, 109
ma-katsuo, 124
maki shrimp, 71
maki sushi
   eating, 267
   history of, 13
   procedure for making, 14
   types of, 13–16
makodai, 118
manekineko, 242–243
mantis shrimp, 36, 163–164
mappa-gani, 113
marlin, 109
maru-gata, 236
maru-saba, 150
maruto-maki, 16
maruzuke, 135
ma-saba, 150
masago, 186
matsuba-gani, 113
matsukasa sushi, 99
matsukawa-zukuri, 174
mazemori style, 223
me-saba, 151
mebachi (bigeye tuna), 139
mebaru, 119

mebuto (bigeye tuna), 139
megai (red abalone), 65
mehari sushi, 17
mejiro, 75
meji, 138
mekajiki, 108–109
mentai, 186
mentaiko, 186
Michizane Sugawara, 185
Mikawa Jiemon, 250
minami-maguro, 138
mirugai (horse clam), 146–149
mirukui, 148
mitama sushi, 17–18
mitsuba, 19, 41
miyakijima-maguro, 137
mizu, 283
modori-katsuo, 125
mojako, 75
momiji oroshi, 88, 209–210
momiji-oroshi-zui, 91
moriawase, 217
moritsuke, 217, 221, 224
mugiwara-dai, 175
mura-choko, 225, 284
murasaki, 284
murasaki uni, 191
murasaki-tade, 158
mure-aji, 55
mushi sushi, 24
mushi-awabi, 66

nagashi arrangement, 224
nakaboushi, 138
nakaochi, 77, 142
nakatsumi, 132
nama uni, 190
nama-nare sushi, xvii
namida, 284
naminohana, 285
nare sushi, xvii
narutodai, 176
natto, 41–43
nebari, 4
negi-hama-maki, 77
Negishi ryu, 250
nei, 77
niboshi, 106, 266
nigemono, 285
nigiri sushi, xix
    composition of order, 271–273
    history of, 8
    procedure for eating, 12
    procedure for making, 11

shapes for, 9–10
Nihon Shoki, 169, 207
ni-hotate, 95
nikimi, 37
nimono-dane, 35–37
ninjin (carrot), 43
nishin, 126
nitsumi, 36
no-no-ji-maki, 16
nojime, 35, 285
noren, 238–239
nori, 46–47
    culture and harvest of, 47
    preparation of, 48
    types of, 49–50
noshi-awabi, 67
nuka, 45
nukazuke, 45

o-aiso, 285
oba, 44
oba-iwashi, 105
oboro, 43
oboro konbu, 40
oboshi, 63
ocean perch, 119
o-cha, 213, 215
ochiayu, 70
octopus, 36, 180–182
    in chirashi sushi, 22
odori ebi, 72
odorigui, 166
ogi-gata, 9
o-guruma ebi, 71
ohashi, 229
o-hashi yasumi, 91
o-hitashi, 39
o-inari sushi, 20
o-inaribukuro sushi, 20
Okakura, Kakuzo, 278
Okame, 245
o-kanjo, 284
oke, 228
omakase, 269–270, 285
o-maki, 13
omiyage, 31
ordering, in sushi ritual, 267–273
    of omakase, 269–270
ori, 227
oroshi daikon, 209
Osaka sushi, 27
osechi-ryori, 127
oshi sushi, 26
    types of, 26–28

oshibori (hot towels), 245–246, 266
oshiki, 227
oshinko-maki, 14–15
oshi-waku, 27
o-te, 181
o-toro, 144
otsubu natto, 42
otsumami, 266

parrot fish, 176
pen shell, 177–179
perch, ocean, 119
perilla, 44
Perry, Matthew, 88
pilchards, 106
plates
    reflective of seasonal mood,
        219–220
    shape of, 219
    texture of, 220
pollack roe, 187
pomfret, 124
pompano, 165
ponzu, 55, 210
ponzu-yaki, 160
porcelain, 225
porgy, 176
presentation, of sushi, 221
    hiramori style, 222
    hosha-mori, 224
    ichimonji, 222–223
    jiro-mori, 224
    kakemori, 223
    kasane-mori, 224
    mazemori style, 223
    moritsuke, 221, 224
    nagashi arrangement, 224
    sugimori style, 223
    tawaramori style, 223
puffer fish, 187
punctatus, 135

quail egg, 193–194

razor clams, 180
razor shell, 179
red abalone, 65
red clam, 56–58
red snapper, 119, 176
renkon, 39
restaurant furnishings, 238–251
rice
    cooking procedures for, 3–4
    types of, 2–3, 5

rikyu-gata, 10
rikyu-style chopsticks, 236
rockfish, 119
rudderfish, 116
ruibe, 157
Ruijuzoyo-sho, 216
Ryoma, Sakamoto, 123

saba (mackerel), 35, 149–153
    in battera sushi, 28
saba no sugata sushi, 152
sabi, 285
sabi-nuku, 285
saeri, 160
saero, 160
Saga nori, 49–50
saiku sushi, 17
sailfish, 110
saimaki-ebi, 74
sai-maki shrimp, 71
sake (rice wine), 211–212
sake (salmon)
    commercial fishery of, 154–155
    dishes using, 154
    history of, 153–155
    skin, 156
    in sushi, 155–158
sake hada, 156
sake harasu, 157
sake no sakana, 212
sake no tsukudani, 212
sake sushi, 25–26
sakui, 103
sakui no medatsu, 103
salmon
    commercial fishery of, 154–155
    dishes using, 154
    history of, 153–154
    skin, 156
    in sushi, 155–158
salmon roe, 100–103
sampuru, 239–240
sand scraper, 131
sandborer, 129
sandfish, 81–84
sanriku-maguro, 137
sansho, 20, 209
sardines, 35, 104–106
sasa-beri, 246–247
sasa-maki sushi, 19
sashikomi, 202
sashimi, 267
Satake, 82
sawara, 152

sayaendo (snow peas), 43
sayori (halfbeak), 158–160
sazae (turbinate shell), 161–162
scad, 53
scallops, 63, 64, 93–96
scup, 176
se-itcho, 141
sea bass, 32, 170–173
sea bream, 35
    kasugo, 116–120
    tai, xi, 28, 173–177
sea urchin, 37, 189–192
seating, in sushi ritual, 265–266
seigo, 173
seiguro-iwashi, 106, 168
seiko-gani, 113
seiyo-wasabi, 205
seki-aji, 55
seki-saba, 151
Sen no Rikyu, 10
sencha, 214
sesame seeds, 39
shad, 35, 131–136, 267
    in battera sushi, 28
shako (mantis shrimp), 163–164
shari, 3, 11
shiba-ebi, 73
shibi-maguro, 137
shichimi togarashi, 93
shiho-zara, 225
shiitake, 43–44
    in chirashi sushi, 23
shikai-maki, 17
shiko-iwashi, 168
shiko-shiko, 3
shima-aji (striped jack), 164–166
shima-aji no kuzu uchi, 166
shime-dai no oshi sushi, 29
shimofuri, xii, 144
shinko, 132, 135
shinmai rice, 2
shinoda sushi, 19
shiokara, 57
shiozake, 157
shiraga daikon, 209
shiraita konbu, 18
Shirakawa-dai, 173
shirako, 187
shirasi, 44
shirasu, 168
shirauo (whitebait), 166–168
shiro-akagai, 57
shiroamadai, 173
shirogisu, 129

shiro-goma, 39
shirohata, 83
shirokajiki, 109
shiro-maguro, 140–141
shiromi, 32–33
    freshness issues, 34
shirouo, 167
shirozake, 156–157
shishi-togarashi, 103
shiso, 20, 44, 210
    in chirashi sushi, 23
shoga, 207–208
Shōgun (Clavell), xvii
shoio-mushi, 168
shokado bento, 228
short-spined uni, 191
shottsuru, 83–84, 199
shoyu (soy sauce), 196
    history of, 198–200
    Japanese vs. Chinese, 202
    manufacture of, 197–198,
        200–201
shrimp, 37, 70, 74
    in battera sushi, 28
    in chirashi sushi, 22
    mantis, 163–164
    types of, 71–73
shun, 220
shun no aji, 124
sillago, 129–131
skipjack, 124
smelt, 130
smoked salmon, in sushi, 156–157
snapper, 174
snow crab, 112, 113
snow peas, 43
sockeye salmon, 156
soge, 90–91
soup bowls, 226–227
soy sauce. See shoyu
soybean pods, 266
Spanish mackerel, 150, 151
spider roll, 15
spinach, 39
spotted shad, 135
squid, 97–100
striped bass, 172
striped jack, 164–166
suarai, 134
sudachi, 210
sudori, 208
suehiro-gata, 9
sugimori style, 223
sujiko, 100

suketodara, 186
sukubi, 160
sumashi, 81
su-mezu, 4, 285
sumikiri bon, 227
sumiso, 172
suna-zuri, 77, 144
surf clam, 91–93
surimi (fish paste), 43, 168–170
surume-ika, 97
sushi
  argot of, 281–285
  condiments for, 196–210
  drinks with, 211–216
  eating order for, 267
  eating procedures for, 273–279
  history of, xviii–xxii
  origins of, xvi–xx
  presentation of, 221–225
  rice for, 2–7
  ritual of, 263–285
  tableware for, 216–221, 225–237
  terminology of, xiv–xv
sushi tsu, xiii–xiv, xxii
sushi-ben, ix, 281–285
sushi-dai, 225, 228
sushi-ko, 4
sushi-meshi, xix, 2, 274
  types of, 5
suwai-gani, 112, 113
suzi, 145
suzu, 160
suzuki (sea bass), 170–173
suzuki usu zukuri, 172
suzuko, 100
suzume kodai, 119
suzume-tai, 119
suzushiro, 209
sweetfish, 67–70
swordfish, 107–110

tabeawase, 61
tableware
  chopsticks, 229–237
  dishes, 225–226
  plates, 217–221
  soup bowls, 226–227
  teapots and cups, 228–229
  trays, 227–228
tai (bream), xi, 173–177
  in battera sushi, 28
tai no oshi sushi, 29
tai no sugata sushi, 177
tairagai (pen shell), 177–179

taiseiyo, 140
taisho-ebi, 71
takara-bune, 228
take chopsticks, 236
takenoko (young bamboo shoots), 44
takinogawa, 43
tako (octopus), 180–182
takobiki-bocho, 14
takuan, 44–45
Takuan Soho, 44
tamago-yaki (egg omelet), 182–185,
  266–267
tamari, 199
tane (toppings), 11
  akami, 32
  hikari-mono, 35
  hokanomono, 37
  nimono-dane, 35–37
  shiromi, 32–34
tanuki, 241–242
tara, 187
taraba-gani, 111, 112
tarako, 187
tare, 37
tataki cookery, 123–124, 140,
  144–145
tatami (floor mats), 247–249
tawara-gata, 9
tawaramori style, 224
tazuna sushi, 31
te-zu, 4, 285
tea, 212
  tableware for, 228–229
  types of, 213–215
tekka-don, 26
tekka-donburi, 26
tekka-ju, 26
tekka-maki, 15
tekone sushi, 25
temaki, 16
temoto, 229
tenka no sanmai chinmi, 192
tensoge, 235
tenugui, 252
tenzen-aji, 55
teppo-maki, 14
tetsubin, 228
tobiko, 186
tobi-tama, 186
tobiuonoko (flying-fish roe), 102,
  185–186
tofu, freeze-dried, 41
toki-saba, 151
Tokugawa (Ieyasu), xviii, 47

tomoe sushi, 17
tomoturi, 68
tonburi, 20, 210
tora maki, 100
torigai (cockles), 187–189
  in chirashi sushi, 22
tororo konbu, 41
Tosa-mi, 123
trays, 227–228
trough shell clam, 62–64
tsubasu, 75
tsubu-gai, 162
tsuke, 285
tsuke-zara, 225
tsukekomi, 134
tsukemono, 45
tsukikomi (tsukkomu), 80
tsukudani, 266
tsuma, 196
tsunashi, 132
tsutsu-gata, 228
tsuya, 3
tsuyukanpachi, 115
tuna, 32, 136–137
  cuts of, 143–145
  freshness issues, 34–35
  technique for cutting, 141
  types of, 138–141
turbinate shell, 161–162

ubagai, 91
uchi-mise, xx
ukai (cormorant fishing), 69
umeboshi (pickled plums), 61
umekyu, 15
una-don, 26
unagi, 59, 60
una-ju, 26
uni (sea urchin), 189–192
ura-maki, 16–17
urume-iwashi, 106
usu yaki, 183
usu-aji, 5
usukuchi, 199
uzuri tamago (quail egg),
    193–194

waka-ayu, 69
wakashi, 75
wakegi, 210
wan, 226
warabi fern, 24
warasa, 75
waribashi, 230
wasabi
  botany of, 203
  chemistry of, 205–206
  preparation of, 204
  proper use of, 273–276
  substitutes for, 205
  types of, 207
wasabi daikon, 205
wata, 162
watari-gani, 113
Wei zhi, 8
white sillago, 129
whitebait, 166–168
whiting, Japanese, 129
wine, with sushi, 215

yakumi, 196
yamagobo, 39
yamaimo-kake, 145, 210
yamakake, 145, 210
yamanoimo, 210
yanagiba-bocho, 14
yari-ika, 97
yatai-mise, xx
yellow aji, 53
yellowfin tuna, 139
yellowtail
  hamachi, 32, 74–78
  kanpachi, 114–116
yodo, 160
yu-buri, 92
yudaki, 3
yuderu, 95, 174
yugao, 40
yunomi, 228
yuzu, 20

zen, 227
zuwai-gani, 112

About the Author

Dave Lowry has traveled extensively in Japan and has written several books on Japanese culture. He is the restaurant critic for *St. Louis* magazine and lives in Missouri.